Restitution

Restitution

Civil Liability for Unjust Enrichment

WARD FARNSWORTH

THE UNIVERSITY OF CHICAGO PRESS   CHICAGO AND LONDON

WARD FARNSWORTH is dean and the John Jeffers Research Chair at the University of Texas School of Law. He is the author of many books, including *The Legal Analyst*, also published by the University of Chicago Press.

The University of Chicago Press, Chicago 60637
The University of Chicago Press, Ltd., London
© 2014 by Ward Farnsworth
All rights reserved. Published 2014.
Printed in the United States of America

23 22 21 20 19 18 17 16 15 14   1 2 3 4 5

ISBN-13: 978-0-226-14402-3 (cloth)
ISBN-13: 978-0-226-14416-0 (paper)
ISBN-13: 978-0-226-14433-7 (e-book)
DOI: 10.7208/chicago/9780226144337.001.0001

Library of Congress Cataloging-in-Publication Data
Farnsworth, Ward, 1967– author.
    Restitution : civil liability for unjust enrichment / Ward Farnsworth.
       pages cm
    Includes bibliographical references and index.
    ISBN 978-0-226-14402-3 (cloth : alkaline paper) — ISBN 978-0-226-14416-0
    (paperback : alkaline paper) — ISBN 978-0-226-14433-7 (e-book) 1. Restitution—
    United States. I. Title.
       KF1244.F37 2014
       346.7303—dc23

                                                                   2014010198

♾ This paper meets the requirements of ANSI/NISO z39.48-1992 (Permanence of Paper).

Contents

Preface

" Restitution" is a word that bears a number of meanings in American law. This book is about restitution in its core sense: the common-law action that a plaintiff brings to recover a defendant's unjust enrichment. Sometimes a plaintiff uses restitution law to make a defendant pay for benefits he has received; sometimes restitution is used to make a defendant return specific property to which the plaintiff has a claim of ownership. Either way, restitution is the body of law concerned with taking away what a defendant has wrongfully obtained (or, in any event, should not be permitted to keep), not with rectifying an injury the plaintiff has suffered. As this brief statement suggests, restitution is not just a remedy, though it is sometimes misunderstood that way. It is a type of legal claim—a cause of action, and an important one. This book explains its workings and rationales. ("Restitution" is also sometimes used to refer to payments that criminals make to compensate their victims. This book is not about restitution in that sense of the word.)

The reader familiar with private law will recognize that restitution in the sense used here is in many ways symmetrical to the law of torts. Tort law governs liability for losses that one person inflicts on another. Restitution governs liability for gains that one person makes at another's expense. Tort and restitution law sometimes cover the same situations, with the choice between them just a matter of which amount is larger (and thus which the plaintiff prefers to recover): the plaintiff's losses or the defendant's gains. But restitution also offers a more powerful range of equitable remedies than are traditionally available at the end of a tort case, and it covers many situations that neither tort nor any other body of law does. Restitution thus is a major division of American private law, one that sits alongside the law of tort and contract and provides a practical and theoretical complement to them.

Restitution has been much neglected by the American legal academy, however, and has in turn become a subject of faint familiarity to much of the bench and bar. If Professor Kull overstated the matter, it was not by much: "American lawyers today (judges and law professors included) do not know what restitution is. The subject is no longer taught in law schools, and the lawyer who lacks an introduction to its basic principles is unlikely to recognize them in practice."[1] This ignorance is a misfortune for the academic; the law of restitution is full of interesting problems and responses to them, and an understanding of the subject is essential to a clear overall grasp of the law of private obligations. A sophisticated mastery of contract law is particularly impossible without a sense of the principles of restitution that surround it. The ignorance is equally unfortunate for the practitioner because the law of restitution provides a highly useful set of tools for analyzing a wide range of cases that are handled less effectively, or not at all, by other bodies of law. A lawyer struggling to fix a problem by use of a familiar but inferior legal method may have no reason to suspect that restitution provides a better way—that a wrench is available, and would work better than the pliers on hand.

Restitution has suffered such neglect in part because it has a reputation as a hodgepodge of leftover doctrines that don't add up to a clear body of knowledge. That reputation has partly been perpetuated, I believe, by the absence of a readable book that explains the topic in one place and shows how its components relate to one another. This book aims to fill that void. The American Law Institute's publication in 2011 of the *Restatement (Third) of Restitution and Unjust Enrichment* is a suitable occasion for a treatment of this kind. Kull's work on that project has been heroic and immensely valuable; the new *Restatement* explains and organizes its subject in a highly comprehensive and convincing manner. At well over five hundred thousand words, however, it serves better as a reference than as a source of instruction. (The same could be said of the only American treatise on the subject, by George Palmer.[2] It is even longer than the *Restatement*.) This book seeks to explain the law of restitution in as concise and lively a manner as the subject will permit, with a somewhat different organization than the *Restatement* and with more attention to the theory behind the rules. Some details are skipped or handled lightly—the inevitable price of a short treatment. But the aforementioned sources can provide additional discussion for readers who are left wanting more.

This book starts with a brief essay on the relationship between restitution and other bodies of law, then proceeds to consider, in a chapter apiece, four major families of liability in restitution (mistakes, conferrings, takings, and failed contracts), the two kinds of remedies available at the end of a case (legal and equitable), and defenses. The aim is to show that restitution law has a moderately coherent structure, that it lends itself to explanation by reference to a fairly clear and compact set of principles, and that it is interesting. If the book fails in any or all of those ambitions, I will settle for at least providing a helpful overview of a significant and underappreciated branch of the law that can be read in a few sittings.

A final note at my copyeditor's request: I sought to write this book in the clearest possible English. I naturally encountered the problem of choosing a pronoun to refer to someone who could be male or female. I dealt with this by treating the masculine pronoun as referring to anyone of either sex; I find the other, newer ways of handling the problem too self-conscious to bear. I know others have different views, and am sorry for the annoyance that my inclusive use of "he" and "him" may cause them.

* * *

For helpful comments and discussion at various stages in the writing of this book, I thank Douglas Baird, Mark Gergen, David Greenwald, Andrew Kull, Doug Laycock, Brian Perez-Daple, Richard Posner, and Henry Smith. Anonymous reviewers for the University of Chicago Press also made a number of helpful suggestions. For research assistance I thank Jeff Cravens, Andrew Dunning, Ben Giumarra, Laura Graham, Max Lee, Evan Panich, Ari Sacharow, Jeanna Simeone, and Jennifer Small. I would also like to express my gratitude to the staff of the libraries at the Boston University School of Law and the University of Texas School of Law for their generous assistance, and to Kelly Finefrock-Creed for excellent copyediting.

CHAPTER ONE

Restitution, Tort, and Contract

Restitution, tort, and contract are related bodies of law, each addressing cases where people's entitlements have gotten out of alignment—cases where one person has caused losses to another or has gained at another's expense, and so is obliged to make things right. Lawyers are trained early to spot such situations by looking for the first pattern just mentioned. They quickly observe that someone has suffered losses for which compensation may be due from whoever caused them. The losses may result in a tort claim if they involve damage to the victim's person or property, or in a contract claim if they arise from a broken promise. This book views the whole spectrum of obligations through the opposite lens, which more often is overlooked: the rights that arise not when one person has caused an unjustifiable loss to another, but when the defendant has unjustifiably *gained* at the plaintiff's expense. Those cases are matters for the law of restitution. Sometimes searching out wrongful gains will catch the same cases found by looking for actionable losses, because a gain to one person is a loss to another (they are just two ways of looking at the same event—say, a theft); but the search for gains also turns up a great many distinctive problems and solutions of its own, which form much of our subject here.

Types of Restitution Claims

Let us begin by asking how it is that one person ever does gain at another's expense. We can divide all such situations into four rough families according to the consent or intent of the parties to a transfer of property; this book is organized mostly around these groupings. Each of them gives rise to its own claims for restitution with their own difficulties, and in each case we can consider how restitution compares to other kinds of lawsuits as a source of relief.

1. *Mistakes.* Neither party might have intended the transfer. This typically results in a case of mistake, as when someone pays money he doesn't owe. The law of restitution is the exclusive source of recovery in all such cases and has a well-developed apparatus for dealing with the complications that can arise—mistakes that are only partial, or a party who makes a payment while assuming the risk that it is mistaken, and so forth.

2. *Conferrings.* The giver might have intended the transfer, but the recipient did not, or in any event didn't intend to pay for it—as when one person confers benefits on another in an emergency where there is no chance to negotiate. Another sort of conferring occurs when one person does something necessary for himself and can't help benefiting another in the process. Perhaps the plaintiff paid a tax bill that could have been collected from either him or the defendant. In that sort of case the benefit might not seem to be conferred on the defendant "intentionally"; it would be more precise, however, to just say that the plaintiff was not *motivated* by a desire to benefit the defendant. The plaintiff's act in paying the bill was deliberate, and the benefits that accrued to the defendant were neither wished for nor accidental. They were side effects of actions the plaintiff took for other reasons. Again the law of restitution is the only source of help in such circumstances and provides doctrines for separating the good cases for recovery from the bad (typically asking whether the giver's failure to seek a contract for conferral of the benefits was excusable or was a foisting that the law should not reward).

3. *Takings.* The recipient might have intended the transfer while the giver did not. In other words, one person takes benefits from the other. In these cases restitution tends not to be the only body of law that addresses the problem. The victim of a fraud, for example, can choose whether to seek return of the benefits that the defrauder obtained (by way of a restitution claim) or damages for his losses (by way of a tort claim). Sometimes the choice may not matter, but in many cases one of those measures will be larger than the other. And even when the victim does bring a claim for restitution, tort law—and for that matter criminal law—will often remain relevant. A taking only entitles the victim to recover in restitution if the taking was in some way wrongful, and much of the time the law of restitution defers to tort and criminal law for answers to that question. Sometimes restitution does go further than tort or criminal law in

recognizing misconduct that requires gains to be returned. We will touch on those cases. But since restitution law makes only modest contributions of its own to the problem of defining what takings are wrongful, the most interesting questions in this branch of the subject tend to involve measurement of the plaintiff's recovery.

4. *Failed contracts.* Both parties might have intended the transfer, but it nevertheless resulted in unjust enrichment because the intentions of either side, or both, were in some way frustrated or contaminated. It was a defective contract or gift. (Using "failed contracts" as shorthand for this category is rough because a gift may be a transfer intended by both sides, and so fit into this category, and yet not involve a contract.) Maybe one side or the other was not competent to execute the transfer or was forced into it by duress. Or the intended enrichment of one side was conditioned on an intended enrichment of the other that did not occur, as when the parties had a contract and one side breached. The right to restitution may then depend on familiar points of contract law, just as it may depend on points of tort or criminal law in a case that involves a taking. But here, as there, restitution has plenty of its own work to do, for in many cases that arise from efforts at trade the point is that there *is* no contract between the parties. Whatever agreement they made is invalid. So contract law is no help, yet one side has been enriched unjustly. The result is a claim for restitution—not as a remedy for breach of contract, but as a freestanding claim of its own.

The categories just offered are informal, and some situations might be sorted into more than one of them. Transfers made under duress could be viewed as extractions made by a wrongdoer without consent (a taking) or as cases where both sides intended the transfer but the consent of one of them shouldn't count (a failed contract). Or cases where the defendant got the plaintiff's assets by fraud or duress could be put with cases where the defendant got them by mistake, because in both cases there was no meaningful consent to the transfer by the plaintiff. (That last pairing is a conventional way for many students of restitution to speak but not the approach used in this book.) Straightening out all these problems conclusively would require precise definitions of "intent," but we don't need to bother about that because in the law of restitution nothing depends on the organization set out above. The actual doctrines used to decide restitution cases are fashioned at a lower level of abstraction than the divisions just shown. In each of the cases just mentioned as ambiguous from the standpoint of intent, for example, there are clear and distinctive rules for decision. The categories merely are convenient for purposes of this book because they organize all gains by one person at the expense of another into typical patterns that are easier to grasp, that tend to be treated according to related principles or logic, and that are useful to learn about together.

With that disclaimer made, the framework just shown does mean to offer a way of looking at restitution that allows the field to be seen more or less whole, and not viewed as merely miscellaneous. Some may insist that the law of restitution really *is* miscellaneous, but it is not a matter for insistence; the question is not whether restitution "really" is one thing or another. It is whether a way of looking at the subject allows the viewer to better understand it, appreciate it, and see a related logic in its various parts. Whether those effects are achieved by the description of restitution sketched here and elaborated in the chapters to come, the reader will judge.

The Scope of Restitution Compared to the Scope of Tort and Contract

In addition to clarifying the different sorts of restitution claims that can arise, the four-part apparatus described above can serve as a helpful starting point in comparing the scope of restitution on the one hand and the more familiar scope of tort and contract law on the other. Notice that we could have asked how *losses* of wealth ever happen, and then made a sorting that looks much like the one just shown: Losses can occur (a) that nobody intends, as by accident. These usually are cases of negligently inflicted injury, but self-inflicted losses, such as property mislaid by the owner and found by someone else, also might go here. Or a loss may occur (b) by giving away wealth deliberately or otherwise conferring a benefit on someone else. This doesn't give rise to a legal claim when viewed as a loss. In other words it is not a source of tort liability, though it may create a good claim for restitution, as noted earlier. Or a loss may occur (c) when one party intentionally takes wealth away from another. These usually amount to intentional torts, so the victim can choose between recovering his losses (in tort) or demanding return of the other side's gains (in restitution). This category also can include extractions by the government that may or may not turn out to be wrongful. Or, last, a loss can occur (d) because a party makes an intentional trade that goes awry in some way. If the attempted trade ripens into a valid and enforceable contract, the loss that results is remedied by a suit for breach of that contract, with recovery usually measured in terms of the victim's damages. When the attempted trade doesn't ripen into a contract, the loss can only be remedied by a restitution claim, with recovery measured in terms of the defendant's gains.

As that exercise shows, most transactions, voluntary or not, can be viewed as occasions for either gain or loss; it just depends on how you look at them. But notice that restitution law gives a more complete account of gains than tort and contract law give of losses. If I defraud you out of $500, you can bring a tort claim or a restitution claim as you prefer. If you mistakenly send me $500 that you meant to send to your plumber, however, there is both a loss to you and a gain to me, but tort law has no comment to make, while the law of restitution is just as interested as ever. The reason for the asymmetry is that restitution is the remedy for unjust enrichment, which is a very broad category, whereas tort is not quite a remedy for unjust losses. It is the remedy for *wrongs* one person commits against another, which is a smaller set of events. Contract law likewise is not about all unjust losses, or even all losses that can arise from voluntary exchanges that go wrong. It is only concerned with losses that arise from properly formed contracts, which again is a smaller category. Contract and tort law can afford to be narrow precisely because the law of restitution picks up the slack in many cases of misallocation that they don't cover.

But it would be a mistake to infer from this that restitution just exists to give plaintiffs some recourse in cases that tort and contract law miss. It might be closer to the truth to think of tort and contract law as exceptional. Recovery is generally available for unjust enrichment that one party makes at another's expense. Granted, "unjust enrichment" is a term with particular legal meaning; there is a great deal of profitable injustice in the world that the law of restitution leaves alone. But principles of restitution law do speak in detail to all four types of problems outlined a moment ago—mistakes, conferrings, takings, and failed contracts—and provide a remarkable array of tools to rectify them. Then come tort and contract law, which provide some special and additional rules that also allow plaintiffs to recover for their *losses*, even without reference to whether anyone else has gained—but only in a fairly narrow set of cases when particular requirements are satisfied, and then usually by a simple remedy. The plaintiff just presents the defendant with a bill.

It would be tempting and tidy to say that restitution law has the potential to speak to every case covered by tort and contract law (if the cases from those areas are viewed from the standpoint of gains rather than losses) and then many others as well. But it would be a little misleading. In theory, any instance of unjust enrichment can indeed be addressed with a restitution claim. In practice, though, there are occasional types of unjust enrichment that never result in restitution claims because our legal traditions have committed the resolution of them to a different rubric. After a breach of contract, the plaintiff might, in principle, be able to sue in restitution, claiming that the defendant was unjustly enriched by the breach. But this never happens in practice because the law handles those problems as "contract cases"—within which, however, "restitution" is a label given to one possible remedy that operates much like (though not exactly like!) a restitution suit would. And if I steal your goods and you want them back, this too might in principle seem to call for a restitution claim. I certainly have been unjustly enriched. But it just happens that these facts traditionally have been addressed by a suit for replevin rather than restitution. Restitution does become relevant if I have sold your goods and you want the money I obtained for them. These wrinkles might make the scope of restitution sound confusing, but the general result they produce can be stated simply enough. Almost any case of unjust enrichment can be addressed with a restitution claim. There are just a few types that are addressed in some other way, and the two most prominent of them have now been mentioned.

While the scope of restitution law is wider than the scope of tort or contract law, tort and contract undeniably have a more constant practical importance. First, in the cases that tort and contract law cover, plaintiffs usually prefer claims under those headings to restitution claims because their losses are greater than the defendant's gains. In a car accident, for example, the gains to the defendant from skipping whatever precautions he should have taken are minimal, while the losses to the plaintiff are large. The same more or less goes for a punch in the nose. So those incidents invariably result in tort rather than restitution claims. Nobody even thinks of restitution as a plausible line of recovery for them.

The other and larger reason for the greater importance of tort and contract law involves the natural incentives of potential defendants, and the problems those incentives create. Skipping a precaution or not keeping a promise—the stuff that tort and contract claims are made of—usually is easier and cheaper than taking the victim's interests to heart. That is why those types of invasions are common, along with tort and contract suits to redress them. Many classic types of restitution cases are less likely to involve temptations of that sort. If I mistakenly pay you money that I owe to someone else, I have blundered at my own expense, not yours, so I have a built-in reason to be careful not to do it. Likewise, a breach of contract is a more common thing than an invalid contract, because a breach is tempting for one side to commit but an invalid contract is not usually tempting for either side to make. If a contract ends up invalid and useless, it is usually in spite of the original intentions of both parties. In short, tort and contract law get used more, despite covering less ground than restitution, because opportunism is a more powerful force than the altruism, self-injuring carelessness, and other forces that give rise *only* to claims of unjust enrichment.

So restitution shows up behind tort and contract law in practical importance, but not too far behind, for its reach is vast and covers a lot of situations that come up often enough. People make mistakes, reasonable or unreasonable, about whom or how much to pay. They perform disputed obligations that turn out not to exist. They confer benefits on others in emergencies. They do things for themselves that incidentally make others better off, too. They steal and then resell property or commit other wrongs and greatly enrich themselves in the process. They exchange things without enforceable contracts. Those all are cases for the law of restitution, and the patterns they involve can arise not only on their own but in the thick of other cases that may appear at first glance to be matters for some other body of law. The seasoned expert on restitution sees occasions for it that are easily overlooked by the lawyer overly habituated to look for losses, who asks when confronted with any misallocation whether it somehow can be crammed into the law of contract or tort.

Roots and Foundational Principles

The law of restitution can be viewed as advancing a number of different values, some of them utilitarian in character and some not. The case law on the subject descends in a line from Lord Mansfield, who regarded the principles governing the subject as "natural justice and equity."[1] John Dawson identified the law of restitution with a maxim that goes back farther—indeed, two thousand years: "For this by nature is equitable, that no one be made richer through another's loss."[2] To this day, the origins of restitution law in notions of good conscience give it a useful flexibility and versatility as well as an attractive moral footing. As a procedural matter, restitution was available from both law and equity courts, and the influence of equity principles still can show up at every stage of a restitution case now. Contract and tort law, by contrast, were primarily matters for law courts, and this is reflected both in the simplicity of the remedies usually available for such claims—that is, money damages—and in the often more clear-cut rules of entitlement and defense that govern them.

One branch of development from those origins has been theoretical, with scholars and some judges attempting to state master principles that explain what counts as unjust enrichment. It would take a different type of book to provide a fair account of those efforts (the interested reader is referred to the sources mentioned in the notes).[3] The other branch of development has been doctrinal and is the primary subject of the chapters to come. We will see that the doctrines are sometimes complex but often follow from a compact set of principles: that defendants should not benefit from their own wrongdoing; that an innocent recipient of a benefit should be protected against a forced exchange; that a party who confers an unrequested benefit on another should recover only when proceeding by contract was not feasible; that stolen or otherwise misappropriated property can be followed into different shapes and forms until it comes into the hands of a bona fide purchaser. Each of these principles, and many others that we will encounter soon, can be explained in terms of fairness and respect for the parties' autonomy. Each can also be explained on functional grounds, of which more in a moment.

The law of restitution, especially on the remedial side, involves an additional recurring theme that is worth mentioning at the outset: the identification and management of property rights. As noted in the preface, restitution claims often demand that defendants pay for benefits they have received, but sometimes such claims are used for the important and distinct purpose of getting back something the defendant has in his possession that belonged to the plaintiff, and perhaps still does. When a wrong involves taking someone's money or other property, it can matter a great deal whether the victim merely has a right to the value of what was taken (like anyone else to whom the defendant owes money), or whether the victim has a property right in what the defendant now possesses—and thus a right to take back that very thing, or to seize whatever money it produced when it was sold, or to force the defendant or someone else to hand over some further thing the money was used to buy. It especially matters when the defendant has other creditors and doesn't have enough money left to pay them all. One would prefer not to get in line with those others in hopes of recovering pennies on the dollar; one would much rather take back the property outright. The law of restitution provides a framework for understanding when that can be done. Those distinctions are another way in which restitution departs from the law of contract and tort, which are mostly concerned with money liabilities and aren't designed to answer hard questions about the meaning of ownership.

Property rights, once recognized, can have rigorous and startling implications. They don't lend themselves to the balancing and inquiries into blame that we often find in tort cases and with which modern legal instincts tend to be more at home. A brief example will make the point more concrete. Suppose that after defrauding Smithers and Jones out of $500 each, you put their money into separate pockets. You spend Jones's money, and then you are caught. All you have left is the $500 from Smithers. Both parties bring restitution claims against you. Should Smithers get the entire $500 back, or should he and Jones get $250 apiece? The latter solution might seem more fair, since the two plaintiffs were (let us assume) equally victimized by you and equally free from any culpability of their own. But traditional rules of restitution would probably entitle Smithers to all of his money and Jones to nothing, because Smithers can make a property claim. The money is *his*; he can point to it in your pocket, say that you never obtained title to it, and insist that it therefore has to be returned directly without any talk about what is fair to Jones. Some courts might insist on a clearer separation of the funds than just putting them into separate pockets, but the principles would still be the same. Then again, a few modern courts have abandoned this logic in favor of pro rata distribution to victims of fraud when the defrauder has spent the money of some of them but not others. We will return to all this later in the book. For now just consider it an example of a general theme: the recurrent tension in restitution law between rules founded in property and more modern tendencies to apportion liability and loss based on notions of relative fault and desert.

Economic Logic

The scholarship on restitution is vastly more extensive outside the United States than inside. The topic hasn't quite caught on here. Some say this is because the scholarship from elsewhere has a prerealist quality. It often is occupied with philosophical puzzles that are conceptually interesting but seem to have modest practical stakes, at least to American eyes.[4] This book will likely have other problems but probably not that one. Its first ambition is to effectively explain how the law works. And while this is not a "law and economics" book, I do like functional explanations where they are possible and so try to suggest at many points how doctrines of restitution serve the cause of efficiency. Scholars who don't like economic accounts may find some of those explanations unrealistic or otherwise unpersuasive, and scholars from other countries may regret my indifference to some definitional conundrums that they consider essential to an understanding of the field. But they have other books to read.

The functional explanations just mentioned will appear as we go along, but a few themes recur often enough to be worth mentioning from the outset. They may serve as complements to the foundational principles of doctrine listed a moment ago; indeed, in some cases the functional principles are the same as the principles of fairness, just interpreted differently. One is that wrongs should be made valueless to those who commit them—a maxim readily defensible as a matter of justice but also as a matter of sound policy. Another is that the law of restitution, like the law of tort, often can be understood as pressuring parties to make contracts when they can, rather than imposing costs and benefits on each other and then calling for judicial valuation of them afterward. When contracts aren't feasible to make, the law of restitution—again, like the law of tort—sometimes can be viewed as creating the outcome that the parties might have reached by contract if one had been possible to make. This can be viewed as a rule of respect for the autonomy of those who receive benefits they didn't ask for. It also can be viewed as good economics.

Another recurring problem is the correct performance of a cost-benefit analysis when private costs are high and social costs are low. Begin by observing that the losses at issue in restitution cases differ in interesting ways from the losses at issue in many tort cases. Usually negligence that results in tort liability doesn't just cause a loss to the victim; it produces a real loss of resources. An accident has occurred, and now some costs exist that weren't there before—medical expenses, repairs, and so on. Cases of unjust enrichment don't as often involve social losses of that kind, at least directly. If I pay money to you that I don't owe, or I pay you money on a contract that turns out to be invalid, I'm poorer but the world isn't, at least not significantly. Rather, I'm poorer and you are richer, maybe to an identical extent. In this case resources haven't been wasted. They just have been moved from one person to another. It is easy to understand why liability should be imposed on someone who fails to prevent a waste of resources, but not as obvious why there is a public interest of any economic kind in a case where one person's wealth merely has been shifted to another.

Perhaps the answer is that the law in this area is best explained by notions of justice rather than utility, but some justifications are available on economic grounds all the same. Some of them resemble the economic account of why we have liability for intentional torts that merely transfer wealth from one person to another (such as conversion—i.e., theft). First, some acts that call for restitution *are* intentional torts. They result in restitution suits just because the gain for the tortfeasor happened to be larger than the loss to the victim (e.g., when the tortfeasor embezzled money and then profitably invested it). Taking away the tortfeasor's gains will make his act valueless to him, and so deters it better than just making him pay for the damage done. In addition, bad transfers—even those that create no loss to the world in themselves—create side costs if they go uncorrected. If you aren't legally obliged to return overpayments I make to you, then we may have to waste time making our own agreements about how to handle that problem if it ever comes up (contracting around the legal rule, so to speak), or taking exaggerated precautions to make sure such an overpayment never happens. So restitution law may not prevent costly accidents, but it sometimes provides a substitute for precautions that the people involved should not be put to the bother of taking in advance. Granted, that gain comes at some administrative cost: we have to entertain lawsuits from time to time. Whether that cost is outweighed by greater benefits of the type just described is hard to say, but it might be.

An Unfortunate Word

A final note is in order on vocabulary. The principles this book explains tend to be old, but use of the word "restitution" to refer to their collective operation is comparatively recent. The word was picked in 1936 by two law professors, Warren Seavey and Austin Scott, to describe the principles they had summarized in their new project for the American Law Institute—one they christened the *Restatement of Restitution*.[5] Their work was marvelous, but their word for it was not. It basically means "restoration." That sometimes describes what happens in a restitution case, as when the plaintiff sues to get his property back from the defendant.

Sometimes it does not describe what is happening very aptly at all, however, as when the plaintiff sues to recover payment for a service that he performed for the defendant—a classic case of unjust enrichment. So the word is an unhappily imprecise fit to the body of law that it labels.

The word is also unfortunate because it can refer to one of two (or three) things. "Restitution" is, as we have been treating it, the name of a certain kind of *claim* a plaintiff can bring, analogous to one brought in tort or contract law: it is a claim that the defendant has been unjustly enriched at the plaintiff's expense. At the same time, "restitution" also is the name of a certain type of *remedy* a plaintiff can seek in other kinds of cases—mostly cases arising under contract law, but sometimes also involving other areas, such as those governed by statutes that may entitle a plaintiff to "restitution" in a specially defined sense. And then more recently the word has also been appropriated to refer to payments that criminals make to compensate their victims, which often have nothing to do with gain-based recovery. These multiple meanings of the word are mostly just an annoyance that the lawyer has to master early in studying the subject. But it has done practical damage, too, because many generations of attorneys have graduated from law school thinking that "restitution" is just the name of a contract remedy (or an idea from criminal law), and having little or no idea that it may refer to an important and useful legal claim of its own.

Some of this confusion could be avoided by changing our use of the word "restitution" so that it never describes a type of legal claim and only is used to describe a remedy—the remedy of taking away a defendant's gains, whether in response to a claim sounding in unjust enrichment or a claim sounding in contract or some other body of law. The *claims* that now go by the name "restitution" would be called "claims of unjust enrichment" from now on.[6] On this view "unjust enrichment" might refer not to every situation that gives rise to restitution but just to a subset of claims with its own set of elements. We thus would have tort claims, for which restitution is a possible remedy, and contract claims, for which restitution is a possible remedy, and unjust enrichment claims, for which restitution is a possible (or perhaps inevitable) remedy.

That solution might have made good sense as an original matter, and might now make life a little less confusing in some ways. But moving to it also would create a series of fresh problems. The claim of "unjust enrichment" would have to be defined to capture a lot of cases that are quite dissimilar—cases involving, say, both mistakes and conferrings. Some claims will fall outside any definition one makes (restitution law currently covers a lot of very miscellaneous fact patterns); they will be left in search of a name, and in a strange legal posture. Meanwhile it doesn't appear that reworking the verbal and intellectual framework in this way would cause any cases to come out differently. So with due regret that the terminology for these cases wasn't chosen better seventy years ago, the case for a fundamental change in it now seems unpersuasive. Lawyers understand that the word "negligence" is ambiguous, as it can refer either to the tort claim one brings in a typical accident case or to one element of that claim—a failure to use due care. They also understand, or can quickly enough grasp, that "restitution" is subject to its own ambiguity, as it can name either a remedy or a freestanding type of legal claim based on unjust enrichment.

CHAPTER TWO

Mistakes

Mistaken Payments of Money

Herbert W. Smith and Huling W. Smith both have rights in the Amoco oil company. Amoco lists them both in its records as "H. W. Smith," and the identical names cause the company to make a mistake: for several years it sends Huling's money to Herbert. When the error is discovered, Amoco wants Herbert to return the money. This is a real case, and an easy one.[1] Herbert has to give the money back. It is the same if Amoco mistakenly sends him more than it owes by mistyping the amount on the check or if Amoco mistakenly pays him twice for the same thing.[2] In all of these cases the recipient is unjustly enriched to the extent of the mistake and is legally obliged to pay back the overage. Or if a claim is brought against Herbert by the person who was supposed to receive the money—say, Huling Smith—then Herbert has to pay it over to *him*.[3] Either party—the one who made the mistaken payment or the one who should have received it—has a better claim to the money than Herbert does, and either can bring a claim for restitution. (If Herbert makes a payment to either of them, his obligations to both are at an end.)

In effect the liability of someone who receives a mistaken payment is strict. If I inadvertently send you money that I do not owe, it does not matter if you were free from blame, or if I was negligent or even grossly negligent[4]—as I probably was, for that is how mistakes typically happen.[5] You have to repay the money the tenth time I overpay it, just as you did the first. The usual judicial account of the rule is that it is a matter of equity or ethics. The recipient of the money has done nothing to deserve it; if he is in a position to give it back, that is obviously the right thing for him to do, or for the law to make him do.[6] He is said to be "unjustly enriched"—a phrase that makes the result seem to be a matter of desert, as perhaps it is. But what of the economic sense of the rule? At first it might seem puzzling. Mistaken payments in themselves don't cost society anything. They are painful for the maker of the mistake but presumably are just about as pleasurable for the recipient. *Returning* the money does cost a little something. So why not let the loss—or rather the gain—lie where it falls? Or we can state the puzzle this way: the legal response to mistaken payments doesn't do much to deter them. If we try to infer how much care the law wants the mistaken party to take, the answer seems to be none. Wouldn't mistaken payments be better discouraged by letting the recipient keep the money?

No doubt they would, but they probably would be *overly* discouraged. The problem is that the actual cost to the world of a mistaken payment—the social cost of it—may bear no relationship to how large a payment it was. Suppose I send you checks routinely. One day I mean to send you $10,000 but put the decimal in the wrong place and send $100,000, which you deposit without noticing (you receive hundreds of checks each day). The error annoys me and might well annoy you, too, if you feel obliged to correct it. But letting you keep the $90,000 excess as compensation for the annoyance is overkill, because the actual costs imposed on you are unrelated to that figure. They are just the costs of finding the money and cutting a check in the other direction, which (let us imagine) might amount to $100 in trouble. To turn the point around, the threat of a $90,000 penalty for such mistakes would cause me to invest heavily in efforts to make sure the mistakes never happen. Those heavy investments in care would probably cost me a lot more than the $100 that my occasional mistakes would cost you if you are required to give the money back.

So the cheaper way to handle mistakes (if we are looking just at total costs to everyone and not worrying about who pays them) is to have you put up with the relatively small bother of returning the money or, if the bother can be quantified, to deduct the cost of the return from what you pay back to me. The right to deduct those incidental damages is implied in the *Restatement*'s assurance that "[t]he liability in restitution of an innocent recipient of unrequested benefits may not leave the recipient worse off (apart from the costs of litigation) than if the transaction giving rise to the liability had not occurred."[7] This creates a reason to be appropriately but not excessively careful about mistaken payments: makers of mistakes have to pay for any costs they create by them. This probably resembles the solution that we would expect parties to reach who do a lot of business and handle by contract the possibility of mistaken payments. The solution that keeps their joint costs the lowest is to simply have such payments returned whenever they are made, less any quantifiable loss the party at fault has imposed on the other side.

And in the background, besides, is the built-in incentive anyone has to avoid these sorts of tangles. A mistake creates a risk to its maker that the money will not be recoverable because the recipient will have changed position in reliance on it, or will have some other defense, or will abscond. (Even apart from those possibilities, the simple risk of having to litigate to get the money back is enough to make anyone strongly prefer not to send it to the wrong place.) The real case we started with is an example. Herbert W. Smith had to pay back some of the money to Amoco, but not all of it; by the time the company noticed its mistake, its right to take back the earliest payments it made had been extinguished by the statute of limitations. So the built-in incentives to be careful are, if not optimal, adequate to prevent mistaken payments from being a chronic source of trouble to anyone.

As was just mentioned, someone who receives a mistaken payment may resist giving it back on the ground that he changed position in reliance on it. "Change of position" is one of the most important defenses to a restitution claim. It is discussed more fully in the last chapter of this book, but a brief account of the idea here will be useful. In the simplest cases of the defense, you receive money from me without realizing it is a mistake, and then spend it on something that you wouldn't have bought otherwise and that you can't return. Imagine for simplicity's sake that you bought a bottle of wine and drank it. You now have a good defense against repayment of the money I accidentally sent. You may have been unjustly enriched by it, but there is no way to undo the enrichment without risk of making you worse off than you were before it happened. Even if the wine was worth every penny you spent on it, you can still object that you would not have chosen to buy it, or to pay what it was worth, if you hadn't received the mistaken payment.

Consider it this way: after a mere mistaken payment, there is no loss that necessarily has to be allocated; in other words, it is not necessary that anyone be left worse off than he was before the mishap. The defendant can simply return the money and thus restore the status quo. But your consumption of the wine changes the case in that very important respect. Now there *is* a loss to allocate between us. You will end up a little worse off than you were before the mistake was made, or I will. Since the mistake was mine, it is better that I should suffer. So your obligation to pay me back is reduced by the price of the wine, perhaps to zero.

The details of the change-of-position defense can wait until later, but seeing the idea now should help clarify the logic of recovery for mistakes in the first place. The theory of liability and the defense to it give effect to similar values and in some ways are mirror images of one another. The party who makes a mistaken payment can ordinarily claim back the money. He didn't mean to pay it, so requiring that it be returned shows respect for his autonomy and is efficient besides, as we saw earlier. But if the defendant who received the money has innocently changed position in reliance on it, now *his* autonomy is at stake as well. Making him return the money forces a kind of transaction on him that he did not want (in effect he will have bought wine with his own money that he wouldn't have bought at all if the mistake hadn't been made). Since the mistake wasn't his, the concern for the autonomy of the recipient prevails over the concern for the autonomy of the party who made the mistake. And the change-of-position defense promotes efficiency as well. It provides a measure of stability and certainty in financial affairs. If you receive money without notice that the payment is a mistake, you can go ahead and spend it without providing against the nagging worry that someone is going to claim the money back later and leave you in a bad spot. The flavor of this reasoning is familiar from elsewhere in law. We might say that once there is a loss to be allocated rather than a mere transfer to be undone, principles resembling those from tort law will assign the loss to the party whose negligence caused it.

Allocating the Risk of Mistake

Defenses to one side for now, there is one great and general limit on the initial principle of restitution for mistaken payments. The defendant's enrichment is not considered unjust, and thus the plaintiff can have no recovery, if the plaintiff assumed the risk of the mistake. Say we sign a contract in which I agree to pay you $10,000 and you agree to dismiss your lawsuit against me, which had sought $100,000 on the theory that my ox gored you. I don't think that I owe you anything, but I would rather pay the $10,000 than continue the litigation. You are sure that I owe you $100,000, but would rather take $10,000 than go to trial and risk ending up with nothing. A few weeks later I find evidence that would have won

the case for me decisively—the ox had an alibi—and now claim that you
have been unjustly enriched by my mistaken payment to you of $10,000.
The argument fails, of course, because our contract implicitly addressed
the risk that other evidence might later appear and make my case stronger. In effect our agreement allocated that risk to me, the mistaken party;
to settle the case was precisely to take that chance in return for an end
to hostilities. We might even have *said* this.[8] But whether the allocation
was explicit or merely the fair implication of our contract, the result is
the same so far as the law of restitution is concerned. These really are not
cases of mistake at all. They are cases of judgments about risk that one
party comes to regret.

Sometimes the allocation of risk when making a contested payment is
not so clear. Some prominent close cases of this type involve decisions by
insurance companies to pay uncertain claims. Thus in *Pilot Life Ins. Co.
v. Cudd*,[9] the plaintiff's husband, Cudd, was a cook on a ship that went
missing during World War II. The navy told the plaintiff that Cudd was
thought to have been lost at sea. The company that insured his life was
sent a certificate of presumptive death, and it paid Cudd's wife the policy
benefits. Then Cudd reappeared as a prisoner of war in Japan. The insurance company wanted its money back and got it, the court concluding that
"acceptance of the death of the insured as a fact was a mutual mistake of
fact equally concurred in by both parties."[10] To this case compare *New
York Life Ins. v. Chittenden & Eastmen*.[11] The insurance company issued
a policy on the life of a man named Jarvis. Jarvis vanished. The insurance
company said it would pay the policy benefits only if the beneficiaries
signed a bond that would cause the money to be paid back if Jarvis reappeared. The beneficiaries refused. The insurer decided to pay them the
benefits anyway. Then Jarvis did reappear. The company was not able to
recover its payment: "Counsel for appellant insist that this payment was
one made under a mutual mistake of fact, and that in accordance with the
well-recognized equitable principle money thus paid may be recovered
back. The rule thus invoked is not applicable, however, where under an
assumption of fact known to both parties to be doubtful there has been a
voluntary payment in extinguishment of a claim."[12]

These two insurance cases reflect the alternative ways of interpreting a
payment that its maker would not have made if better informed. It can be
viewed as a mistake or as a calculated risk. Deciding which pattern a case
follows can be difficult in practice. If the assumptions behind a payment
are not made explicit, the court has to consider whether the party mak-

ing it stood in conscious ignorance of some feature of the facts. A more recent application of the principle is furnished by *Tarrant v. Monson*.[13] A jeweler lost a customer's ring and so offered to let her choose a replacement from his collection. Later the jeweler found the original ring; the customer preferred to keep the replacement, which was more valuable; the jeweler sued and lost. His replacement of the ring was viewed not as a mistake but as the settlement of what otherwise would have been a dispute: "Since respondent at time of agreement knew that the ring might later be found, respondent bargained with conscious uncertainty and not under a mistaken belief."[14]

Whatever its difficulties in practice, the theory of this "voluntary payment" rule is easy to understand. If the parties are aware that the premise behind a payment may be wrong, the size of the payment will reflect the payor's judgment about that possibility, his willingness to risk litigation by holding out until the unknowns are cleared up, and his assessment of other such uncertainties. He is consenting to a particular allocation of risks and presumably knows better than anyone else how he values them. If a court were to undo that allocation later by awarding restitution, payors in the same position would not be able to credibly commit themselves in the future. A defendant would offer a plaintiff a certain sum to settle a case; the plaintiff would be distrustful, worrying that if facts were to later turn out the defendant's way, the defendant could claim the plaintiff had been unjustly enriched by the earlier payment. So the plaintiff would refuse the offer. The result would be litigation that neither side wanted.

The risk of a mistake also can be allocated to a claimant in subtler ways that don't involve the consciousness of risk we saw in the cases just described. In *United States v. Systron-Donner Corp.*,[15] the federal government gave Lockheed a contract to build missiles. Lockheed's price was based partly on the bid of a subcontractor, Systron-Donner. That bid turned out to include mistaken double charges. The government sought to recover its payments for those charges, claiming that the payments were based on a mistake: the government had thought that it owed the money but it "really" didn't. But it really did; the claim was rejected. There had been a mistake in a sense, but not (the court thought) in the sense relevant to restitution. Even if the risk of this error had not been the subject of any conscious awareness on either side, it was assigned to the government anyway—"as a matter of law," as the *Restatement* puts it,[16] which essentially means that the allocation serves the interests of public policy.

The result in *Systron-Donner* might seem questionable. The government had agreed to pay twice for the same thing and would not have consented to the contract if it had understood that. But the mistake made by the bidder can be viewed as just an extreme example of a familiar enough pattern in which the price a seller proposes turns out later to be higher than it would have been if he had shown more care or foresight in calculating it. More commonly this will be true because performance simply ends up being cheaper than the bidder had expected. In *Systron-Donner* it was true for a different reason: in effect the bidder had gotten its math wrong. It was like a case where you see a used car advertised for $10,000 and agree to pay that price without discussion; you then discover (somehow—perhaps the seller imprudently admits it) that the seller's calculations of the car's value had mistakenly counted the radio twice. This does not entitle you to have some of your money back. Your agreement to pay $10,000 was an assumption of the risk that the seller came to that price by mistake, or by throwing darts, or in any other way, so long as he made no misrepresentations—an important qualification. These are not cases where one side pays the other an amount that everyone can agree was not owed.

The point of the rule is that contracting parties seem best served when the prices they agree to pay and accept for things are treated as final and opaque unless stated otherwise. Bidders get no relief if they make mistakenly high price quotes that prevent them from winning contracts, or if they make other mistakes that cause their performance to be costlier than they had estimated. Buyers likewise get no relief if they agree to prices that they later learn were higher than they could have been. Parties that want different allocations of risks are free to offer (or demand) prices that are explicitly subject to reduction if it turns out that the estimates or calculations behind them were higher than necessary. Such contract provisions evidently are unusual. Part of the reason probably is that bidders and sellers already have enough incentive to avoid these sorts of mistakes; after all, they are trying to win a bidding contest or to sell a car. But more generally it would create uncertainty in commercial life if an agreed-upon price could be attacked later by showing that although neither side said anything false, one of them made a mistake in figuring out how much it should offer.

Now a final type of mistake. I sell you a horse because you seem to be an upright sort of person. Later I discover that you are a scoundrel—a felon, even—and I want to unwind the transaction, regarding it as a great error; I would not have made the sale if I had known your true character. More likely variations involve gifts made to friends or relatives who turn out to be unworthy—and this is a more interesting version of the problem, too, because one cannot just say the risk of the recipient being a scoundrel was impounded in the contract. There was no contract. It was a gift. But I still can't recover it or demand payment.[17] There is always a risk that the recipient of a gift, or the partner in any transaction, will turn out to have bad character or make the other side sorry for some other such reason. Once those qualities have been revealed, it is too hard for a court to figure out how important they really are, or were, to the unhappy party, how much investigation of them would have been worthwhile beforehand, and so forth. The answers to those questions will vary a lot from person to person and depend on testimony given in hindsight that will tend to be self-serving. If one prefers a forward-looking explanation, not letting the giver reverse the gift gives him a good incentive to check out the recipient's character in advance if he cares about it, rather than trying to undo the deal at a later point that causes more disruption and doubt.

The line between mistakes of fact and of judgment cannot be made entirely precise, and it is pliable in the face of other considerations besides the ones just mentioned. It makes a great difference if the recipient hid things from the donor or otherwise engaged in conduct the court regards as "inequitable." So to the disappointed gift giver discussed a moment ago, compare *Hutson v. Hutson*.[18] The plaintiff married a woman and made a gift of property to her before discovering to his surprise that she was still married to someone else. The gift was held to be recoverable in restitution. The misapprehension was a matter of fact that the plaintiff had no reason to doubt and that anyone would regard as important. It wasn't a judgment that might have idiosyncratic importance to him and that he should have understood himself to be making at his own risk when he entered into the marriage. Yet in *Mott v. Iossa*,[19] a plaintiff likewise was duped into marrying a woman, one Filomena, who was already married to someone else, but he was not allowed to recover gifts he made as a result—because the gifts were made not to Filomena but to her son. The court defended the result by saying that "the cause of the gift was his affection for the boy himself and not his belief that Filomena was his lawful wife." This reasoning seems wrong; there were many "causes" of the gift, and it seems highly doubtful that it would have been made if the plaintiff had known the truth about his wife. Probably a better explanation of the result is that the son was innocent and the court was loath to upset his expectations.

Benefits Other Than Money Generally

The next series of problems is best pursued through a stylized example
that can illustrate them all. Instead of mistakenly sending money, suppose
you send me an order and payment for ten thousand bricks. I mistakenly
send twelve thousand. Without counting them, you use all the bricks to
build a wall. Then I discover my mistake and demand payment for the
extra two thousand bricks. Notice first that if the mistake had become
apparent before you built the wall, it really wouldn't be a problem. You
would simply be obliged to return the extra bricks. A mistakenly delivered thing, like a mistaken payment of money, unjustly enriches whoever
receives it; if the thing can be returned, the plaintiff is entitled to that remedy—a case of "specific" restitution.[20] The brick wall is a harder case because it isn't feasible to return the goods. The bricks are *in* the wall. They
could be removed, but only at considerable cost to you. So you undoubt-
edly have been enriched by the extra bricks—let's assume they made the
wall stronger—and I have suffered a loss, but there is no way to rectify
the situation cleanly. And let us assume that whatever contract we had did
not speak to this possibility.

The basic problem would be similar if, instead of sending you extra
bricks, I were to mistakenly plow your field, thinking it belongs to someone else who had hired me. In either case the benefit cannot feasibly
be returned, and in either case it will probably be hard to say what you
should pay for it. The law deals with problems of this kind by applying two
fundamental principles.

The first is that recovery in restitution is measured by the defendant's
provable gain (the benefit he received from the extra bricks) and not by
the plaintiff's loss (probably the cost of the bricks).[21] Notice that the plaintiff's loss usually will be greater than the defendant's gain; after all, the defendant didn't want, or at least did not ask for, whatever the plaintiff sent.
If the plaintiff's loss is *smaller*—as in the rare case where a mistaken improvement is made that is worth a great deal to the recipient of it—then
the defendant can just pay those costs. In other words, the measure of recovery is the *lesser* of the costs to the plaintiff or the gain to the defendant.[22] (We are speaking now of the rules when the defendant is innocent.
The principle just shown is reversed when the defendant is a wrongdoer,
as we will see in the chapter on takings.)

This "whichever is less" principle didn't make a difference in the earlier cases where one side paid too much to the other. If you mistakenly send me a hundred dollars, my gain and your loss are the same, so it doesn't matter which way we look at it. But the difference in perspective can matter a lot when anything other than money is involved and can't be returned. We are then likely to find a discrepancy between the value the two sides put on whatever changed hands. The "whichever is less" approach protects the autonomy of the innocent defendant and ensures that the mistaken party does not benefit by forcing a transaction on the other.

The second major principle relates to that final point. If the defendant—that is, the recipient of the benefit—has done nothing wrong, a restitution claim cannot be used to make him any worse off than he was before the mistake.[23] He cannot be made poorer and should not have a forced exchange imposed on him; in other words, he shouldn't be made to buy things that we are not sure he otherwise would have bought—not even if making him a little worse off in these ways would make the plaintiff much better off, or be simpler for the courts, or create rough justice. This principle has great practical importance because it often rules out solutions to a case that might otherwise seem tempting. (Some of those solutions are so tempting that the rule gets relaxed slightly. We will see an example soon.)

Though the law is very protective of the innocent defendant, it takes a quite different attitude toward the defendant who bears some blame for the mistake, either because he caused it or because he knew it was happening but said nothing.[24] In that case he will have to bear a share of the loss that reflects his share of fault for it. "Loss" here means any losses the plaintiff still may have after collecting whatever gains he can prove the defendant had from the mistake. For example, if I mistakenly provide you with $1,000 worth of bricks (or a plowed field at a cost of $1,000, etc.) and the provable benefit to you is $600, you can be made to pay me the $600. That still leaves a loss of $400 that must be apportioned somehow. It will be allocated to me (the maker of the mistake) if you are innocent. I simply won't collect it. But you will share liability for the $400, or pay all of it, if responsibility for the mistake was partly or wholly yours, as in a case where you overlooked obvious early hints that it was happening, or did worse. Depending on the extent of a defendant's blameworthiness, he may be required to go further and disgorge other gains from the transaction, but this point can wait until the chapter on monetary remedies.

Let us move from those first two principles to the problem of valuation. We just spoke of the "provable" benefit to the defendant. Provable

benefit is the limit of the plaintiff's recovery of a mistaken transfer, and
if the size of the benefit to the defendant cannot be proven, the plaintiff
generally cannot recover anything at all.[25] But how is that proof to be
made? Presumably the bricks were worth *something*. You used them, and
the wall was stronger as a result. But since you had not asked for them,
we can't assume that they were worth their market price to you. The obvious inference is that they weren't; if they had been worth their market
value to you (or a little more), you likely would have asked to buy them,
which you didn't. It would be different, too, if you asked for the bricks
or the plowing job but we never settled the price. The law will then typically assume that you were prepared to pay market value for what you
received—the measure known as "quantum meruit." But that assumption
doesn't make sense, and so this theory is generally off-limits, when the defendant received an unrequested benefit.

(This discussion just made reference to "quantum meruit"—literally,
"as much as he deserved." That is a slippery phrase in law. It can refer to
either of two things: [a] A party's recovery on an implied contract; the
court assumes the recipient meant to pay the market value of whatever
he had asked for. [b] A party's recovery in restitution when there is no
enforceable contract between the two sides but one has conferred benefits on the other. The performing party, again, sometimes may collect the
market value of those benefits. In a case of an innocent defendant who received unrequested benefits, however, recovery in quantum meruit is not
available in either sense.)

So forget the market value of the bricks. What about the market value
of the wall? Suppose the wall were appraised and its value were found to
be $100 greater because of the added strength provided by those extra
bricks. Couldn't you then be required to pay me $100? No, because that
appraisal only shows how much the market values the stronger wall. It
doesn't show how much *you* value it, or whether you value it at all. True,
the appraisal might show that if you ever sell the wall, it will fetch $100
more than it otherwise would have. But notice that there are problems
here not only of valuation but of liquidity. The money value of the thing
cannot be realized without selling it, and a forced sale is not generally an
option allowed by the second principle outlined above. Ordering you to
pay $100 would force a transaction on you—the purchase of the bricks—
that we have no reason to think you wanted to make.

With market value unavailable for use, there remain a few other ways
to show that the recipient valued an unrequested benefit at some par-

ticular amount. First, sometimes it can be shown that the plaintiff's mistake saved the defendant an expense he otherwise would have incurred. That approach seems unlikely to help in the case of the bricks, but it works if my mistaken plowing of your field allows you to cancel similar work you had ordered by someone else. A related approach is to show that the benefit supplied by the plaintiff was something the defendant had offered to pay for on this or on other occasions, thus revealing his valuation of it. So suppose it were shown that after you originally ordered the ten thousand bricks from me, you offered to buy another two thousand for $100. I refused, saying that I would accept no less than $200—but then I mistakenly sent them anyway. Your offer to pay $100 for those two thousand additional bricks is evidence that you value them at least that much and is a good basis for requiring you to pay me $100 now.

These principles are illustrated well by *Mich. Cent. R. Co. v. State*.[26] A railroad mistakenly delivered to a prison a carload of coal that had been meant for another buyer. The prison, accustomed to receiving the same sort of coal on cars from the same railroad, accepted the shipment and burned it before the mistake was discovered. The railroad sought recovery in restitution in the amount of $6.85 per ton, which was the market value of the coal. That was not allowed; for while it was clear that the prison needed coal, there was no proof that it valued the coal at its market price when delivered (indeed, there was evidence that it did not). But the prison did have its own long-term contract to receive the same type of coal at $3.40 per ton, and this provided a basis for recovery on either of the principles put forward a moment ago. The contract showed how much the prison valued coal, and it showed what expense the prison had been spared by the railroad's mistake. So the railroad collected $3.40 per ton, a sum that plainly did not cover its losses but that did reflect the maximum provable value of the benefit to the prison.

Sometimes the benefit to the defendant will later be reduced to cash because he will choose to sell whatever the plaintiff gave him (or he will sell some larger thing in which the plaintiff's benefit was mixed). The defendant can then be made to give the plaintiff a share of the money, which serves as a solvent of their difficulties. The brick wall and mistaken plowing may be less helpful as examples than a case of mistaken improvements that result in a long-lasting benefit to the property, such as a re-roofing job that I was supposed to perform for someone down the street but mistakenly did for you instead. If you were then to *voluntarily* sell the house, and an appraisal showed that the sale price was $5,000 greater because of my mistaken contribution, I would have a good claim to that amount (so long as it cost me at least $5,000 to put on the roof).[27]

Suppose, finally, that you never offered to pay me anything for the extra bricks and that you never sell the wall—what then? You probably owe me nothing. My claim against you fails because there is no way to prove how much you valued the extra bricks or that you valued them at all. And requiring you to give them back would make you worse off than you were before the mistake was made, since you would have to build the wall twice. Sometimes that is the result in a case of mistake. The plaintiff eats it.

The logic just pursued represents an orthodox view of restitution law and follows the *Restatement*, but courts do not always adhere to it rigorously. When the stakes of a case are modest, it is easy to say that a plaintiff who mistakenly confers a benefit on the defendant should collect nothing if the value of the benefit cannot be specifically proven. But as the stakes increase, the equities of a case can put pressure on the orthodox logic. If it becomes evident that the benefit conferred on the defendant was large, courts are reluctant to turn away the plaintiff with no recovery, even if the size of the benefit is hard to pin down. This tendency emerges most clearly when the unrequested benefit consists not of simple goods or services but of improvements to real property. Let us turn to them.

Mistaken Improvements to Property

As just noted, large-scale improvements are of particular theoretical interest because the equities of them put pressure on the usual principles of restitution and sometimes cause them to buckle a bit. We again can start with stylized facts. A builder mistakenly erects a house on someone else's vacant lot. He was confused about which lot he owned, or he bought the lot from someone he mistakenly thought had authority to sell but didn't, or he had a deed but the deed was defective. The owner of the lot discovers this, moves into the new house, and posts a guard dog outside to prevent the builder from trespassing. The builder brings a restitution claim against the owner. What is the result?

Under the principles seen so far, the outlook for the builder seems grim. Assume the owner hadn't previously planned to build a house on his property but has no plans to sell the house now that it exists. On those facts it will likely be impossible to prove how much the owner values the house. The fact that he chooses to live there is interesting and might suggest that he should at least pay some sort of amount for the pleasure—maybe something like its rental value each month. But this would force a transaction on him that he might not have wanted. What if he only likes living in the house because it is free? Of course the builder is likely to be allowed whatever specific restitution he can get without violating our second principle shown earlier (that the defendant should not be made any worse off by the plaintiff's error): if the house can be removed without damaging the owner's land, the builder will probably be allowed to come take it away.[28] (Sneaking onto the property to destroy the improvement is a very different thing and may result in an award of damages against the destroyer.)[29] But often it will not be movable and the builder will be able to salvage only a bit of his work. So he seems likely to receive nothing or close to it. If the builder is entitled to demolish and remove the house, the result might be a negotiation in which he agrees not to do that in return for some small amount—anything more than what the builder would net from the wreckage after he carts it away.

This analysis is, again, what would follow from the simple principles introduced earlier. The result—a blundering builder puts up a house, perhaps at enormous cost, and receives nothing in return—is very harsh, and intolerably harsh in the view of most courts today. Not that the courts set rules about when the harshness becomes too much to bear; they just look at each case and try to come up with solutions that seem reasonable based on all the facts, constrained only by the idea that the remedy must not impose undue prejudice on the recipient[30]—a standard that provides much flexibility and a long menu of solutions to consider. Those possible solutions include forcing an owner to choose between buying the house from the builder or selling the underlying land to him, in either case at a market rate.[31] Or the court can give the builder an equitable lien on the house, possibly in a conditional form that allows the value of the improvement to be collected from rental payments produced by the property or by a later sale of it.[32] Or the court can order a simple payment of the value of the house or other improvements to the builder.[33] Or it can always follow the older rules and just let the builder remove whatever parts of the house he can carry away, with nothing more.[34]

All these options are available in principle. Whether a court is willing to use them in practice will depend on the equities of the situation. First, of course, there is the simple question of good faith. The builder who knew he was outside his rights—an unusual character, but not unheard of—will be out of luck entirely[35] (he probably does not belong in this chapter, since strictly speaking he did not commit a mistake). Likewise, the owner who knew of the builder's mistake but kept silent will not be heard to complain later when the builder is granted liberal relief.[36] Then come related matters of negligence. We saw earlier that a claimant's negligence usually is not relevant to whether a defendant is found to have been unjustly enriched; it becomes very relevant, however, at the remedial stage of a case. A builder who was negligent about where to build will be entitled to less solicitude than one who did all that could be asked but was the victim of a bad surveyor.[37] The general idea from an economic standpoint is to preserve good incentives by denying some benefits to anyone who had a chance to avoid the fiasco but didn't.

Finally, a court choosing a remedy will be interested in the relationships between the parties and the property at stake. If an innocent owner lives on the land that was mistakenly improved, the costs of a forced sale are at their highest. No court will oust him. At the other end of the spectrum, where unoccupied land is held just for the sake of investment, a court is more likely to be creative in fashioning relief. The old example was wooded property on the frontier. A more modern version is *Voss v. Forgue*.[38] The parties owned different plots in a subdivision that was under construction. One of them mistakenly put up a house on the square of land owned by the other. After finding that the two squares of property had the same value and no intrinsic advantages relative to one another, the court simply ordered the parties to trade lots. The remedy didn't really cost anybody anything, and it probably increased the overall value in the situation because the house the builder had created was no doubt more valuable to him than it was to the owner of the underlying land (who presumably had a different design of his own in mind). And the solution still leaves the mistaken builder with an ample incentive to be careful, since he can't count on being so lucky next time: the law's usual presumption is that every parcel of land is unique, meaning the owner attaches special value to whichever one he has, so a forced trade of the kind used in *Voss* is rarely going to be an attractive remedy.

The shift just described, from clear rules (don't force a transaction on the owner) to standards that are less protective of the innocent recipient (just don't inflict undue prejudice on him), also reflects a shift in time. Common-law courts in the nineteenth century usually stuck to simple rules; in the settings we are examining here, those simple rules generally left mistaken builders without much recourse. That pattern was reversed by legislatures in almost every state, which passed various sorts of "better-ment acts" that give broader rights to mistaken builders who have acted in good faith, often including the right to force a sale on the landowner or collect the market value of the improvements. The new rules reflected sensitivity to the position of builders on the frontier, who were adding a lot of value to empty land, and for whom exact information about land boundaries was not as easy to come by as it is today. Those statutes are still the starting place for analysis of any such case now. They tend to be limited in scope and to coexist with the state's common law, but they still have their effect.[39] And in any event the courts have gradually followed suit on their own.

The result in this area bears some resemblance to the tort rules gov-erning liability for encroachment. If I mistakenly build a house that ex-tends a foot onto your property, there is no possible claim that I have en-riched you, unjustly or otherwise. Instead you have a tort claim against me for trespass and can ask a court to order the house removed. That re-quest typically will be granted; removal is the usual rule in a case of en-croachment.[40] But most courts are willing to make exceptions when the builder acted in good faith and the equities are very lopsided, as when a whole house would have to be torn down because it encroaches just a little. The mistaken builder may then be allowed to just make a payment to the neighbor for the value of the property—a forced transaction.[41] The resemblance to restitution law in cases of mistaken improvement is evi-dent. In both cases a formal rule works best most of the time, and in both cases the formal rule is relaxed when its application would work great hardship and the courts are satisfied that the transgression was innocent. In most of these cases the courts may just find the equities unbearable. It bothers them to see a massive punishment befall a party as the result of a relatively minor act of negligence. But that reluctance also has the eco-nomic basis mentioned earlier. It relieves parties of an incentive to over-spend on precautions to prevent small invasions of the rights of others.

Mistaken improvements can be made to chattels as well as to land. The largest set of cases in this branch of the law involves automobiles. A thief steals your car and resells it to an innocent buyer. The buyer rebuilds the engine and replaces the tires—and then you appear and demand the return of the car. Your claim to the car cannot be questioned. It is yours; the thief acquired no title to it, and so could pass none to the buyer. But the buyer still might assert a restitution claim against you, for again he is as much a mistaken improver as the builder who puts a house on the wrong lot. Here as there, the buyer will be allowed specific restitution to the extent it can be easily made. In this case that means he can take back the new tires he added, since they can be removed simply enough (but he also has to put back the old ones).[42] As for rebuilding the engine, his only hope for compensation is probably a finding that you had already commissioned similar work when the car was stolen, for then there is evidence that you valued it and by how much. Otherwise the buyer (or more typically the repair shop) is just another plaintiff who, by rebuilding the engine, made a mistaken but irreversible transfer of unknown value to the defendant—in which case the improver ordinarily loses.

So far this is just like the case of the brick wall, the plowed field, or any other mistakenly conferred benefit. When does it become parallel to the mistaken construction of a house—in other words, a case where the equities require some flexibility in the application of basic principles? The answer is illustrated by *Ochoa v. Rogers*.[43] Ochoa's car was stolen and sold at an auction to one Rogers, by which time it was a wreck with no top, no tires, an engine that had been removed, and so forth; as the court put it, what Rogers bought "was no longer an automobile, but a pile of broken and dismantled parts of what was once Ochoa's car." Rogers used the parts to build a delivery truck. A year later, Ochoa saw the truck Rogers had built and recognized the hood and radiator cover as his own. He demanded the truck. Rogers resisted on the ground that he had contributed most of its value. Notice the analogy to the case where a developer builds a house on a vacant lot and thus may be responsible for most of the lot's value in the end. Courts often balk at throwing the developer out of court on those facts, and the court balked in the case of the rebuilt car as well. Rogers was held entitled to it by the doctrine of accession—but he still had to pay the plaintiff the scrap value that the car had when he first bought it. That is what the remains would have been worth to Ochoa if he had come upon the wreck himself before Rogers went to work. It is analogous to letting the builder of the mistakenly placed house force the owner of the underlying land to sell it to him.

Mistaken Payment of Another's Debt or Performance of Another's Obligation

Suppose I mistakenly pay a debt that you owe. Maybe it is a tax bill that I thought was mine but actually is yours; the town wrongfully added some

of your property to my assessment. Or an insurance company pays someone for damage done by its insured, but then discovers that the insured's
policy did not cover the incident. Those situations are structurally the
same. One person has paid money that was owed by another. Such cases
usually produce restitution claims that really are no different from the
other cases of mistaken payment discussed already. You have been unjustly enriched to the extent that I paid off your obligations and saved you
what would have been a necessary expense. This usually means that you
now owe the money to me instead of to the original creditor. I become
subrogated to the creditor's rights. (That term has no important practical implications here, but it will later.)[44] Since our concern is with unjust
enrichment, the amount that I mistakenly paid on your behalf is not the
important point. What matters is the amount that you avoided paying because of what I did. These might be different amounts. Imagine, for example, that since I paid your tax bill, you are now unable to deduct your
payment of it (because you made no such payment) from your federal income taxes. That fact reduces the net benefit to you, and it consequently
reduces the amount that you owe to me.[45] Or I paid the full bill for whatever it was, but you would have been able to get a discount because you
are a regular customer. The lesser amount that you avoided paying is all
that I can collect from you.

The same sort of restitution claim arises if I mistakenly pay off a lien
on your property. You sell me property encumbered by a mortgage, I pay
off the mortgage, and then it turns out that your sale of the property to me
was invalid. I have a claim against you for the enrichment you received
when I paid off the lien, and your defenses are the same as they would
be if you were confronted by the original lienholder.[46] Other complications may arise, as usual, when we stop talking about mistaken payments
of money and start considering nonreturnable benefits that I provide to
others but that should have been provided by you. If I perform a job that
you were obliged to do (by contract or law), you owe me, of course—not
the amount I spent, but the amount you saved by not having to do the job
yourself, which again may be something less.

So suppose that, as in *Sykeston Township v. Wells County*,[47] a township and county both think the township is responsible for putting gravel
on a road. The township does so. Then the parties discover that the law
is otherwise: putting down the gravel was the county's job. The township
is entitled to restitution. But since the case did not involve a mistaken
payment of money, the measure of recovery would have to account for

the difference between what the benefit cost the plaintiff and what it was worth to the defendant. Suppose the county could have done the paving job more cheaply than the township. If so, that fact will reduce the township's recovery. It is entitled to collect the amount it spent laying down the gravel or the amount the county would have needed to get it done— whichever is less.[48]

The policy behind all of these applications is generally the same. Letting the mistaken performer of another's obligation recover "whichever is less" (what he paid or the amount he saved the party who should have done it) gently deters these mistakes, since the maker of them risks being undercompensated for his costs. And it probably resembles at least roughly the outcome the parties would have reached by contract if they had seen the risk of such a situation coming. To be more precise, if one imagines the range of terms that the parties might have agreed to, the law chooses the set of terms most favorable to the party who was supposed to pay the obligation. He pays whatever amount he was saved, but not a penny more. In effect he had the transaction foisted on him by the party who performed his obligation by mistake. That party should not be able to do any better by his error than he might have done if he had proceeded (as we would generally like him to have done) by an open negotiation in which he offered to pay the bill or do the work for the other side and the parties finally consented to terms that we know made them both better off.

The mistaken payment of an obligation owed by someone else can raise a special difficulty. I mistakenly pay X the money that you owed him—or that you seemed to owe him; but actually you *deny* owing him the money. And maybe you have a good argument. Perhaps I inadvertently paid your tax bill, and now you tell me that you thought the bill was erroneous and that you had planned to contest it. Do you owe me the full amount that I paid? Not necessarily. You are free to argue that the tax bill was wrong.[49] I, in turn, will argue that the bill was valid. It might seem odd that I end up arguing the government's position in the lawsuit between us, but that is what can happen when one party pays an obligation owed by another. To state the point more generally, the beneficiary of a mistaken payment to a creditor has all the same defenses against the plaintiff that he would have had against the creditor who was mistakenly paid. And now suppose those defenses succeed, so you don't have to repay me. Do *I* now have a claim against the town for reimbursement? So it might seem. After all, I paid money to the town that a court has said was not due. But the town fairly can claim that it hasn't had its own day in court yet. It can't be bound by the finding in my lawsuit against you, because it did not participate—a necessary condition of collateral estoppel.[50] So I will have to bring a fresh lawsuit against the town, arguing that the tax bill it sent you was wrong—after I just finished, in my suit against you, arguing that the bill was right. What fun!

Temporal Mistakes: Expectations of Ownership

The mistakes examined so far have been of a straightforward variety. Someone made a payment or improvement that he would not have made if he had understood the facts. We now look at a couple of other situations that also can be classified as mistakes in a less conventional sense: benefits conferred by people who had mistaken expectations about what was to come next.

We have talked about gradations of good faith and negligence that may bear on the remedy in a restitution case. On occasion those considerations are powerful enough to affect the basic finding of liability. An important category of case like this involves a frustrated expectation of ownership.[51] The claimant buys a piece of land, makes improvements on it, and then the original sale of the land to him is unexpectedly rescinded or the claimant is otherwise ousted from the property. Courts are quite sensitive in these cases to the reasonableness of each side's behavior. The outcome depends on just *why* the sale was reversed. Suppose I bought the piece of land from you, and you later sued to rescind because you lacked capacity to make the deal;[52] or it turned out that the land did not match the deed description you gave me, and so I was the one who sued to rescind;[53] or we shared a misunderstanding about the property's suitability for the purpose I had in mind, a misunderstanding so fundamental that a court declares our contract void on account of mutual mistake.[54] In any of these situations the contract may be rescinded. And in any of them I have a solid argument for recovery of the value that I added to the property that is now being returned to you. (You may well have a claim of your own that partly offsets mine—say, for the rental value of the property during the time I enjoyed it.) But my claim fails if I made the improvements to the property while at the same time failing to make the required payments on it, for in that case any expectation of future ownership I had was not reasonable. The allocation of the loss follows the parties' fault, and thus their capacities (or the capacities of others situated the same way) to prevent similar losses next time.

The argument for recovery is particularly easy to make when I went forward with improvements to the property on the basis of a promise you made. Maybe you assured me that the sale would go through or that I would be allowed to stay. In that case a claim for restitution and a claim based on estoppel may well produce the same result.[55] I have no claim if my expectation was not so reasonable, as when I buy property at a judicial sale and begin to improve it despite knowing that the original owner of the land may be able to redeem it—that is, get it back—upon payment of his taxes.[56] If he does, then my decision to improve the property will be viewed as a calculated risk similar to an insurance company's decision to pay a claim that it knows is questionable. There is no restitution for the company or for me when our gambles turn out badly.

Temporal Mistakes: Unmarried Cohabitants

The cases just discussed involved "mistakes" about what the future would hold. A similar logic is one way to understand restitution claims between unmarried former cohabitants—couples who were engaged but then called off the marriage, for example, or couples who lived as though they were married without ever tying the knot,[57] or same-sex partners who lived together in a state that would not recognize their marriage and then separated.[58] Sometimes one party to such an arrangement will sue the other to recover for benefits conferred while they were together. Perhaps one of them always paid the rent during the relationship, or one paid the other's tuition expenses, or one spent money to improve the house where they lived,[59] which increased its resale value later on. Or in an extreme case one of them might simply have deeded property to the other.[60] In any of these cases the parties might separate, with a claim for restitution then made by the party who paid against the party who did not.

These cases are an awkward fit to usual principles of restitution law because at the time the payments are made they typically are meant to be gratuitous. Neither side expected them to ever create any legal obligations. In most other settings, as when similar arrangements occur between family members or friends, this would spoil any possible restitution claim made later. The payments would just be considered either gifts or subjects of implied contracts. There would be no room between those options to squeeze in a restitution claim, because there would be nothing to excuse the claimant's failure to make a contract if he wanted legal obligations to arise from his payments. But the law of restitution handles unmarried cohabitants a little differently. It often lets the claimant collect if the benefits can be clearly proven and quantified.[61]

The reason the law sometimes honors these claims can be viewed as analogous to its reasons for allowing recovery in cases where a party improves property with the reasonable expectation that he owns it, or soon will, but turns out to be mistaken. The unmarried cohabitants in a restitution case likewise had an expectation that their lives would continue in a certain way. In some of these cases one might question how reasonable that expectation really was, but let that point pass. The parties committed a temporal mistake. Nobody is likely to blame them for failing to make a contract for the benefits involved, because it was reasonable for them to suppose that no contract was needed. Enrichment that seemed just at the time it occurred thus comes to seem unjust in retrospect.

Principles of restitution law will not apply to cases like this if the state has chosen to handle such disputes altogether differently, as by adopting the American Law Institute's *Principles of the Law of Family Dissolution*. That framework provides its own set of rules for claims between people who lived together without being married. If the state has not gone that route, courts hearing restitution claims still are reluctant to turn themselves into family courts by conducting a full accounting of all the ways in which one party benefited the other during a relationship. People who live together exchange benefits informally all the time; thus claims based on restitution for cooking and other such domestic services usually do not succeed, because they are viewed as the sorts of benefits that cohabitants routinely provide to each other as in-kind compensation.[62] In cases where courts find that restitution law does apply, the facts and equities vary widely. Courts exercise much flexibility in meeting them, and this makes it hard to generalize much about the results one can expect.

The most common case of successful recovery for unjust enrichment involves a clear trade of benefits that never gets completed or is lopsided in some other obvious way. Suppose a claimant pays $100,000 in tuition bills so that the defendant can go to medical school while they are living together. They expect that the defendant will go on to a lucrative career as a doctor and support them both in high style. And the defendant does begin a lucrative career, but then the parties end their relationship. Now what? Assuming liability for restitution is established, the claimant might

seek a share of the income that the medical degree will entitle the claimant's former partner to earn. After all, both parties had expected those
earnings to be enjoyed by both of them. Wouldn't allowing the graduate
to keep all the earnings now amount to unjust enrichment? Probably not;
the *Restatement* would limit recovery, in cases of this type that succeed,
to the actual amount spent on tuition.[63] The larger amount the claimant
seeks—not just compensation for the services rendered, but a piece of
their "traceable product"—is commonly awarded only against defendants who are guilty of wrongdoing.[64] The defendant who went to medical
school and then broke off the relationship is regarded as the beneficiary
of a noncontractual transfer, and perhaps the beneficiary of a mistake, but
not as a wrongdoer (at least not without more facts).[65] The wrongdoer—
especially the conscious wrongdoer—needs a stronger deterrent, and gets
it in the form of a more generous measure of his enrichment. The difference between these two types of recovery comes up a lot in restitution law
and is considered in the chapter on monetary remedies.

CHAPTER THREE

Conferrings

In a case of mistake, a benefit moves from one person to another without either party intending it. A *conferring* differs because the claimant has a different state of mind. He often confers the benefit intentionally, usually confers it knowingly, and in any event he would not have acted differently if he had known that the benefit would land where it did. Sometimes this difference in state of mind leads to different outcomes, with recovery made more difficult. If you mistakenly rake my leaves, you can recover from me in restitution if you can prove that your work saved me an expense that I otherwise would have been sure to incur. (Maybe I was able to cancel a visit by my usual leaf raker. In that case you are entitled to your usual rate or his usual rate—whichever is less.) But if you *deliberately* rake my leaves without asking, you cannot collect anything no matter how clear it may be that you saved me an expense. The law will not reward a claimant who, in conferring a benefit, knowingly and without excuse bypassed the chance to make a contract.

We say "without excuse" because sometimes the law *does* allow a claimant to collect for a benefit deliberately or knowingly conferred on another without a contract. Here, as with recovery for benefits transferred by mistake, there are easy cases for recovery and hard ones, and in some respects they are the same here as they were there. If the unearned benefit conferred on the defendant takes the form of cash or other property that can easily be returned to the claimant, then it often does have to be returned, as we will see; this principle makes such minor demands on a defendant that it generally holds whether the benefit was conferred by mistake or through some deliberate act. The difficult cases are more common—those where the claimant has conferred a service on the defendant or discharged a debt for him, in either case bestowing a benefit that cannot be returned. The defendant either will get to keep a benefit for nothing or will have to buy something he did not bargain for. This dilemma is similar to the one created by the mistaken improvements discussed in the previous chapter. The claimant's right to collect generally depends on two showings: that he had a good reason for conferring the benefit on the defendant without making a contract, and that the benefit to the defendant has a clearly ascertainable value.

The principles just sketched can be explained as matters of autonomy that are now familiar. As in the previous chapter, the law carefully protects the right of a party to say no when giving him a chance to say it is feasible. But when viewed from an economic standpoint, the challenge presented by a deliberately conferred benefit is distinctive. The problem typically is that when the plaintiff acts for his own good, he creates external benefits—that is, additional benefits for others that he does not fully enjoy himself. Those benefits may well have social value. Still, if the plaintiff could have made a contract with the beneficiaries but did not, he should not be allowed to collect from them; we want to force him to make that contract, since it will produce a cheaper and more accurate assessment of the size of the benefit (and a surer sense of whether the benefit was wanted, all things considered) than a lawsuit would. On the other hand, if making a contract would have been expensive or impossible, and there is no doubt that the plaintiff's acts did produce benefits, then the law needs to do something to let the producer of the benefits "internalize" them—that is, to benefit from them himself—so that he and others like him will go on producing them in the future. In effect the law allows a restitution claim to serve as a kind of substitute for the contract that the parties could not feasibly make, and thus prevents the defendant from free riding on the plaintiff's labors.

Money Benefits Deliberately Conferred

If I deliberately do something that happens to generate money for you, it might seem sensible enough, and efficient enough, for you to give the money to me. Handing over cash isn't too much trouble, and you didn't do anything to earn it (or if you did have a good right to some of it, you can just give back the rest). But we should start by asking how such a situation would arise in the first place. *Mistaken* payments are easy enough to understand; anyone can send a check to the wrong place or make a bookkeeping blunder. But what could I possibly do on purpose that would cause checks to arrive at your house and then be claimed by me? The list of such situations is short. The most notable of them occurs when a claimant brings a lawsuit that generates a cash recovery for others as well as for himself—a so-called common fund from which the claimant demands some payment for his labors.

Suppose, for example, that I sue the state where I live, claiming it collected a tax that was illegal in some way. (My suit might be a class action, but not necessarily.) I win the case or settle it favorably; the state is found to have unlawfully collected a big pot of money from its taxpayers, including me. The court might order that the pot be distributed in the form of refunds to everyone who paid the bad tax. But the court also might order that some reasonable share of the pot be set aside to compensate me and my lawyer for the costs of bringing the suit.[1] That order would be a form of restitution. Notice how the basic elements of recovery are satisfied. First, I had a good excuse for not making contracts with everyone who benefited from the suit. Getting consent from all of them would likely have been impossible. Second, it is obvious that they did benefit and to what extent: they all are receiving cash, which everybody likes, and after paying me they still will have more than they did before I brought the suit. A possible objection to recovery is that my action preempted a suit by others that would have produced even better results. If not, though, the main hard question will involve the fee my lawyer should get. Unless resolved by statute, that issue will be resolved by judicial discretion without much help from the law of restitution.[2]

The case just described is a classic and straightforward one for recovery from a common fund. It also illustrates the economics behind this corner of restitution doctrine. By bringing the lawsuit I created an external benefit. The incentives to bring such suits will not be as large as they should be unless I end up with all of my costs covered (as well as my share of the benefits as a class member). Ideally I would have solved this problem by making a contract with all the other taxpayers in which they agreed to cover my fees if I collected benefits for them as well as for me. But the transaction costs involved in getting all the beneficiaries to agree to this in advance are too high, so the law provides a substitute by means of a claim in restitution.

More interesting problems arise when one or two of the reassuring features of the case just shown are relaxed or absent. If the number of other beneficiaries is small, for example, the claimant might be faulted for not seeking a contract with them after all. Still, this problem can usually be overcome by simply giving those other parties a way to opt out of the arrangement in advance, and by inferring their consent to pay reasonable fees if they don't. The harder cases are those where the beneficiaries neither consent to support the claimant's efforts nor repudiate the benefits that result from them. Thus in *Felton v. Finley*,[3] two nephews of one Coleman hired a lawyer to contest Coleman's will. The nephews had other relatives who stood to benefit from the lawyer's efforts but who declined to sign contracts authorizing the lawyer's work; their sister said, "What you boys do is your business, but I will have nothing to do with it." The lawyer's efforts were successful, and the nephews and their relatives all received money as a result. The lawyer sought to collect from the relatives who hadn't signed contracts. The court refused to allow it.[4]

The result in *Felton* might seem to be bad policy. One judge registered this objection, which has the ring of rough justice about it: "The acceptance and receipt by appellants of their share of their enhanced inheritance were entirely voluntary, because there is no law which required them to accept the greater amount; they could have taken only the $500.00 which the will initially gave them and refused the additional sum. Whatever scruples or feelings they had about not signing contracts, taking a dead man's money or interfering with his will, had thus evidently disappeared when the money was made available to them, even though without their active participation."[5] In other words, the sister can be viewed as free riding on the efforts of others. Whatever she was or wasn't thinking, look ahead to other cases like this. If it is clear to the sister (or future parties in her position) that her brothers are going to litigate the will no matter what she does, and she knows she will collect a share of the winnings whether or not she contributes to the effort, why should she agree to pay anything? ("Familial obligation" evidently is not a satisfactory answer.) And knowing this, perhaps the brothers would like to be in the sister's position—so in a future case they might *all* wait for others to take action, with the result that no one does anything.

But the majority's position in *Felton* has much sense in its favor as well. The sister's objection to hiring the lawyer was entitled to respect, whether it was based on a distaste for litigation or a judgment that the expected likelihood of the suit being worthwhile was low. To again put the point in economic terms, only a contract provides complete assurance that the parties all view the benefits of hiring the lawyer as greater than the costs. The sister might reasonably have felt that she would be happy to have any money she was due but didn't consider the lawsuit a good gamble. Or she might have objected to the size of the contingency fee the lawyer had arranged for himself: a rather startling 50 percent of any recovery. And the lawyer, for his part, was not obliged to get involved in the first place unless he was satisfied with the compensation that his actual clients had agreed to pay him. Evidently he was.

The dilemma presented by *Felton* epitomizes the conflicting policies that are the basic problem of this chapter. Courts resolve it, in the part of the world *Felton* represents, by bearing down hard on the particular facts of each case to see which policy predominates. Assume again that I hire a lawyer to contest a will and you stand to benefit from his labors. If you know this but never say anything one way or the other about getting involved, I probably will be able to claim some of your share of the winnings to contribute to payment of my attorney's fees.[6] The court reasonably infers your consent to pay from your silence. But if I could have notified you of the litigation yet didn't,[7] then you can't be held liable after all for any of the costs—and you still get your share under the will. This time consent cannot be inferred, and I can be faulted for not trying to proceed by contract when it would have been feasible.

There are other constraints on common-fund recovery. The interests of the claimant and the other beneficiaries have to be closely aligned. Suppose we both are shareholders in a corporation. I bring a suit against the corporation that challenges a bad practice by its directors. I win my suit, and this saves the corporation a lot of money. A bit of that money can be diverted to me to cover my expenses of suit. The rules governing such recovery are likely to be settled now by statute, but otherwise they can still be viewed as matters for the law of restitution.[8] From that perspective we would say the "common fund" is the corporation itself, the value of which has been preserved or increased by my efforts. The restitution obtained comes, in effect, from you and the other shareholders. So far, so good— but now notice that my victory might also be good news for the corporation's creditors. Maybe some of them were nervous about getting paid, but now the corporation can cover its debts with no trouble. Yet I can't collect any restitution from them. Recovery from a common fund is limited to cases where the claimant and the beneficiaries all have parallel interests in the pot that has been recovered, probably because the benefits to other, less similar parties too quickly become speculative.

The Problem of Nonmoney Benefits in General

The more common sort of "conferring" does not bestow cash on the defendant that he can hand over to the claimant painlessly. Instead the claimant has performed a service that cannot be returned or has paid an obligation that was rightfully the defendant's in whole or in part. The question then becomes whether the defendant will keep those benefits for free or be forced to pay the claimant for something he did not request. Since neither alternative seems very fair on its face, courts decide which result is better by using principles that are tailored to more specific patterns in the cases. We can make a few useful generalizations about the results. As noted earlier, recovery in restitution for conferring a benefit on a defendant generally requires two things: a good excuse for not making a contract and proof that the defendant valued the benefit at a certain amount. The first criterion—the good excuse—is satisfied in this setting by showing either that an emergency made it impractical to seek a contract or that the claimant acted reasonably to protect his own interests or the interests of others regardless of the defendant's wishes or willingness to agree to anything. The other criterion—certainty of value—is generally satisfied either by showing that the benefit conferred on the defendant was something everyone obviously values (having one's life or property saved from destruction, though even this is not foolproof) or by showing that the claimant saved the defendant an expense that he would or should have been obliged to pay later to someone else anyway.

We will walk through some situations where these criteria are met, but it will be instructive to start with cases where they aren't. The most prominent set of "near miss" cases, where a restitution claim of this sort might seem attractive but fails, arises when the claimant takes an action to benefit himself that also happens to create a benefit for someone else. A classic instance is *Ulmer v. Farnsworth*.[9] Ulmer and Farnsworth owned adjacent limestone quarries that both had too much water in them. Ulmer drained the excess water from his quarry at some expense. This had the useful effect of also draining excess water from Farnsworth's quarry. But Farnsworth wouldn't pay any of Ulmer's costs. The case for restitution seems intuitive. Ulmer was doing something reasonable and couldn't help himself without helping Farnsworth at the same time; Farnsworth was getting a benefit that (let us assume) was undeniably valuable as a result. Yet Farnsworth won and wasn't required to pay anything.

The result in *Ulmer* is easy enough to defend from the standpoint of protecting the parties' autonomy. An arrangement between them could have been made by contract, and Farnsworth's refusal to make one (assuming he did refuse) does not entitle Ulmer to create benefits for Farnsworth and then expect to be paid. A restitution suit cannot be used to make a defendant buy something if he could have been asked and would have been free to refuse. Maybe the defendant didn't want his quarry drained; maybe he liked to swim there. Or maybe he did like the idea of having his quarry drained but couldn't afford it, or would have wanted it drained by some other method that was cheaper. In any event, nothing depends on proof of those possibilities. They are just mentioned to help explain the real point: courts are highly reluctant to let anyone force a transaction on anyone else when an unforced one was possible. This value runs strong in the law of restitution.

From an economic perspective the result in *Ulmer* might seem less appealing because it invites free riding. It amounts to a rerun of *Felton v. Finley*, the case of the contested will discussed a moment ago, but in a factual contest not involving money. Parties in Farnsworth's position can calculate that if they do nothing and agree to nothing, parties in Ulmer's position may eventually take care of their drainage problems (or whatever else) for free. Relying on such parties to solve the problem by making contracts may not be reliable because they are locked into a bilateral monopoly. They can only bargain with each other, so each may be more stubborn than he would dare if he were bargaining in a market where there were lots of competitors making better offers to either side. But there is no way to avoid this problem without also letting parties force transactions on each other that they may not want. And *Ulmer* presents the additional problem, not present in *Felton*, of deciding just how much Farnsworth valued the benefit he received. In *Felton* the benefit to the defendant was a cash distribution under a will, so valuation was not a problem. If the benefit is a drained quarry, the value of it is not self-defining in the same way.

When restitution law does not provide a satisfactory solution to these dilemmas, legislative or regulatory answers may be possible. If neighbors should have a claim to contribution from one another for their drainage efforts, for example, then perhaps the best solution is a regulation requiring the drainage and requiring contributions to it from both of them. A near analogy, though opposite in character, is furnished by laws that take oil fields lying under multiple properties and "unitize" them into a single resource to be drawn out from one point. Instead of several owners all having an incentive to race against each other to draw the oil out too quickly, the law creates a single incentive to extract the resource efficiently.[10] Those laws solve a type of cooperation problem in which everyone is consuming a resource faster than is best. A comparable regulation on facts like *Ulmer*'s would solve a reverse sort of cooperation problem: free riding in which nobody wants to be the first to do the work.

In the absence of such legislative solutions, results like *Ulmer* are common enough. One party builds a road that benefits itself and its neighbors, or makes some other improvement that benefits the whole neighborhood, and yet the neighbors are required to pay nothing.[11] Or, to switch to a different sort of circumstance, you and I negotiate over a project, and you spend a lot of time coming up with plans and good ideas for it. Then our negotiations fall through—but I use your good ideas to carry out the project with someone else. Still no recovery.[12] We could have made a contract but didn't, and I would have been free to refuse the benefits if asked, so there is no basis for requiring involuntary payment now. The result in all these cases is enrichment of the defendant at the plaintiff's expense, but it is not deemed unjust in the sense relevant to the law of restitution. The simple spectacle of one person benefiting from someone else's labors, and paying nothing for them, is part of life and is tolerated all the time.

Intervention to Protect Life or Health

Now consider the other end of the spectrum, where one party deliberately confers an unrequested benefit on another and does have a right to recover for it. A simple instance of such a case, and a strong one, involves medical emergencies. Thus in *Cotnam v. Wisdom* a man fell off a streetcar and lay unconscious on the ground. A doctor rushed to his aid. The court said that the doctor had a good claim afterward for the market value of his services.[13] (Occasional references to such a case as involving a contract "implied in law" are misleading and now best avoided. It is a matter of restitution, not contract.) What is the distinction between this case and one where I wash the windshield of your car while you are stopped at an intersection, then demand money? The differences are obvious but worth recounting because they help resolve harder cases that lie between the easy ones. First, there is good reason to excuse the failure to make a contract. One party is unconscious; the situation is an "emergency," meaning for these purposes that waiting will be very costly; and there is no plausible room for doubt about what the recipient's wishes would be if he were conscious. A stranger's demand for payment after washing your windshield is offensive precisely because he could easily have asked you whether you wanted it done, and because the value of the benefit conferred is open to dispute.

It might seem that the presumption in favor of awarding the doctor his market rate could be rebutted by showing that the treatment failed—for how was the decedent enriched then? Indeed, the patient in *Cotnam v. Wisdom* never regained consciousness; the doctor's claim was against his estate. The reason for allowing recovery anyway, of course, is that medical services are not priced according to their outcome. The economic logic is plain enough. The treatment provided in *Cotnam* improved the patient's odds of survival, and that improvement was very valuable to him at the time of his non-negotiation with the doctor.[14] Besides, denying recovery because there was no "actual" value realized from the treatment would not give doctors the full incentive the law ought to provide to help in such cases. They would know that they stand to be paid nothing unless their intervention turns out to be successful, the odds of which might be low.[15]

This discussion shows that allowing a doctor to recover at his market rate is sensible enough, but what if the provider of the emergency services has no market rate? Suppose he was a passerby who does not normally provide medical treatment to anyone and for whose services no market would exist. Valuation of such treatment is difficult and prone to error, and the law deals with these problems by simply denying any recovery to the nonprofessional rescuer.[16] The result is sometimes defended as well by saying it is unclear whether amateur efforts at rescue generally do more good than harm (sometimes such attempts endanger both parties), so the law is reluctant to push for them. When viewed that way, the rule in restitution is like the tort doctrine that refuses to impose a duty on people to rescue strangers from distress, even if they seem able to do it easily.[17] Consider whether this rationale is consistent with a rule we will encounter soon: the amateur who intervenes to protect property rather than life does have a chance of recovery against the defendant who benefits from the efforts. Perhaps an amateur's efforts to save property are not as likely to result in disaster all the way around as efforts to rescue the drowning.

We can see the force of some of these rationales by observing what happens in a case where they are weaker. In *Webb v. McGowin*,[18] Webb worked in a lumber mill. He heroically diverted a heavy block of wood that was falling toward McGowin. Webb was injured in the course of the rescue. Afterward McGowin gratefully promised Webb $15 per week for the rest of Webb's life—something like $200 per week today. McGowin made these payments for many years until he died, at which point his executor stopped them. A lawsuit resulted, and the court held McGowin's promise enforceable. The case is sometimes regarded as a chestnut of contract law. It is said to show that the consideration needed to make a promise enforceable can consist of an act done before the promise was made if the act bestowed a benefit on the promisor.[19] That line of reasoning reduces "consideration" to a fiction, since Webb's act was finished by the time McGowin made his promise; McGowin got nothing back in return for it. Consideration may be a largely fictitious requirement in any event, a possibility the *Webb* case helps illustrate. But the outcome might also be explained in a more straightforward way as a matter of restitution. McGowin was greatly enriched by Webb's rescue. Normally the law would not permit recovery by an amateur rescuer like Webb, but the strongest usual reasons for that rule aren't present on these facts. When McGowin announced that he was prepared to pay Webb $15 per week, he provided an unusually solid basis for estimating the value of the rescue to him. It is like the cases in the chapter on mistakes in which the defendant had revealed the value of a benefit mistakenly conferred on him by offering to pay some price for it on another occasion. And recovery here is not the kind of reward that would encourage dangerous efforts of the same kind by others. They wouldn't be able to count on the beneficiary of their efforts being as generous as McGowin was to Webb.

Intervention to Save Property

Acts to save property in an emergency, as when I make heroic efforts to save your boat rather than your life,[20] are governed by the same general principles just shown, but their application is a bit more complicated. As ever, the first question is whether the facts excuse the plaintiff's failure to obtain consent in advance. When property is at stake, the justification for bypassing the owner often involves a transaction cost that may be hard to prove: it is not feasible to identify the owner of the property or to contact him. When it's simply the owner of a house who is out of town, that element seems easy enough to satisfy.[21] But property takes various forms, and sometimes the feasibility of approaching its owner can become controversial.

Thus in *Trott v. Dean Witter & Co.*,[22] an employee of Dean Witter invited Trott to join a scheme to defraud the firm. Trott did not report the matter to Dean Witter because he worried that he would not be believed (he did not work there himself) and because he feared reprisals from the employee, whom he thought was involved in organized crime. Instead Trott went along with the scheme until he had solid evidence of a crime, *then* reported it to Dean Witter and to the government. The corrupt employee went to prison; Trott went into a witness protection program with a notably reduced income. Trott brought a restitution claim against Dean Witter. It failed. The problem was not that Trott was an amateur rescuer. As noted a moment ago, courts are willing to allow recovery by amateurs who rescue property (in many such cases there may be no relevant professionals to whom one can defer). Nor was there any doubt that Trott had saved Dean Witter a great deal of money—had in fact "rescued" the firm's property. But the court held that Trott did not have a satisfactory excuse for failing to talk to Dean Witter before undertaking to collect the evidence. Since Trott had a chance to proceed consensually but didn't, he was simply a volunteer.

In medical cases the courts typically are quick to order restitution because it is obvious that the recipient of the treatment would have wanted it on the spot if he could have been asked. In property cases it may not be so clear because the costs and benefits of urgent efforts to preserve property vary in ways that the costs and benefits of urgent efforts to save life do not. Here is an example less colorful but more common than the previous one: a garage that takes in a stolen car found by the police can, once the owner is found, collect restitution from the car's owner for any costs of towing and storage.[23] But the garage generally cannot collect for repairs it performed, because it will be impossible to show that they needed to be done before the owner could be found.[24] The repairs may have been needed; they may even have saved the owner an expense he would have found necessary soon enough. It does not matter. The owner may have his own preferences about whether or when or where to do the work. The garage has no right to force a transaction on him if waiting until he appears will do no harm.

On the other hand, suppose the owner then sells the car. And suppose the price he gets in return for it is improved by the repairs that the garage performed without his consent. The garage may then have a good claim to those extra proceeds that were produced by its labors. The owner of the car is not being forced to buy repairs he did not want. He is merely required to pay back the benefits that the repairs generated once those benefits are reduced to a form that is easily returned—namely, the cash received when the car was sold.

A restitution claim for medical benefits fails if the recipient made clear that he didn't want them or wouldn't pay for them; the same principle applies to owners of property and is more likely to be of consequence for them. In *Bailey v. West*,[25] the defendant bought a horse but rejected it upon delivery because it was lame. He sent the horse back to the seller, who refused to accept it. The driver of the delivery truck deposited the horse at a nearby stable. An ostler there took care of the animal and sent bills to the buyer and seller, both of whom refused to pay and denied that the horse was theirs. After several years of this, the ostler sued the buyer of the horse, seeking to collect in restitution for his expenses in maintaining the animal. The ostler pointed out that the seller had since won a judgment upholding the sale and awarding contract damages against the buyer. It might seem to follow that the buyer had responsibility for the animal and should be obliged to pay for its upkeep, but the court nevertheless denied the claim. The buyer had told the ostler that he would not pay for the animal's care, so the care was provided at the ostler's own risk.

The parties' intentions can be relevant to a restitution claim in a more surprising way as well. Suppose the ostler had, at the time of performance, no plan to charge anyone for the upkeep of the horse. The thought of being paid only came to him later. Perhaps he originally regarded the buyer as a friend but later changed his mind about that. He then has no restitution claim. The services must be provided with the intent to charge for them,[26] as well as with no reason to doubt that the benefits are wanted.[27] The rule likely expresses concern about the use of restitution to disruptively undo gifts and other gratuitous transfers when the transferor has second thoughts. But of course proving the first thoughts may be no easy matter.

Rescues of property can also lead to restitution claims of a different kind. My boat runs into yours, which begins to sink. A rescuer arrives and tows your boat to safety. The rescuer has a good restitution claim against me because he reduced my liability to you; if your boat had sunk, my exposure to damages would have been much greater.[28] Claims of this kind are rare but interesting. An example is *McNeilab, Inc. v. North River Ins. Co.*,[29] where the claimant was a pharmaceutical company that recalled one of its products at great expense. Had it not done so, it would have been subject to tort liabilities that its insurer would have been obliged to cover. Should the insurer therefore be liable in restitution for the expense of the recall? This case, like most others of its type, turned largely on interpretation of the contract between the insurer and the insured.[30] Contracts of that kind naturally impose certain duties on the insured to avoid running up costs that the insurer will have to pay. One question in the pharmaceutical case was whether the efforts taken were within that duty or beyond it. Yet even if they were beyond the requirements of the contract, the court was not inclined to award any recovery to the insured. The plaintiff here, like the plaintiff in the Dean Witter case, had plenty of time to discuss its course of action with the beneficiary of its "rescue"— the insurance company—before going through with it. Those chances for a voluntary deal scotch the claim for collection when the plaintiff proceeds involuntarily.

Performance of Another's Obligation

The claims just discussed resemble another family of restitution claims that involve three parties: those where the claimant has carried out someone else's legal responsibilities. Many conferrings arise in cases of that kind; the claimant has performed an obligation that the defendant owed to someone else, usually by paying a debt—either a bill or a legal liability that hadn't yet matured into a bill. This simplifies the showing that the plaintiff's act had value to the defendant (since the defendant avoided a legal obligation), and sometimes makes the value of the act to the defendant easy to quantify. But these situations vary in the kinds of justifications the claimants can offer for acting without a contract. The stronger the claimant's own legal duty to act in the circumstances, the wider the range of payments he can make on behalf of the defendant and still collect in restitution afterward.

When the Claimant and Defendant Have a Shared Duty

The most straightforward cases for recovery are those where the claimant has performed a duty that he shared with the defendant. Suppose you and I are joint tortfeasors, having both contributed to an accident that injured someone else. Our obligations are evenly shared. The doctrine of joint and several liability allows the tort plaintiff to collect all of his damages from either of us—and he decides to collect them all from me. Now I have a good claim for restitution against you, though the claim also can go by other more specific names. It may be called a claim for "indemnity" if you are obliged to reimburse me in full, or a claim for "contribution" if you just need to reimburse me in part.[31] Or suppose you and I jointly guarantee payment of a note by someone else; when he defaults, I end up paying the entire amount, either because I step forward to do so or because the creditor makes me the target of his collection efforts. My subsequent claim against you would arise from a combination of restitution and contract law (or restitution and tort law in the case of the accident). The contract and tort rules, or rules from suretyship or whatever other body of underlying law may be involved, set the terms on which we share responsibility and the extent of my right to collect restitution from you after I have paid for both of us. (Sometimes a claim for indemnity amounts to a claim for equitable subrogation. I'm arguing that you should have paid the entire amount. We will return to this idea in a moment.)

To take a more complex example, suppose we are sued together for $100,000 after an accident and I settle the claims against both of us by paying the plaintiff $80,000. I may have rights of restitution against you even if you disliked the settlement and wanted nothing to do with it. The reason is that I might have paid an amount you would have been obliged to pay sooner or later, which leaves you no reason to complain about the amount; and I paid it because I was protecting my own legitimate interests in avoiding a lawsuit, which leaves you no reason to complain that I was meddling. We said that I "might" have paid money that you owe, because that point now has to be proven. To win a restitution claim I have to show how much the tort plaintiff would have won against you if his case had gone forward, or what share of responsibility you would have been assigned for the accident. Those matters are governed by the law of tort, not restitution. But restitution law does have this to say about the substance of the outcome: whatever I may prove about your possible exposure to liability without the settlement, I cannot collect more than $80,000 from you. Allowing me to do so would violate the principle of restitution law that limits a plaintiff's recovery against an innocent defendant to the defendant's gains or the plaintiff's costs, whichever amount is less. And my right to recover from you is limited, as usual, by any defenses you could have raised in the suit brought by the original plaintiff, even if those defenses wouldn't have been available to me.

An illustration will make the operation of these points clearer. In *Yellow Cab of D.C., Inc. v. Dreslin*,[32] one of the defendant's cabs hit a car driven by Dreslin. The collision injured Dreslin's wife, who was a passenger in the front seat. She sued the cab company and won a jury verdict. The jury found that both cars had been driven negligently, however, so the cab company sought restitution from Mr. Dreslin for his share of responsibility. It was a standard application of the logic of this chapter. The cab company and Mr. Dreslin both had obligations to his wife, both had breached those obligations, and the two breaches had caused injury to her—but the cab company had paid for all the harm. Yet the cab company's claim failed. The reason was that local law provided for "interspousal immunity" in such a case. This meant that Mr. Dreslin could not be held liable to his wife. It followed that the cab company, in paying all of Mrs. Dreslin's damages, had not reduced Mr. Dreslin's potential liability (he had none anyway) and so had not enriched him. Another way to put the point is that the cab company, when it sought reimbursement from Mr. Dreslin, had to overcome all the same defenses that he would have had against the claim that the cab company paid off. In this case Mr. Dreslin would have had an insurmountable defense if sued by his wife. The outcome might seem unjust, since two parties were responsible for the accident and only one of them ended up paying for it. But that result is a consequence not of the law of restitution but of the law of interspousal immunity, which still exists on facts like these in a majority of American jurisdictions.[33]

Claims fitting the pattern of this section can also arise where the two of us are co-owners of a piece of land.[34] I pay the taxes on it myself, or the insurance bills. You can be required to contribute your share in restitution. And the co-ownership can go beyond the obvious case where both parties have the same active stake in the property (as joint tenants or tenants in common). The same rules apply if I have the property now but you will take it after my interest expires,[35] or if I pay bills on the property while we are disputing ownership of it and you eventually win the fight.[36] And the property itself can take more exotic forms. One of us makes payments due on an insurance policy that will benefit us both—and not necessarily home owner's insurance; it might be a life insurance policy on a parent or some such thing.[37] Again the party who paid has a claim for restitution against the party who did not, though these more complicated ownership interests may also lead to more complicated disputes about the size of each side's share. In their economic logic these situations are much like the common-fund cases discussed earlier in the chapter. One party created a benefit for another and had a good reason for failing to proceed by contract. The law provides a restitution claim as a substitute.

We have seen that in some cases one co-owner of a piece of property can seek reimbursement from the other for bills paid—but which bills? The test in a property case is not quite whether the expense was legally required. It is enough that the expense was "necessary." So if the roof of our building is torn off by a hurricane, I can have it replaced and collect your share from you later. I was not under a legal duty to have the work done, but it was fairly considered necessary to preserve the value of the property as a practical matter.[38] A requirement that work on the property be "necessary" is not as clean as a requirement that the payment be legally compelled. It leaves a little room for judgment, and the difference between necessary and elective maintenance of a house can be hard to state. The courts typically manage the problem by drawing a line between *repairs*, which can be paid for by one tenant and then collected from the other without his consent, and *improvements*, which cannot.[39]

The policies behind this distinction are the usual ones in this branch of restitution law; they are matters of autonomy and efficiency. The courts do not want one party to be able to force a transaction on another when negotiation between them is a possibility. But they also don't want one party to be able to free ride on payments by the other that obviously would have to be made by one of them eventually. A party who rakes the leaves without asking and then demands compensation from a cotenant is, perhaps, a problem at the seam between these principles. The leading case on the question denies recovery, finding that consent to the work might have been sought in advance and that the plaintiff's "failure to communicate prevented [defendant] from maintaining the property herself or having it done by someone else at a lower rate."[40]

When the Claimant Has an Independent but Secondary Duty

Now suppose that two parties have overlapping legal obligations to a third, but the obligations are not the same. I am your insurer. You are hit by a car. The driver now has a duty to compensate you and so, let us suppose, do I. But the driver's obligation seems greater; he is the one who did the actual damage, whereas my duty arises just because we have an insurance contract. So if I pay your bills, I now have a right to seek restitution from the driver. To state the reasoning more formally, we say that the driver and I both had obligations to you, but that the driver's obligation was primary. So he was unjustly enriched by my payment of it, and I can collect it from him in a restitution suit.[41]

Restitution of this kind is often called "equitable subrogation." "Subrogation" generally means "substitution." If I am "subrogated" to your rights, I can press whatever claims you might have had against the defendant (and with the same priority among his creditors), and the defendant—the driver of the car, for example—can raise any defenses against my claim that he could have raised if you had sued him directly. The "equitable" part of the term refers, historically, to the origins of the device in courts of equity. As a more practical matter it refers to the result the suit seeks, which has been aptly described as "securing the ultimate discharge of a debt by the person who in equity and good conscience ought to pay it."[42] In equity and good conscience, the driver of the car, not your insurance company, should have the ultimate responsibility to pay for the damage inflicted on you. And the word "equitable" has still another significance. It means that my right to sue in this way arises not from contract but from law. I may also have rights of subrogation under our insurance contract; that would be "conventional" subrogation rather than the equitable variety. My rights then would be defined by whatever the contract says, though principles of restitution law may be used to fill in gaps. (Whether the suit is "equitable" in the additional sense that the plaintiff gets no jury trial is a separate question of constitutional law that depends on other details of the case.)[43]

The size of the driver's possible liability in a suit of this kind is just what you would expect from the principles already considered in this book. He can't be forced to pay any more to me than I paid to you; he is potentially on the hook for either the amount that he saved by my payment to you or the amount that I spent on it, whichever is less. And of course I first must show that the defendant's obligation to pay really is "primary" compared to mine. That seems intuitive enough here. The driver caused the harm. But reducing that intuition to a rule for other cases turns out to be difficult. If one party is guilty of some sort of fault and the other is not, then the party in fault will typically be said to have the primary obligation to pay for the result. The other party has what is sometimes called the "superior equity."[44] This explains the case against the bad driver. But sometimes an insurance company competes for "secondary" status with a party who has some legal responsibility for a bad outcome but isn't culpable in any sense. It may be another insurance company or some other such party who also has a merely contractual duty to compensate the victim of the loss. In these sorts of cases an insurer who pays the victim and then seeks reimbursement from the other responsible party may not be able to collect. The results in such disputes are hard to predict in a general way. They require a close study of the contracts involved to see who most clearly agreed to cover whatever situation has come up.

A different complication can arise in states that adhere to the "collateral source rule," which holds that if the victim of an injury receives compensation for his bills from an insurance company, he can still bring a suit for the full amount against whoever inflicted his injuries.[45] The rule has the potential consequence of letting a victim collect twice for the same injury—once from the insurance company and then again from the injurer. It is defended on various grounds, but our concern here isn't with the merits of the rule. Our concern is with the consequence of it for the logic of unjust enrichment. Suppose a driver runs you over and your insurer writes a check to compensate you for the costs of your injuries. That compensation does not reduce the liability of whoever hurt you (because the collateral source rule still allows you to sue him). So he wasn't enriched by the insurer's payment to you. But *you* will be unjustly enriched if you collect both from him and from the insurer. So restitution law (probably along with your insurance contract) allows the insurance company to bring a claim against the driver in your place. This will cause all parties to pay what they should. The insurer will pay you once. The driver will pay the insurer once, since the insurer is your subrogee; the driver will not then have to pay you again; and in the end all parties will have either paid or been paid just what they should. But the details of the recovery allowed to the insurer vary a bit according to the facts and the jurisdiction. And note that this logic is not applied to every sort of insurance contract. If you are killed by the negligence of another, your survivors may collect both the benefits of your life insurance policy and damages from the tortfeasor. It is always a question of what the point of the insurance contract was.

So far we have been talking about equitable subrogation as a tool for insurance companies. They are the most common users of it, but there are others. Thus in *Rawson v. City of Omaha*,[46] Rawson's car hit a pothole and then collided with a car operated by another driver. Rawson settled with the other driver, then brought a suit against the city; she claimed the city was to blame for the accident because it should have fixed the pothole. The court held that the city was indeed entirely to blame. This sounded like good news for Rawson, yet it raised a potential problem for her. She was now entitled to collect from the city for the damage to her own vehicle, but could she get restitution for the amount she had paid in settlement to the other driver? The court's finding that it was all the city's fault meant that Rawson hadn't really owed that other driver anything. In days of yore this might have meant that Rawson was a "volunteer" when she made her initial settlement and spoiled her ability to recover it. But not anymore. She was held entitled to seek recovery of her settlement—not from the other driver, but from the city by way of equitable subrogation. The modern result is the same in most states.

The *Rawson* decision illustrates a general point. Claimants using equitable subrogation need not have any actual obligation, in the end, to the party whose damages they initially paid (and for which they are later seeking reimbursement by restitution). It is enough if they paid damages to someone out of fair concern that they might be held liable or because they were trying to protect their interests in some other legitimate way.[47] This doctrine makes good sense. If parties like Rawson were not able to recover restitution from the city, they would have an incentive to delay in settling with anyone else before the city's liability is resolved. Giving Rawson the right to seek restitution from the city means that the other driver will get paid earlier (by Rawson) and that the party in Rawson's position will avoid large litigation costs (by settling). Meanwhile the party in the city's position is not made to pay any more than it owes; it merely pays it to a different party: the equitable subrogee.

Finally, restitution claims with the structure just shown can also take forms that have nothing to do with reimbursement of accident costs. You ask a bank teller for $100 and he mistakenly gives you $150. The extra $50 does not rightfully belong to you. You owe it to the bank. But in a sense the teller also owes it to the bank. You both have obligations, though yours might be considered primary since you are the one who actually has the extra money. So while this case does not, on its surface, seem to resemble the insurance cases we have been discussing, it is similar in structure and in outcome. The teller can pay the bank the $50, then seek to recover it from you in a suit for restitution. It is a simple matter of equitable subrogation.[48] Or suppose a town is required by statute to remove asbestos from inside the walls of its school buildings, and the tort law of the jurisdiction would require the manufacturer of the asbestos to remove it as well. Again the town and the manufacturer both have obligations. It might be argued that the obligation of the party who made the asbestos is primary. If the argument succeeds, the town can remove the asbestos and then seek recovery in a restitution suit against the manufacturer.[49]

When the Claimant Has No Duty of His Own

Sometimes a claimant discharges a defendant's duty despite having no legal obligation to do so. He freely decides to pay a bill that needs paying or to build a bridge that needs building, though in either case the defendant should have done it. Since the claimant acts freely, there are dangers in such cases that he will meddle in the affairs of others and foist benefits on them that would better have been made the subject of a contract. So in keeping with the pattern now familiar to us, the claimant needs a good excuse for not proceeding in that way. Here the law addresses these concerns by requiring two elements for recovery: the need for the claimant's intervention must be strong, and the defendant must have had some sort of obligation to do the act that the claimant performed. This requirement of an obligation on the defendant's part is meant to remove the worry that he received a benefit he did not really value.

The cases that typically satisfy those requirements come in two basic varieties. In the first, the claimant pays for someone else's "necessaries" that the defendant should have provided. In the second, the claimant has performed a duty that the defendant owed to the public. These two categories can be viewed as differing mostly just in scale. Something small or large needed doing and the claimant did it. A matter from the small end of the scale, which creates a minor liability in restitution, requires less urgency by way of justification, as when a claimant pays funeral expenses for a family member and then seeks restitution from the decedent's estate.[50] Or suppose a niece or some other appropriate party—a stranger would not qualify—pays a utility bill for an aunt who is in the hospital, and does so without asking.[51] This is likely to produce a successful claim when later pressed against the aunt's estate, even if the payment was a matter more of convenience than of necessity. But the scale slides only within limits. The niece will lose if she seeks restitution for the wages she lost while paying those bills and otherwise managing her aunt's affairs.[52] That sort of reimbursement requires a contract, express or implied.

Matters larger in scale and greater in urgency will justify more aggressive and expensive intervention by a claimant, as when the United States supplies electricity to customers of a utility whose generator has failed;[53] or as when the defendant is a governmental body that refuses to discharge a duty to the public (a duty to fix a sewer or a bridge, say), forcing the directly affected parties to hire a private contractor to do the work;[54] or as when a corporation's agent causes a spill of toxic chemicals, and the police summon a local specialist to clean it up.[55] Because the welfare of people besides the defendant depends on swift action in such cases, a claimant may be able to carry out the defendant's responsibilities and still be awarded restitution at the defendant's expense afterward—despite the defendant's perfect availability and refusal to consent. Since the need for

the claimant's intervention was created by the defendant's inability or un-
willingness to take care of its responsibilities, the measure of recovery in
such a case is likely to be liberal, perhaps reimbursing the plaintiff for his
full costs even if a less expensive response might have been possible.[56]

A mixed case will show the difference between facts that satisfy these
principles and facts that do not. In *Hazelwood Water Dist. v. First Union
Management, Inc.*,[57] the defendant was a shopping mall. The plaintiff was
a utility that decided the mall needed new water meters and backflow-
prevention devices. The mall refused to pay for either of those things, so
the utility installed them and sued to recover its costs. The court refused
to allow recovery for installation of the meters, because they did not serve
the interest of public safety; the court said that if the mall would not pay
for appropriate meters, the utility should simply have shut off the flow of
water until the mall took a more flexible view. But the court did allow recovery for the backflow-prevention devices the utility installed, because
they served the general interest in a necessary way. They ensured that pol-
lutants from the defendant's buildings would not find their way into the
general water supply. The defendant had a duty to protect the public from
that risk, and the utility had taken care of that duty on the defendant's
behalf. Put differently, the utility's acts created important external benefits (i.e., benefits not just for the utility), the provision of which should not
have been dependent on the defendant's willingness to sign a contract.

Payment to One Party of an Amount Owed to Another or to Both

At the start of the chapter on mistakes, we saw that a mistaken payment
can be recovered in a restitution suit brought either by the person who
made the payment or by the person who was supposed to receive it. A
similar logic applies here and produces a rule to complement the ones
just shown. We have seen that if I pay an amount that should have been
paid partly or entirely by you, I can bring a restitution claim to make you
pay your share. We can now add that if you *receive* an amount that should
have been partly or entirely received by me, I likewise can bring a restitution suit to recover it.[58] This is not an example of a "conferring," so in that
sense the pattern makes a questionable fit in this chapter; the intent behind the payment and your receipt of it could take many different forms.
But this is still the best place to discuss such recovery because it so closely
mirrors (i.e., reverses) the doctrines of indemnity, contribution, and equitable subrogation that we have just considered.

The flip side of contribution, for example, would be a case where a debtor owes money to you and me jointly. The debtor pays you, and this discharges his obligation to both of us. Now you owe me half the money, at least in the absence of any evidence that one of us was entitled to a greater share than the other. This makes easy sense but does not arise terribly often. The more common and difficult problems arise from the flip side of equitable subrogation. You receive a payment, and we both have rights to it, but I claim that my rights are superior to yours. So suppose Buyer purchases cider from Seller and includes a specified amount to cover Seller's payment of taxes on it. Then the tax is declared illegal and Seller gets a refund. Seller has a perfectly fair claim to that refund; but Buyer has a better claim, because his money was used to pay the tax. So Buyer can recover the refund from Seller in a suit for restitution.[59] (On these particular facts it is important that the taxes were originally billed and paid as an item distinct from the thing taxed. The result can quickly become different if Buyer's payment to Seller was an undifferentiated lump sum.)[60]

Or consider *Gutierrez v. Madero*.[61] As part of a divorce settlement, Gutierrez promised to continue naming his children as beneficiaries of his life insurance policy. Later he changed the policy to make his mother, Madero, the sole beneficiary. After Gutierrez died, the insurance company paid out on the policy to Madero, but his children were able to collect the benefits from her in a suit for restitution.[62] Madero had a right to the benefits under the insurance policy—but Gutierrez's children had a better right, because their father had promised, in the decree resolving his divorce, that he would not do what he later did. Allowing the children to proceed directly against Gutierrez's mother deters the double cross by people in the Gutierrez's position. For those who regard ex-husbands as hard to deter, the economic explanation can focus on a different point in the timeline. If the children were not entitled to collect the money from Madero, it would be harder for future parties in the position of Gutierrez to make credible promises when trying to work out a divorce settlement in the first place.

When the Claimant Has a Duty by Contract with a Third Party

I am building a house for Smithers and I hire you, a gardener, to install the shrubs. After you have finished the work, I vanish without paying you.

Can you bring a claim against Smithers to collect for the value of what you did? Probably. Smithers has been enriched to the extent of the value of the shrubs to him. He expected to pay for them (let's assume he hadn't yet paid *me* for them when I disappeared), and if Smithers doesn't pay you, nobody will. When conditions like these all hold, a claimant has a good claim for restitution.[63] Such claims are a close relative of the ones just considered at some length where the claimant performed an obligation to a third party that was owed by the defendant. This new case, too, is a three-party problem. The general pattern here is that the claimant conferred a benefit on the defendant, and both of them expected the claimant to be paid by someone else—but the payment was not made.

The illustration just drawn is typical. A general contractor goes bankrupt (or dies, or absconds) without paying a subcontractor. The subcontractor will often have a right to collect from the owner of the project under statutes that allow mechanics' or materialmen's liens. But if he cannot or does not take advantage of those, he has a common-law right to restitution. The right is limited. If the owner has already paid the full contract price for the work the subcontractor did—whether it was paid to the general contractor or to a replacement the owner found after the general contractor defaulted—the subcontractor is out of luck. He can't make the owner pay twice, and indeed the owner cannot be made to pay a penny more than was called for by the original contract to which he agreed for the total project.[64] And there are other limitations. *Callano v. Oakwood Park Homes Corp.*[65] involved a variation on the gardener's story offered a moment ago. The owner of a project hired a developer and gardener to work on it. The owner died. The developer agreed not to sue the owner's estate, and the owner's estate agreed to give the developer rights to what had been built. The developer sold it all off to a third party, and the amount he received was increased by the work the gardener had done. So did the developer owe the gardener anything? No—because the gardener had a good contract claim against the owner's estate. He didn't need a restitution claim against the developer in order to get paid.[66]

These restrictions on recovery are meant to advance a simple idea. If the owner of a project is getting a benefit for free that he had expected to pay for and the subcontractor who provided it is not getting paid by anyone, the law of restitution will fix the situation by making the owner pay the subcontractor directly. Notice that the recovery in restitution will often leave the subcontractor with less than he expected under his contract, for he is not suing on his contract (because his contract, let us assume, was not with the owner). He is entitled to the value of the benefit to the owner *or* to recovery of his own costs, whichever is smaller.[67]

To the case just described, compare a near miss that is superficially similar. A tenant in a building hires a contractor to do some work in his apartment. The tenant then goes bankrupt. The owner of the building knew about the work, approved of the work, and will benefit from the work, so the contractor sues the owner for its value—but loses, because the owner didn't *ask* for the work.[68] His tenant did, but the tenant was not an agent of the owner and had no right to bind him. The landowner here, unlike the landowner in the case of the shrubbery, never expected to pay for the work, directly or indirectly. For all we know, he was happy to see the work done or not done and wouldn't have dreamed of commissioning it himself. This case ends up being like *Ulmer v. Farnsworth*, where one neighbor's efforts to drain his quarry also drained the quarry of his neighbor. In this case, as in that one, the claimant could have made a contract with the defendant but didn't. He cannot force an exchange on him afterward. (But if the improvements are easily taken back, the contractor is welcome to come get them.)[69]

CHAPTER FOUR

Takings

Relation to Tort

Thus far we have considered cases where one person has given benefits to another. Sometimes the benefits were given by mistake, as when the plaintiff sent money to the wrong person or improved someone else's property because he thought it was his own. Sometimes the benefits were conferred in an emergency, or as a side effect of the claimant's efforts to protect his own interests, or in other such circumstances that do not involve mistakes but also do not involve a consensual exchange. Now we turn to an altogether different pattern: benefits that are taken from the owner rather than mistakenly given to him or deliberately conferred on him. Another way to describe the cases we will examine here is that they involve wrongs. We will see that the measure of recovery for them in restitution depends in interesting ways on the defendant's culpability—a point that we will pursue further in chapter 5, which covers the calculation of money remedies.

Every case of liability in this chapter will feature a defendant who violated the rights of a plaintiff and thus committed a wrong in the eyes of some source of law. That source may be a criminal statute. It may be the common law—usually the law of torts. Or the defendant's conduct may be viewed as wrongful in equity; in that case we might now speak of it as recognized as wrongful by the law of restitution itself. These different sources of condemnation make this branch of restitution law conceptually messy in two ways. First, it means that a plaintiff often has a choice between bringing a restitution claim or a claim based on some other body of law. Compare a case where I *mistakenly* send money to you: the legal analysis usually can have nothing to do with tort law, with contract law, with statutes, or with anything else except the common law of restitution. Now suppose instead that I enter your land, cut down your trees, and take them away to make furniture. I committed a trespass and an act of conversion—two torts. You can sue in tort to collect your damages or in restitution to collect my gains. In olden days a plaintiff who chose restitution for whatever reason was said to "waive the tort," but this expression is misleading and best avoided. The plaintiff really isn't "waiving" anything.[1] He is just choosing a legal theory—though it is true that he must pick one or the other and cannot have both tort damages and a recovery in restitution. So how does a plaintiff decide which to try?

The answers are matters of strategy. Of course restitution may be preferable, first, because it leads to a larger recovery. This may be the case if the defendant has gained more from the wrong than the plaintiff lost, or if the thing taken has since grown in value, or if the defendant's gains are easier to prove than the plaintiff's losses. Or the plaintiff may prefer restitution because the remedies it offers will allow him to recover property directly without competing against other creditors of the defendant. Or a plaintiff may prefer restitution because the limitations period for such a claim usually is longer than for a tort and sometimes may be set flexibly by the doctrine of laches.[2]

There is a second way that this branch of restitution can be complicated by the other sources of law bearing on it. Sometimes restitution will borrow a conclusion of wrongfulness from one of those other bodies of law; in other words, it will regard the defendant as unjustly enriched because he obtained his gains in a way that is said to be wrongful by tort law, or criminal law, or a statute. (In the latter case the statute has to be examined carefully to see whether it allows restitution by its terms, and if not, whether it leaves room for a common-law restitution claim in the event of a violation.) As noted a moment ago, however, there also are a few areas where the law of restitution itself identifies the wrong—and is quicker to recognize the wrong than the law of tort or any other branch of law would be. These sometimes are matters that historically would have been considered wrongful as a matter of equity. A breach of the duty of loyalty owed by a fiduciary is an example. That sort of wrong is always a good basis for a restitution claim. Many such cases would provide a good basis for a tort claim, too,[3] but the restitution law on point borrows nothing from the law of torts, and restitution more easily captures cases in which the fiduciary made wrongful gains but the plaintiff suffered no injury. Historically the correction of such misconduct was secured by a device that is one of the predecessors to the modern law of restitution: a bill of equity that sought an accounting from the defendant or some other specific relief. The practical result is that restitution law tends to be more hospitable than the law of torts to claims that involve breaches of trust. The same could be said about the sensitivity of tort and restitution law to some types of deceit.

Kinds of Wrongfulness

What do cases of restitution for wrongs look like, viewed generally? Let us begin by putting to one side some situations that are not included. The law of torts defines wrongs of all sorts, but most often they do not give rise to restitution claims. The most common kind of tort is the negligent infliction of a personal injury—one car hits another, or a sponge is left inside a patient on the operating table. In these cases the plaintiff has obvious damages, and the defendant has no gains; or if the defendant does have gains, they consist of the tiny savings from skipping a precaution that would have spared the plaintiff some grief. Whether those sorts of gains can be the subject of a restitution claim might be of some theoretical interest, but in practice that question does not come up. The reason is that the defendant's savings will invariably be smaller than the damages suffered by the plaintiff. If the savings were *larger*, the plaintiff's negligence claim would be at risk of failing because the accident was not worth preventing—the implication of Learned Hand's formula for measuring reasonable care.[4] In any event, victims of negligently inflicted injuries generally do not choose to bring restitution claims against their injurers. They are better off recovering their damages.

To find restitution claims arising from wrongs we must look elsewhere—away from personal injury cases and toward notably profitable wrongdoing, which generally involves taking or using the plaintiff's property. So let's put onto a spectrum all the ways that one person can wrongfully gain property by invading the rights of another. At the most culpable end would be theft, followed by embezzlement and fraud; these all are made wrongful by the criminal law as well as the law of torts. Next might come wrongs such as unfair competition, tortious interference with contract, and exploitation of the plaintiff's intellectual property, which are usually either tortious or violations of statute but not criminal. Then there are transfers induced by improper pressure within a fiduciary relationship, or pressure applied against someone vulnerable in some other way (in a "confidential" relationship—typically between family members or close friends), or transfers caused by some other intentional act that equity will not tolerate. And at the least culpable end of the spectrum we have the innocent converter of goods who mistakenly takes your umbrella instead of his and the good-faith purchaser of stolen goods. Here we also find the innocent maker of a misrepresentation that causes a transfer to be made.

Of course the scale just sketched is informal, and one might debate the placement of some of the wrongs. It doesn't matter. The point is to observe that a very broad range of acts can cause property to move wrongfully from one person to another, that the word "wrongfully" hides many differences of degree, that wrongfulness may be established by quite diverse sources of law, and, finally, that every one of those wrongful acts can be made the subject of a restitution claim. Indeed, the law of restitution reduces that unruly list to a set of common problems that are addressed by a manageable set of principles. The principles are sensitive to some differences in the facts, but they cut across the different sources of law that make a taking wrongful. Granted, in some cases a wrong will be defined by a statute that also sets out the available remedies, which may or may not include rights of restitution; the field of intellectual property provides notable examples.[5] (Some more detailed notes on intellectual property appear at the end of chapter 6.) But unless such contrary indications exist, any wrongful movement of assets from one person to another—in other words, any movement made wrongful by any source of law—can give rise to a restitution claim if the victim wants to get his assets back or go after the defendant's gains. This usually makes the basic question of liability for a taking simple enough. The harder and more interesting questions involve the value of the defendant's enrichment and the ways that judgments about that question of value are affected by the defendant's culpability.

Innocent Defendants

Again: the defendant enters the plaintiff's land, cuts down his trees, and hauls them off to make chairs. The defendant's enrichment may be measured in many ways: by the market value of the trees before they were cut or after they were chopped down; or by that value less the value of the time the defendant spent doing the chopping; or by the cost the defendant would have had to pay to buy the logs elsewhere if the plaintiff refused to sell them; or by the value of the chairs made out of the wood; or by that value less the cost of the labor and other materials spent in building them.[6] The choice among these measures is made by the use of general principles, not rules.[7] The most important principle involves the distinction between the innocent and the conscious wrongdoer.

Let us begin with the innocent defendant. If I cut down your trees while under the reasonable impression that they were on my land, I did commit a wrong but without a culpable state of mind. The standard measure of recovery on such facts is simply the market value of the plaintiff's property—here, the market value of the trees before they were cut down (known as "stumpage").[8] I might value the trees less than that (I wouldn't have cut them down at that price). And you might value them more than that (you wouldn't have sold them for the going rate). This latter possibility is especially likely. After all, your trees weren't "for sale," which is another way of saying that you probably valued them more than the market did.

In other cases the award of restitution may be considerably greater than the plaintiff's actual damages. In *De Camp v. Bullard*,[9] the defendants were harvesters of timber. They sent their logs down a portion of the Moose River, thinking that this was lawful; in fact that portion of the waterway was the plaintiff's property, and the defendants had committed a trespass. The question was what they owed the plaintiff for it. The defendants argued that they should pay the plaintiff's damages, which were merely nominal. She hadn't been harmed by the defendants' use of the river. But the court allowed a restitutionary approach to recovery, measuring the gain to the defendants by the market value of a license to use the plaintiff's property. The court noted that the defendants' theory of recovery "would place a premium on trespassing, because it makes the position of the trespasser more favorable than that of one lawfully contracting. If a man's house is vacant with no prospect of a tenant and no intention on his part of occupying it himself, and a trespasser occupies it, he must pay as damages for the trespass the value of the use and occupation, for this would be the duty of a tenant contracting upon a quantum meruit for the use, by consent, of that which the trespasser uses without consent."[10] Restitution as a measure of recovery works here only because the defendants did get benefits from the river's use. Compare a hypothetical second case in which that isn't so: An employee instead sends the logs down the river because he misunderstands his instructions. The defendants actually wanted the logs to stay where they were. An appeal to restitution would fail, and the plaintiff would have to settle for damages after all. As a formal matter, the differences between these two versions of the logging case have nothing to do with culpability. Both situations involve mere mistakes. The difference, rather, is that in the second case the defendants were not enriched by their use of the waterway.

Conscious Wrongdoers Generally

Suppose that instead of cutting down your trees by mistake, I did it on purpose. I hoped you wouldn't notice they were gone, but you did. Or I send my logs down your waterway, again hoping you won't notice; no such luck. We thus move from a case of innocent mistake to a case of conscious wrongdoing, a major divide in the law of restitution for takings. If the defendant is a schemer, payment of restitution measured by market value may not be enough to stop him. Upon learning that the waterway is owned by someone else, he might decide to take his chances and use it without permission. Either he gets away with it and pays nothing, or he gets caught and pays market value, which is probably what he would have had to pay anyway if permission had been sought. He also has forced a transaction on the plaintiff that the plaintiff might not have wanted.

The law provides an assortment of ways to stop a defendant from acting like this and to force him to channel his behavior into the market—that is, to ask permission and make contracts. In a tort suit the solution would be an award of punitive damages against him as an intentional tortfeasor. The law of restitution does not typically resort to punitive damages to supplement a recovery based on unjust enrichment (though there is no insuperable objection to such a combination). Instead it is likely to use aggressive measures of enrichment that can have a subtly punitive character. While the innocent converter generally has to pay just for the value of what he took, the conscious wrongdoer also has to disgorge all profits that resulted from his wrong, including consequential gains (a category discussed in more detail in chapter 5).[11] Behind this rule lies the general proposition that a defendant should not be allowed to profit from his conscious wrongdoing—an attractive notion as a moral matter but also as a matter of incentives. The courts aim to make the wrongdoer's conduct valueless.[12] But defining a defendant's gains can be a complex matter.

Forfeitures and the Problem of Proportion

First, courts sometimes have to make hard judgments about which of the defendant's assets were derived from the wrong committed against the plaintiff and what deductions should be made to reflect legitimate contributions the defendant added to the property in the meantime.[13] The more egregious the wrongdoing, the more aggressive the courts will be in forcing the defendant to disgorge. To start with the simplest point, a conscious wrongdoer must turn over not only what he took but what it has produced for him. If I somehow get hold of your money inadvertently, I am liable for the return of it with interest, but not for investment income. But if I *steal* your money and invest it, I must return to you not only the amount stolen but the dividends that it produced.

Or to return to our earlier example, it is not enough for a defendant to pay for lumber he knowingly took from the plaintiff. He must give the plaintiff the chairs made from the wood, or their value if he has already sold them. But weren't the chairs built not only out of trees that were the plaintiff's but out of labor that was the defendant's? Yes, and the chance that the defendant would lose the value of his labor was a risk he took when he wrongfully converted the trees to his use.[14] Again, an innocent converter who is required to pay back money in these circumstances would be entitled to a credit for improvements made to the wrongfully obtained property—that is, for the labor spent turning the wood into chairs. He might even get to keep the chairs and just pay for the wood. Thus in *Silsbury v. McCoon*,[15] the defendants stole corn from one Wood and turned it into whiskey. The question was whether they had good title to the whiskey. The court said no, and its reasoning offers a useful account of how the relevant principles operate against different sorts of defendants:

> The thief who steals a chattel, or the trespasser who takes it by force, acquires no title by such wrongful taking. The subsequent possession by the thief or the trespasser is a continuing trespass; and if during its continuance, the wrongdoer enhances the value of the chattel by labor and skill bestowed upon it, as by sawing logs into boards, splitting timber into rails, making leather into shoes, or iron into bars, or into a tool, the manufactured article still belongs to the owner of the original material, and he may retake it or recover its improved value in an action for damages. . . . [T]he trespasser loses his labor, and that change

which is regarded as a destruction of the goods, or an alteration of their identity in favor of an honest possessor, is not so regarded as between the original owner and a willful violator of his right of property.[16]

But the rule is different when the same transformation is made by an innocent party:

> [I]f the chattel wrongfully taken, afterwards come into the hands of an innocent holder who believing himself to be the owner, converts the chattel into a thing of different species so that its identity is destroyed, the original owner cannot reclaim it. Such a change is said to be wrought when wheat is made into bread, olives into oil, or grapes into wine. In a case of this kind the change in the species of the chattel is not an intentional wrong to the original owner. It is therefore regarded as a destruction or consumption of the original materials, and the true owner is not permitted to trace their identity into the manufactured article, for the purpose of appropriating to his own use the labor and skill of the innocent occupant who wrought the change; but he is put to his action for damages as for a thing consumed, and may recover its value as it was when the conversion or consumption took place.[17]

When a court confiscates the defendant's labor in the course of taking back property that he has stolen and improved, in effect it is making a punitive exaction. The plaintiff is getting back more than was taken from him, and this demanding remedy is mostly for the sake of deterring the defendant and others like him. Cases to test a court's severity arise when the defendant has mixed the property he took not just with his labor but with other property. If the defendant is innocent, of course, a court will make the allowances suggested in the passage above and illustrated in *Ochoa v. Rogers*, which was discussed in the chapter on mistakes: when the innocent buyer of stolen parts turned them into a car, he was obliged to pay the plaintiff the value of the parts, not to give him the car or the car's value.[18] But if the defendant was a deliberate wrongdoer, the court has to weigh different considerations in deciding how great a forfeiture to tolerate. In *Jewett v. Dringer*,[19] Dringer fraudulently obtained large quantities of scrap iron, brass, and copper from the plaintiff, and then mixed those metals in piles with his own. The court held that Dringer could not be allowed to benefit from the mixing and invoked some older language from Lord Brougham: "When did any wrong-doer ever yet possess the hardihood to plead, in aid of his escape from justice, the extreme difficulties he had contrived to throw in the way of pursuit and detection, saying, you had better not make the attempt, for you will find I have made the search very troublesome? The answer is, the court will try."[20] It was concluded that if Dringer could not separate his own metals from the plaintiff's, the plaintiff had a right to all of them.

At some point the comfort of a court with such a remedy, like a court's comfort with a large award of punitive damages in a tort case, will no doubt be exhausted. Thus the artist who steals a paintbrush and uses it to paint a masterpiece need not forfeit the painting, the *Restatement* assures us[21]—though alas, there has not yet been a case quite like that, nor the tantalizing variation in which the painting was made on a stolen canvas. What one might like as a more plausible test case is a defendant who stole the plaintiff's wood and used it to make joists for a good-sized house, which he built for himself and from which the joists cannot be extracted. Would a court allow the plaintiff to take the whole house? Such extreme questions only ever have been addressed in hypothetical form.[22] Some fact patterns not far from that one are discussed in the chapter on failed contracts, however; and it does seem clear that if a deliberate trespasser builds a house on the land of another, he loses the house—but because his own restitution claim fails, not because the owner has a restitution claim against him.

Imaginative Measurement of Gains

What if a deliberate wrong produces no damages or consequential gains? In *Jacque v. Steenburg Homes*,[23] the defendant sought to deliver a mobile home to a neighbor of the plaintiffs. The easiest way was to convey it across the plaintiffs' land. The alternate route was covered with seven feet of snow and contained a turn that would have required expensive equipment to navigate. The plaintiffs refused to permit the defendant to come onto their property. The defendant did it anyway. The plaintiffs sued for trespass, and the defendant replied that the plaintiffs could show no actual damages. The court agreed that the plaintiffs' damages were nominal but awarded them $100,000 in punitive damages anyway. The court noted with apparent disapproval that the defendant had considered the affair a laughing matter. The *Restatement* suggests, plausibly, that the case might as easily been dealt with as a matter of restitution.[24] How to measure the defendant's gains? Not just by awarding the market value of a license to cross the plaintiffs' property, for that would put the defendant on the same footing as someone who did the right thing by bargaining for permission (and also on the same footing as someone who committed the mistake innocently).[25] A more suitably aggressive measure would account for what the defendant would have had to spend if the plaintiffs' property had not been available: the cost of plowing through the snow and using pricey equipment to get around the bend in the road.

This general approach to valuation—making the defendant pay the cost avoided by invading the plaintiff's rights—is an especially attractive measure in a case like *Jacque* where the plaintiffs had specifically denied permission to the defendant to take or use the property in question. It also can serve as a fallback measure in cases where consequential damages exist but can't be calculated with confidence. It might seem more direct to treat such a case as a matter of tort law and award punitive damages, especially since the punitive award is more likely to not only make the defendant's conduct valueless to him but to ensure that it has a negative expected value. Restitution, however, has the advantage of being less arbitrary (in *Jacque* there was no particular basis for the $100,000 the court authorized; it was a round number). And awards of punitive damages are, partly on account of that sort of arbitrariness, subject to constitutional challenges that are not likely to be an issue in a restitution case.[26]

Or perhaps there is yet other evidence of how much the defendant valued the use made of the plaintiff's property. In *America Online, Inc., v. Nat'l. Health Care Discount, Inc.*,[27] for example, the defendant got customers of America Online to send out spam on its behalf and paid those customers a fee anytime a spam message they sent provoked interest on the part of a recipient. After finding this a wrong against America Online, the court awarded the company a sum that was about the same as the total amount the defendant paid out in fees to its helpers. It was hardly a perfect measure of what the defendant gained by its wrong, but it was difficult to find a proxy that was more precise. Rough justice is a common enough outcome in restitution cases.

Semiconscious Wrongdoing

We have been speaking of conscious wrongdoing as a clear-cut category. Sometimes it isn't. A defendant might inadvertently invade rights of the plaintiff that are defined ambiguously by statute and end up sued—for example, for infringing some aspect of the plaintiff's intellectual property.

The law's usual response to such cases is to label as a "conscious wrong-doer" anyone who knew that his acts *risked* being wrong.[28] This definition resembles the distinction in tort law and elsewhere between recklessness, which typically is defined as the conscious disregard of a known risk, and negligence, which entails a mere misjudgment and need not involve any awareness of risk. Once an actor perceives a risk, the law puts strong pressure on him to assess it and, if he cannot be sure what is lawful, to err on the side of prudence.

We also have spoken as if a defendant's obligation to disgorge all consequential gains strictly tracks his consciousness of wrongdoing. That is usually true, but not always; courts can extend the aggressive disgorgement to any case where policy requires it. Suppose you have abused a fiduciary relationship with the plaintiff. You were a lawyer and took commercial advantage of knowledge gained in that role,[29] or you took actions to compete in some way with your client.[30] You committed no tort, let us suppose, but your receipt of the money is recognized as a wrong in equity and creates a basis for a restitution claim. Sometimes it is possible to commit acts of these kinds without being conscious of wrongdoing. You think you have the right to use what you learned from your client to inform your own investment decisions, but it turns out that you were wrong. The law in such a case will treat you as if you were a conscious wrongdoer and require you to account for any consequential gains—not because you were conscious in fact of any risk that you were in the wrong, but because a fiduciary occupies a position of trust, and the client tends to be in a position of vulnerability.[31] This creates easy opportunities and natural temptations for abuse. The law helps to offset them by requiring complete disgorgement of gains from any breach of the fiduciary's duty.

Money

Put aside logs, oil, and spam e-mails and take the more common case where the defendant simply takes the plaintiff's money. We should start by asking why a plaintiff would bring a suit for restitution in such a case rather than a tort claim. The reasons were clear enough in some of the cases discussed so far; restitution makes natural sense if the plaintiff has trouble showing substantial damage, as when the defendant trespasses on the plaintiff's river or sends e-mails on the plaintiff's network. But if you steal $100 from me, my loss and your gain are the same, so the typical outcome of a tort suit or a restitution suit in response would seem to be the same as well. Sometimes a claim for restitution nevertheless has advantages because, first, it can include specific relief—in other words, a demand for the return of the very thing taken. This might mean taking back checks or identifiable cash the defendant obtained by fraud, or seizing property the money was used to buy. So if I take your money and buy a car with it, a restitution claim (but not a tort claim) allows you to claim the car. And if I use the money I took from you to buy stock, or to buy lottery tickets, or to bet on a horse race, the result under the law of restitution usually is the same. You are entitled not just to the return of your money but to the return of anything I made by my use of it. If my investment of the money went badly and I *lost* it, of course, I receive no credit. You can simply demand the amount originally taken.[32]

Second, restitution offers additional advantages when suing a defendant who is insolvent. Consider the thief who owes money to many victims and other creditors and is unable to pay them all. The normal result is a bankruptcy or receivership proceeding in which the thief's assets are divided among his creditors, with each receiving cents on the dollar. A plaintiff who sues the thief in tort has to get in line with those other creditors and receive a partial recovery. But if the plaintiff can use the law of restitution to make a *specific* claim to the money taken from him or to its "product" (in other words, to something that was bought with it or that it became), he may be able to get back all of it. The plaintiff steps in front of the other creditors, in effect, by claiming not that the wrongdoer owes him money but rather that the wrongfully taken property still belongs to him and thus cannot be sold to satisfy the wrongdoer's debts.[33]

It is a harder question whether the victim is entitled not only to the return of his property ahead of the wrongdoer's creditors but also entitled to all *proceeds* of it ahead of them. The facts of *G & M Motor Co. v. Thompson*[34] illustrate the problem. Thompson embezzled money from the plaintiff and used some of it to help pay premiums on his life insurance policy. The truth came out after he died. Normally the victim of a wrong like this can trace the money taken from him into the results of any investment it was used to make, which would include the proceeds of an insurance policy.[35] But this assumes the contest is between the wrongdoer and his victim. If the embezzler's estate has other creditors, or if the embezzler left behind a wife and child who were counting on the insurance money (as was true in Thompson's case), what then?

Part of the answer is easy. The victim is entitled to reimbursement of whatever the embezzler took; he gets it ahead of any other creditors and ahead of the embezzler's family. He can take it back, with interest, by means of an equitable lien on the insurance benefits, even if some of the embezzled money wasn't used to pay for the policy (though the victim can reach only that share of the insurance proceeds that corresponds to the share of premiums demonstrably paid with the embezzled funds). But once the victim has been made whole in this way, his right to also collect additional proceeds from the policy must yield to the right of other creditors to first ensure that *they* are made whole.[36] And often a court will then prefer to let the surviving family receive the remaining policy benefits—as the court in *Thompson* did.[37] The choice between these outcomes can depend on such detailed equities as whether the family seems to be well provided for without the insurance. Allowing the family to keep the proceeds—or whatever is left of them after the decedent's victims are reimbursed—might be described as kind hearted but troubling from the standpoint of policy, since it means that Thompson's perfidy was partly rewarded. In effect he was able to extract an involuntary loan from his employer to pay for an insurance policy that helped his family.

The Slayer Rule

So far we have been occupied with cases where one person uses or takes the property of another in some way. But property can end up in the wrong hands through less direct means. In *Riggs v. Palmer*,[38] Elmer Palmer was the largest beneficiary named in the will of his grandfather, Francis Palmer. Worried that the grandfather might change his mind, Elmer poisoned him. It might seem obvious that a party in Elmer's position cannot be allowed to have the money that the decedent's will leaves to him. The bad incentive it would create is plain enough, though letting Elmer collect would seem intolerable even if his motive hadn't been to obtain the money (e.g., if he hadn't known about the will when he poisoned Francis). But just *how* a party like Elmer Francis is to be denied the inheritance has caused occasional puzzlement. The slayer is criminally liable for the murder, obviously, but the consequences of that liability are set by statute, and the statute may just call for a prison sentence and say nothing about money. Meanwhile other parts of the statute law, not to mention the decedent's will, may indicate that the slayer is entitled to the money and contain no qualifications or exceptions to cover the problem of the murdering heir.

The court in *Riggs* held that since the legislature would not have wanted the murderer to gain from his crime, the statutes should be construed to forbid that result.[39] *Riggs* has played a part in debates about whether and when courts have to step beyond the authoritative legal materials bearing on a case to reach a just result in it.[40] But when viewed as a restitution case, the correct handling of *Riggs* is not so remarkable: declare that the grandson has been unjustly enriched and that he holds the money in constructive trust for the proper beneficiaries.[41] Or use the same principles to prevent the murderer from ever acquiring legal title to the assets in the first place. On this view the difficulties associated with *Riggs* merely illustrate the limits of law as distinct from equity.

The particular doctrine of restitution that prevents the murdering heir from profiting is sometimes called the "slayer rule." Identifying and proving the unjust enrichment in such a case tends to be simple so long as the defendant's criminal liability is clear enough. If he has been convicted of murder, the findings in the criminal case probably will be regarded as conclusive in the civil suit under the doctrine of collateral estoppel.[42] But who gets the money if the slayer doesn't? The answer usually will be the other beneficiaries in the decedent's will, or the other payees of his insurance policy, or any alternative or contingent beneficiaries named in the will or policy—in other words, those whom the decedent thought should receive his property if the slayer were unable to receive it or, where none of these sources of guidance are helpful, whoever would succeed to legal ownership in the slayer's absence (perhaps some distant kin of the decedent).[43] If there are no heirs in view, the state can take title to the decedent's property by escheat.

The approach just described, rather than the approach of *Riggs v. Palmer*, has been the most common judicial handling of the murdering heir, at least until the jurisdiction adopts a statute that directs a similar outcome without need for help from judges. Most states do now have statutes of that kind,[44] but they do not always cover all the variations that can arise on this fact pattern. When they don't, traditional principles of restitution continue to fill the gaps—some of those principles being matters of common law, some of equity. For example, a restitution claim usually is the only way to reach any money the slayer *saved* by his crime, as when he owed money to the decedent.[45] And the statutes are likely to speak of inheritance by the slayer without addressing the problem of insurance benefits payable to him. Restitution reaches all such cases, because they all involve unjust enrichment.

CHAPTER FIVE

Failed Contracts

The Problem Generally

We have seen how the law of restitution responds when a benefit changes hands in a way that neither side intended (cases of mistake), or in a way that the giver intended but the recipient did not (conferrings), or in a way that the recipient intended but the giver did not (takings). It remains to consider cases where a transfer is intended—initially, at least—by both sides. They attempt to make a contract, but it fails in some way and so leaves one side unjustly enriched at the expense of the other. Some cases of this kind involve mistakes of various sorts by either or both parties. But it won't do here to say that the plaintiff collects his cost of performance or the value received by the defendant, whichever is less. That approach to recovery has much power when the defendant is the innocent recipient of a benefit mistakenly conferred. In the settings considered here, however, the transfer between the parties is a joint enterprise to at least some extent. Deciding which side is more "innocent" (if either is), or which should otherwise be favored by the rules of recovery, thus becomes a good deal more complicated.

Cases that call for restitution after a failed attempt at a contractual exchange follow one of two general patterns. First, the parties might have had an agreement that never turned into an enforceable contract. They tried to make a contract but it was illegal, or it didn't comply with legal formalities, or it was tainted by fraud. Some of those cases might be viewed as part of the previous chapter (on takings), of course, if they involve wrongful conduct. But when fraud or duress or some other misconduct results in a contract that turns out to be invalid, it can present special problems that are best treated at the same time as other reasons why contracts may become impossible to enforce.

In some of these cases, half a trade (more or less) has been made, but the other half is not going to happen. The one who has performed seeks recovery from the one who has not. In other cases, the trade has been carried out in its entirety but one side wants to undo it—to rescind the contract, return any benefits received, and get back whatever benefits were passed to the other side. Restitution law can be used to address any of these situations. (Some details of how rescission works will be left for the chapter on equitable remedies, but the occasions for it will be discussed here.)

Second, the situation is different if the parties *do* have a valid contract and one side breaches it. The other side now has a straightforward claim for breach of contract and can seek restitution as one kind of remedy for it—not as a separate cause of action. The injured party might want to recover the value of his services rather than the usual expectation damages, or he might want to rescind the contract and seek a return of benefits received by each side.

These last possibilities are the uses of restitution that have caused the most confusion in discussions of the subject. To clarify, "restitution" is the name of a cause of action a plaintiff can bring (which is how the word is used at most points in this book). The word is also used to name one kind of remedy for the different cause of action known as breach of contract. It might seem that we could avoid any trouble by just saying that if a plaintiff wants restitution as his remedy in a contract case, he should bring suit based on the law of restitution rather than the law of contract. But that doesn't quite work. If the parties have a valid contract, it leaves little room for restitution as a cause of action. The contract itself, along with the surrounding default rules of contract law, defines the parties' rights to relief. But contract law happens to provide certain remedies that are at least somewhat restitutionary in character, which explains the survival of the word in that setting. (To compound the confusion, however, we will see that there remains one instance where a true restitution claim *can* be brought after a defendant breaches a valid contract: a case where the defendant's breach is opportunistic and profitable.)

We return later to restitution as a remedy in a contract case and begin here with restitution as a cause of action to redress unjust enrichment that results from a failed attempt to make a contract. Suppose you perform your side of a contract only to discover that there *is* no contract; the agreement you had is unenforceable. Clearly you cannot sue to force the other side to perform, nor can you sue the other side for breach of con-

tract. What remains is a suit for restitution that seeks to recover the benefits you conferred on your trading partner. Having received something
for nothing, he would appear to be unjustly enriched. But whether the
suit succeeds will depend on why the contract failed in the first place. The
general rule is that the performing party can get restitution so long as it
would not violate any policy behind the rule that made the contract unenforceable. But recovery is also affected in more subtle ways by whether
the law is indifferent to the transaction the parties attempted, hostile to
it, or especially sympathetic to the position of the plaintiff or defendant.

When the Law Is Indifferent to the Parties' Transaction

The law sometimes declines to enforce a contract while having no hostility to it. Things simply did not work out between the parties for reasons
to which the law is indifferent. The parties did not follow certain rules or
labored under misunderstandings, but no larger public policy is offended
by the behavior of either of them. In these cases restitution tends to be
unproblematic. Typically one side enriches another and expects that a
counterperformance is forthcoming. It turns out not to be forthcoming, so
the transaction is unwound, with all benefits returned from the defendant
to the plaintiff. In effect the law shrugs, unwilling to enforce the parties'
original agreement but happy to help return the parties, if it can, to the
positions they had before. An exchange of promises may be unenforceable in this way, for instance, because it was made orally and so failed
to comply with the statute of frauds, which requires contracts of certain
kinds to be evidenced by a signed writing—contracts for the sale of land
or that cannot be performed within a year, for example.[1] Or the contract
may be too indefinite to enforce because details about the price, duration,
or other features of the arrangement were not specified clearly enough.[2]
Though the law may refuse to enforce the agreements in these cases, a
party who has performed, entirely or partly, still can recover the market
value of any benefits received by the defendant.

Recovery in restitution is likewise available when a contract is set
aside because some basic assumption behind it has failed. If one side performed—or performed more than the other side, at least[3]—before the
failure of assumptions became clear, the side that received benefits can
be made to pay for them. Thus suppose an insurance company sells its
customer a policy on the life of X, then the parties discover that X was

already dead when the contract was made. The contract will be set aside and the customer can get back whatever he paid to the insurer.[4] Sometimes a contract can even be set aside on this rationale, and restitution ordered, after both sides have completely performed their agreement. Go back to the insurance policy issued on the dead man, and this time suppose the insurance company pays out on the policy before discovering the mistake. A restitution claim can be used to unwind the transaction and secure the return of all payments made in either direction—the premiums paid to the company and the benefits paid to the client.[5]

Or perhaps *future* events were contrary to some fundamental expectation that both parties had. Thus in *Parker v. Arthur Murray, Inc.*,[6] the plaintiff paid in advance for thousands of hours of dance lessons at the defendant's studio, then was disabled in a car accident that finished him as a dancer. The defendant pointed to language in the contract that said no refunds could be made, but the court would have none of it; a basic assumption behind the agreement had failed, so the contract was subject to avoidance and the plaintiff was allowed to get back the payments he had made for lessons that he hadn't taken and never would. What to make of the "no refunds" language in the contract might have been a hard question, but it was a question of contract law. Having resolved it in the student's favor, the application of restitution principles is simple (and describing the return of the plaintiff's money as following from contract or restitution law is a formality without importance).

In the most typical case of a failed assumption, the performing side has partly or completely performed and the paying side has not paid— and won't. So the performing party can recover, but not the contract price and not his costs. He can recover the benefits received by the other side, which may be something less. Granted, the best measure of how much the recipient valued the plaintiff's performance will normally be the contract price. But that is only a starting point. Suppose the defendant had spent money in reliance on the contract that he thought he had with the plaintiff. Or suppose the plaintiff only performed part of the agreement the parties had made, and now the defendant will have to get someone else to finish the job at greater expense than the contract had provided. In either of these cases, the defendant really has not benefited from the plaintiff's performance to the full extent of the contract price, and he gets an offset to reflect this. He pays the contract price for the work the plaintiff did but minus whatever he spent in reliance on the agreement. And at the end of the day—after the recipient has paid to have the work finished by someone else—his payment to the plaintiff for his mistaken labors cannot cause the defendant to pay out, in all directions, more than the contract price for the work. In effect the losses caused by the mistake thus are borne by the party who unluckily performed before the mistake was discovered.[7] It might seem a hard result, but it is consistent with the usual focus of restitution law on the defendant's enrichment rather than the plaintiff's costs.

Notice that recovery on the theories discussed here assumes the parties did have an agreement, just not one that was enforceable. But now suppose that they merely negotiated without ever reaching conclusions, and then the plaintiff went ahead and performed the version of the agreement that he was hoping for. Clearly the defendant does not owe him any counterperformance. But assuming he doesn't perform, does he at least owe the plaintiff reimbursement for benefits received? It might seem that he does, since otherwise he gets something for nothing. Yet a defendant in this position is not liable.[8] Without an agreement between the parties of some sort, even if not legally enforceable, the plaintiff amounts to nothing more than a volunteer. In effect he took the chance that he and the defendant would fail to come to terms, and they failed to come to terms. So the defendant keeps the benefits and owes nothing.

When the Law Is Hostile to the Parties' Transaction

In the cases just examined, contracts failed for reasons to which the law was indifferent. The parties may have blundered, but neither was blameworthy in a sense that the courts would want to punish. But sometimes the law is hostile in some way to the agreement the parties tried to make (or maybe hostile to one of the parties); something in what at least one of the parties tried to do offended a public policy. That same hostility may make a court hesitate before ordering restitution if one of the parties performed and got nothing back.

In *National Recovery Systems v. Ornstein*,[9] for example, Ornstein borrowed thousands of dollars from a pair of casinos, lost the money, and did not repay it. The plaintiff sought to collect Ornstein's debts. The court held that while Ornstein's gambling was itself legal, loans made to finance gambling by the debtor are not enforceable. But shouldn't Ornstein at least be obliged to give back the money, since otherwise he would be unjustly enriched? No, because making him give back the money is too close to enforcing the loan agreement. In other words, allowing restitution would undermine the policy that caused the parties' contract to be unenforceable in the first place.

A similar analysis applies to *Womack v. Maner*.[10] Womack paid a bribe to a judge, and then—perhaps after the judge defaulted on his performance—sued for the return of the money. Their contract was illegal, of course, so the judge had no need to fear that he would have to pay expectation damages. But nor could the plaintiff even get back his money. This time it is not because restitution would circumvent the prohibition (it wouldn't). It is because the plaintiff's conduct is so bad that the law is not interested in helping him—a case of "equitable disqualification" for relief, where the claimant is said to have unclean hands and so is barred from seeking a remedy.[11] This is the usual result when a claimant has made a contract in pursuit of some criminal design. Note that the defense of equitable disqualification is not limited to claims seeking equitable relief. It is potentially available to fend off a restitution claim of any kind when the plaintiff committed misconduct in the transaction that gave rise to the suit. Its most common application is to cases where the plaintiff wants restitution of benefits received by the defendant under an illegal contract.

This is not to say that restitution can never be had when a party has performed under an illegal contract. Sometimes it can. In *State v. Pettit*, Pettit sold cocaine to undercover police officers.[12] He was later arrested, and the state sought restitution of the amounts they had paid to Pettit for the drugs. The court naturally allowed the recovery. The contract was illegal, but its illegality was no bar to restitution. On the contrary, the illegality of the contract *requires* restitution, and this regardless of whether the defendant was unjustly enriched. Letting him keep the money would frustrate the statute that makes the deal illegal.[13] Or go back to the case of the bribed judge. Change the facts only slightly and it becomes a case of extortion in which the plaintiff felt obliged to pay the judge $10,000 or else be punished with unfavorable rulings. The payment was unrecoverable when it was a bribe. But in this variation the plaintiff *is* entitled to restitution because any other result frustrates the law forbidding the extortion.[14] The right to restitution is determined by the policies that made the contract unenforceable in the first place.

Between the extreme cases shown so far are many others with no general rules to govern them. They require a hard look at the policies behind the statutes involved, the defendant's culpability, and other policy considerations at stake, including the law's simple distaste for unjust enrichment. In *Cohen v. Radio-Electronics Officers Union*,[15] the plaintiff was an attorney who made a retainer contract with a union. The contract provided him with a set fee of $100,000 per year and a right to six months' notice before the arrangement could be canceled. The union fired him with three days' notice. The contract was held unenforceable because it unduly constrained the client's right to discharge its attorney. But the lawyer could still collect restitution—or recovery in quantum meruit, as the court styled it—for the services he had provided. If (as in *Cohen*) the lawyer had earned the entire $100,000 envisioned by the retainer, then he would be entitled to that full amount. The contract, even if not itself enforceable, would provide the best evidence of how much the union valued his services, and letting the lawyer collect that amount would offend none of the policies behind the unenforceability.

Some similar issues can arise when a contract is held unenforceable not because it is illegal in what it tried to achieve but because the defendant did not have the legal capacity to sign it. Perhaps he was too young or was mentally incompetent, though cases of this kind can arise any time a party tries to make a contract without authority—even when it is a city that borrows money beyond what statute allows. If you make a contract with such a party, perform it, and then find that the contract cannot be enforced, allowing you to collect restitution might seem to defeat the purpose of the law by effectively forcing the defendant to pay an obligation that he was not supposed to be able to acquire. Yet if you can't have restitution, the defendant might end up unjustly enriched at your expense. What to do?

The law's typical answer is quite favorable—maybe surprisingly favorable—to the restitution claimant. Courts do award restitution in cases where the plaintiff has dealt fairly and reasonably with (and provided benefits to) someone who is a minor or is mentally ill—even if the plaintiff knew it.[16] But this approach does not necessarily gut the rules about incapacity. Suppose a minor makes a contract to lease an apartment for a year, then quits the premises after a month without paying anything at all. He will be held liable in restitution for the rent specified in the lease during the month when he actually used the place (or for the fair market value of the benefit received, whichever is less).[17] But since the contract is unenforceable, he will not be held liable for the remaining eleven months. That executory portion of the contract cannot be a source of liability to the defendant in any sense. This evidently is the core purpose of legal incapacity: protection of the incapacitated party against improvident commitments that he later may want to avoid, not protection from creditors who want payment for benefits that the "infant" has actually received.

The law's answers are slightly different when the defendant is not a child or lunatic but is instead a town that has entered into a contract beyond its legal authority to make. Under statute the amount of the contract was too large, or it was supposed to be put out for open bidding but was not. The other party, say a business, performs its side of the contract, finds that the town will not perform, and so brings a restitution suit to collect for the benefits it supplied. Allowing that suit to succeed might permit the parties an end run around the statute that forbids contracts to be made in these circumstances. The town would get its performance and the contractor would get paid—a bad result. And yet the contractor is owed protection against the risk that it will be hired to do work by the town and then be told later that their contract counts for nothing. This tension might appropriately be resolved by examining the plaintiff's good faith—meaning, here, that the plaintiff might collect if it had no notice of the town's lack of authority to make the contract.[18] If the plaintiff did know about it, then it was a party to an effort to circumvent the statute. The statutory requirements were at least largely for the protection of the taxpayers, whose interests may have been betrayed by collusion between the parties. So on those facts the contractor collects nothing, regardless of what benefits it has conferred.[19]

When the Law's Sympathies Are with the Plaintiff: Misrepresentation

In another set of cases, a contract is subject to avoidance because the plaintiff's agreement was induced by misrepresentation, or duress, or undue influence. A transfer caused in these ways generally can be rescinded, and benefits recovered, at the instance of the victim. The sympathies of the law are with him, and the protections offered by way of restitution are strong. Again, some of the relevant principles here were noted in the previous chapter, but we should mention a few others that become particularly important when the result of the wrongdoing is a contract.

Transfers caused by misrepresentation present the most complexities, and working through them will make some of the problems of duress and undue influence easier to understand as well. When one thinks of a misrepresentation inducing a trade, the image that comes to mind most immediately might involve a seller lying about the goods he offers to the plaintiff. But misrepresentations can occur in a variety of settings and with different degrees of culpability, and the differences have consequences.

First, a misrepresentation can be innocent or deliberate. The distinction affects how easily the plaintiff can undo the result. Any transfer can be rescinded on a simple showing that it was induced by fraud. But if the misrepresentation was innocent, the plaintiff must also show that it was *material*.[20] The meaning of "materiality" is generally a subject for the law of tort and contract rather than for restitution, but we can note a practical point: decisions about what is material often seem to be affected by the outcome that the decision would produce. The easier a transaction would be to undo, the easier it tends to be to convince a court that the transaction was founded on a "material" misrepresentation. To turn the point around, courts are reluctant to order transactions unwound on the basis of innocent misstatements made in the course of negotiations, especially if the unwinding would be messy or create hardship because circumstances have changed.

Second, different kinds of misrepresentation will occasionally give the victim different rights to seize property from third parties who end up with it. It is a familiar and useful rule of thumb that the victim of a theft can always recover stolen property, even from someone who bought it in good faith from the thief, but that the victim of a fraud cannot recover what he lost once it passes into the hands of a bona fide purchaser. The thief obtains no title (or "void" title), while the defrauder is sometimes said to obtain title that is merely "voidable." But that rule is not absolute. Sometimes a sufficiently egregious fraud will cause a court to call the result not mere "fraud in the inducement" of the contract but "fraud in the factum" (or "fraud in the execution")—a fraud that goes to the fundamental character of the contract and causes the party to agree to something entirely different than he intended. The defrauder's title is then void and he has nothing to transfer to anyone else. The classic example is the blind or illiterate victim who is presented with papers to sign that say one thing when he is told another,[21] or the party who means to sign one document but is surreptitiously slipped a different one.[22] In effect the decision about how to classify the fraud allocates responsibility between the victim who originally lost the property and the third party who later buys it. The economically sensible line, tracked a bit roughly by the cases, is thus between fraud the victim can be faulted for not detecting and fraud he couldn't feasibly have caught.

Third, fraud differs from the related problems of duress and undue influence (discussed below) because fraud entitles its victim to restitution without any showing that the defendant has been unjustly enriched. The purpose of restitution here, as the *Restatement* puts it, is to "vindicate the transferor's transactional autonomy," which may be compromised without any pecuniary injury to him or gain to the defendant.[23] An interesting example is *Gray v. Baker*,[24] in which the claimant sold some property to a church, and the church immediately resold it to the claimant's archenemy. The claimant alleged that the identity of the ultimate buyer had been concealed from him deliberately, and the court held that this stated a good claim for rescission of the sale. Notice that both the church and the final buyer might have paid full price. No matter. The plaintiff has a general right not to sell to someone he does not like for whatever reason. If that right is compromised by fraud, the transaction can be undone without a showing of further injury to the plaintiff or enrichment of anyone else.

Finally, compare a restitution claim based on fraud to actions of other kinds that may lie on similar facts. Suppose you enter into a contract on the basis of fraud and therefore receive less than full value for your money; the house you bought is a disaster. There are options available to you under contract, tort, and restitution law. If the fraudulent statement that caused you to buy the house amounted to a warranty—that is, to a guarantee about properties of the house—then you can sue to enforce that warranty like any other promise and seek damages to put you in the financial position you would have had if the contract had been performed. Or you can bring a tort suit and collect damages to restore you to the financial position you had before the transaction was made. Punitive damages may be a possibility as well. (In some jurisdictions the remedies available in tort may go further, including recovery of the benefit of the bargain.) Or—of greatest interest to us here—you can bring a restitution claim that seeks to rescind the contract and collect any gains the other side obtained from it.

At first that final option might seem less attractive than the first one and maybe less attractive than the second. Why just seek to unwind the transaction when you could sue for the gains you expected to receive from it? One answer is that those gains may be hard to prove, whereas reversing the transaction, and getting back whatever was passed to the other side, may be simple. Second, your expectations from the contract may have turned out to be negative. You were defrauded, but the deal—if honestly made and carried out—would have lost money for you. So you don't want to be put into the position you would have had in that case, and you may have no tort damages, either. You would rather just reverse the transaction and get your money or goods back, or recover the market value of the goods if the original deal called for something less than that. A restitution claim founded on fraud thus can allow a plaintiff to escape the consequences of a losing contract.[25]

An example is furnished by *Farnsworth v. Feller*.[26] The plaintiffs bought a sand and gravel concern from the defendants. The sale was based on a fraudulent appraisal that overstated the value of the business. The plaintiffs successfully rescinded the transaction and got their money back. The defendants protested that the plaintiffs' "real reasons" for wanting rescission involved the money the business had been losing since the plaintiffs acquired it, but the court wasn't interested: "Whatever may be [the plaintiffs'] ulterior motive in escaping from what had probably proved an unprofitable venture, it cannot affect their equitable right to rescind on the ground of the misrepresentation."[27] In a situation of this kind, both sides may have behaved in less than commendable ways—the defendant by lying and the plaintiff, perhaps, by showing bad business judgment. Letting the plaintiff recover might give him a kind of windfall, since he is freed from the consequences of his bad judgment by the defendant's lie (and there may have been no causal connection between the lie and the judgment). But this seems better than the alternative, which is to inadequately deter the defrauder by letting him use the plaintiff's misjudgment as a way to avoid responsibility for his wrong. These points are similar to the tort rules that generally forbid contributory negligence to be used as a defense against a claim of intentional tort and that say tortfeasors take their victims as they find them.

There is another strong and common reason—by now familiar—to prefer restitution to a claim sounding in contract or tort. A winning suit for tort or contract damages makes the plaintiff a creditor of the defendant. He is simply owed as much money as the court awards. If the defendant is insolvent, the plaintiff will have to get in line with all of his other creditors and receive something less than full payment. As noted in the chapter on takings, that is a common enough outcome when suing someone who has been perpetrating frauds. But a restitution claim brought against a defrauder can have different consequences. It always begins with rescission of the parties' agreement, and this equitable step does not make the plaintiff a creditor of the defendant; it makes the plaintiff the owner of whatever was transferred on account of the fraud. So long as he can still find it, or its product, he takes it back directly—whether the "it" consists of goods or money—and ahead of the defrauder's ordinary creditors, through the imposition of a constructive trust or similar remedy (discussed in chapter 6).[28]

We have been speaking of cases where a plaintiff can choose between a restitution suit and a claim for breach of contract. But sometimes only one of those choices is possible, and it is worth pausing to clarify the scope of each type of action. If you are induced by fraud to make a contract but discover the problem before either side has performed, you have good ground for seeking rescission of the agreement but no claim for recovery in restitution, because (of course) the other side has not yet obtained any benefits. But now suppose that *both* sides perform, so that the transfer is entirely complete when the plaintiff discovers the fraud. This is an obvious occasion for rescission accompanied by restitution, and thinking of the case that way makes more sense than regarding it as a case of promissory liability that calls for application of contract law, for the promise was not broken.[29]

Note, too, that while our focus in this chapter is on contracts, the rules of restitution we have seen (unlike the rules of contract law) apply as well to so-called gratuitous transfers, or, in other words, gifts.[30] Thus suppose someone tells you a series of lies, and the lies convince you to give them some property or to give the property to someone else. Again you can avoid the transaction, this time by rescinding the gift. Contract law is of no use.

When the Law's Sympathies Are with the Plaintiff: Duress and Undue Influence

Fraud is not the only wrong that can cause someone to agree to a transaction. There are two prominent others worth mentioning, and they are related: duress and undue influence. Both types of pressures are recognized grounds for invalidating a contract, gift, or will. The rules involving restitution on these grounds are especially important because duress and undue influence (and abuse of a confidential relationship, a related idea discussed below) are traditionally considered equitable rather than legal wrongs. As a practical matter that means they are a good basis for avoiding a contract or reversing a transfer, but in themselves they don't provide a basis for recovering damages in tort or by other means. Restitution is the primary legal mechanism for responding to them.

Duress refers to a wrongful threat of some sort. Typical cases involve threats that are themselves criminal or tortious ("your money or your life," or less extreme variants in which the defendant forces the plaintiff to agree by detaining property wrongfully); demands made in bad faith, as when one threatens a lawsuit known to be groundless; and threats of criminal prosecution, embarrassment in the community, or other such unpleasantness, though the threat in itself may not be tortious. The pressure in cases of undue influence need not be as great. Such cases arise when parties are in a relationship that allows one to dominate the other. Usually it is a relationship that the law regards as "confidential" (an unfortunate term referring not to secrecy but to the confidence reposed in one side by the other).[31] Indeed, transfers between parties to a confidential relationship often are presumed to be the result of undue influence until proven otherwise.[32] The arm twisting can occur in informal settings, as between family members. Recognition of claims arising from such facts sometimes seems to be a little broader in restitution law than in the law of contract.

A good example of a close case is *Webster v. Lehmer*.[33] Webster was a handyman. Lehmer was a lawyer. They were neighbors for many years and sometimes exchanged favors: Webster would do repairs for Lehmer, and Lehmer would give legal advice to Webster. A day came when Webster was unemployed, behind in paying his taxes, and struggling with a drinking problem. Meanwhile Lehmer had learned (but Webster had not) that Webster may have had valuable rights of adverse possession against the company that owned the land on which Webster's house sat. Without mentioning this, Lehmer invited Webster into her house and offered to buy Webster's interest in the property where he lived for $5,000, with Webster retaining a life interest. Webster agreed. Lehmer wrote out a contract on the spot and both parties signed it. When it later became evident that Webster's interests had probably been worth at least $240,000, Webster sought to rescind the agreement, arguing that it was a case of undue influence. The hard question was whether the parties had a confidential relationship. The trial court found that they did, citing Lehmer's occasional legal advice to Webster, Webster's desperate condition at the time of the sale, and the parties' disparate knowledge of the value of the property. This by itself didn't make the sale invalid, but it created a presumption that any benefits Lehmer received were the result of undue influence. Lehmer was unable to rebut the presumption. She needed to show that she had paid Webster what his land was worth, and she couldn't do it. Webster won rescission.

Much of what was said about fraud applies to contracts and gifts made under duress or undue influence as well, but there are a few differences and other points of interest to note here. First, we saw that the title obtained by a crooked defendant may be either void or voidable depending on the severity of the deception and the victim's ability to have detected it. This determines, in turn, whether the victim can reclaim the property from a later good-faith purchaser of it. In a case of duress, the difference between void and voidable depends on the extent of the duress. A transfer induced by physical force or threats tantamount to it is void.[34] The recipient is a thief, or close enough to being one, and gains no title to the property that he can pass to anyone else.[35] Transfers induced by duress of lesser varieties—or by mere undue influence—are voidable. A good-faith purchaser who comes into possession of the property can keep it.

Second, we observed that a plaintiff can rescind an agreement induced by fraud without showing any pecuniary injury to himself or gain to the defendant. Duress and undue influence do not work in quite that way. If a payment is made under duress, its maker is entitled to recover it in restitution—but only to the extent that the payment unjustly enriched the recipient.[36] The usual application of this idea comes in cases where the defendant accuses the plaintiff of embezzlement, threatens him with prosecution and ruin, and so induces the plaintiff to pay what the defendant says he owes. This is duress, and the plaintiff can rescind and have restitution to the extent that he didn't owe the money. If he *did* owe the money, he cannot get it back, and this no matter how repulsive the defendant's threats. It is the same if I pay you because someone else puts wrongful pressure on me. You cannot be made to disgorge money to which you were properly entitled, because you were not unjustly enriched by the receipt of it. (If you *defraud* me into paying money, the transaction can be rescinded even if I did owe it to you.)

These results might suggest that the rules about duress do not protect the plaintiff's autonomy as strictly as the rules about fraud, but the actual reasons for the difference are probably more practical. Claims of duress often arise in gray areas of business dealings between parties, as when one is a creditor of the other and makes threats of various kinds—perhaps some that are proper and some that may not be—to try to get paid. If the recipient receives money he is not due, the wrong is clear and the law of restitution is quick to supply a remedy. If the recipient receives money that he *is* due, then ready access to a restitution claim by the party who made the payment could too frequently interfere with the negotiated settlement of disputes. It might seem troubling that one party could demand, at gunpoint, the payment of money he is owed without incurring liability. But of course the only liability that he escapes is restitutionary. The threat itself would be illegal and would subject him to the penalties of tort and criminal law.[37]

When the Law's Sympathies Are with the Defendant: Restitution to a Party Who Breaches a Contract

We conclude this part of the discussion with cases where the position of the plaintiff who brings the restitution claim is peculiarly unattractive. He has breached a contract and now seeks to use the law of restitution to help himself. A plaintiff in that posture may succeed but will encounter some difficulties that we have not previously seen.

Suppose, then, that you and I have a valid contract. I breach it—and then I sue you to recover for whatever performance I rendered before breaking my promise. In this case, unlike the others we have discussed, the contract itself is unproblematic; it is untainted by mistake, fraud, or other such defects. But I still cannot sue under the contract, because in this example I am the one who breached it. My only recourse, then, is restitution. To be sure, not every suit by a breacher follows the reasoning just outlined. Rules of contract law sometimes show mercy to a party who partly performs and then breaks a contract. I might be found to have performed substantially enough to recover on the contract even though I didn't finish. Or if the contract can be severed into parts, I might be able to win damages for the part that I performed and that you didn't.[38] But in other cases my breach might be sufficiently "material" that I have no such rights. It was a large breach, or a breach that was small but violated a clear condition, so you have no obligation to perform and I have no rights recognized by the law of contract. Yet I did provide you with some benefits, so I can sue in restitution to recover for the value that you got from my partial performance. Since you are the victim of a breach of contract, however, the law will be protective of your interests.

The easiest cases of this type involve the return of money, but even these can present some complications. I promise to buy a house from you and I make a down payment on it; then I repudiate the contract and want the down payment back. This first raises an issue of interpretation. Maybe the point of the down payment was to give you something to keep if

I tried to back out of the deal: a kind of liquidated damages.[39] If so—and if the amount is upheld as reasonable—I have no right to its return. You haven't been unjustly enriched. But even ignoring that argument, getting my money back is not as simple as pointing out that you have received a payment for nothing. You have rights under the contract. You are entitled to damages for my breach. Those damages are the difference between our contract price for the house and the amount you can sell it for after I cancel (its market price—plus additional costs of resale even if you suffer no loss in the market). For all we know, those damages may consume much or all of the down payment—"for all we know" because the burden is on me (the restitution claimant) to show otherwise. If I want my down payment back, I have to prove that you were enriched by it, even taking into account the damages you suffered from my breach. In other words, I have to show that the down payment was greater than any actual injury you sustained. This often will be difficult.[40]

Restitution becomes still more complex when the claimant, rather than just wanting the return of money paid, seeks payment for work he has done or other nonreturnable benefits the defendant has received. Since the defendant asked for whatever he got, it usually will be clear that he valued it and should pay something for it. But here again the law is protective of his interests. After all, once the plaintiff has breached by making either an incomplete performance or a defective one, the defendant continues to have the right to a complete performance at the contract price. He thus can hire a replacement to finish the job. The defaulting plaintiff gets paid for his partial performance out of whatever money is left over after the replacement has been paid—and there may be nothing left over. Indeed, the defaulting plaintiff will have to pay the costs of completing the job to the extent those costs exceed the contract price. To put the point another way, the contract price is a ceiling on what the defendant can be made to pay out in all directions, both to the breaching plaintiff and to whoever is completing the contract instead, and the breaching plaintiff gets paid last. The defendant will not be permitted to suffer a net loss. The burden of showing his net gain is on the plaintiff. And the defendant's cost of getting the job done or done right will be estimated generously, with doubts resolved against the breacher.[41]

And if the plaintiff's breach is tainted by fraud he may recover nothing in restitution at all.[42] In *Dodge v. Kimball*,[43] Kimball hired Dodge to construct a building for $96,500. The contract called for a particular type of mortar to be used in the plastering and said that "this mixture must be strictly adhered to without any deviation whatever." Dodge intentionally departed from those specifications and used a somewhat less expensive mortar. The cheaper mortar caused the building to be worth $800 less than it would have been if the contract had been obeyed. The cost of removing and redoing the plaster would have been $7,000. Kimball had made progress payments to Dodge but had yet to pay him $9,215 of the contract price. So what did Kimball owe Dodge? The court's answer had the charm of simplicity: Kimball owed nothing. It is a case of equitable disqualification; the law of restitution will not recognize a claim by a plaintiff who has committed a fraud of this kind.[44]

This is a striking result to modern ears because it imposes a potentially massive forfeiture on the breacher. It seems to imply that if the defendant had not yet paid anything for the plaintiff's construction work, he would end up paying nothing for it at all, ever, because the plaintiff cannot sue for breach of contract (since he is the breacher) and his hands would be too unclean to permit him to sue in restitution. That penalty for the plaintiff's fraud bears no relation to the actual damages suffered by the other side. The harsh result is tolerated to punish the contractor for trying to slip one past the home owner. But courts nowadays do not often tolerate forfeitures of quite such an extreme kind, and it is not clear that they would do so here. The new *Restatement* takes the same hard-line position as *Dodge v. Kimball*, but the cases it relies on—the only good cases out there—are old.[45] And the possible forfeiture on facts of this kind is generally limited as a practical matter by progress payments the plaintiff made while the house was under construction. Even in the old cases (including *Dodge*), the usual result of the fraud is that the buyer just withholds the last payment for the work, not *all* payment (nor does he sue to get back the payments already made). These patterns keep too much pressure from being put on the rule.

A useful last example of these principles can be fashioned from the facts of the well-known English case of *Ruxley Electronics & Constr. Ltd. v. Forsyth*.[46] Forsyth hired Ruxley to build a swimming pool in his yard and specified that its maximum depth should be seven and a half feet. Ruxley mistakenly built a pool that was never more than six feet nine inches deep. Forsyth refused to pay Ruxley the remaining balance due, which was most of the contract price. The House of Lords decided that Ruxley had performed "to a substantial degree," that the pool was "perfectly serviceable," and that Forsyth was entitled to a relatively small amount as compensation for his loss of amenity in not having a pool quite as deep as he would have liked.

Ruxley was decided as a contract case, not as a matter of restitution.

But there are many ways to argue for a different result. Most of them start by questioning the decision that Ruxley substantially performed the contract. Some critics, including some of the judges who heard the case, would say that Ruxley didn't. This would make the case, and the payment due to Ruxley, more a matter for restitution law than contract law. The *Restatement* suggests that damages of the kind the House of Lords awarded are wrong because they force an exchange on the owner that the original negotiations show he did not want. Obviously this judgment depends on the finding that the owner made his views perfectly clear in advance and that the discrepancy in the pool's depth was a serious matter to him. But supposing we do reach those conclusions—what then? A rather meager measure of restitutionary recovery from Ruxley would be whatever amount Ruxley saved by building the shallower pool.[47] Another possibility, suggested by the *Restatement*, would be to make Forsyth pay to Ruxley just the amount by which the pool increased the overall assessed value of his property (which of course may be less than the contract price).[48] Notice that these two proposals involve restitution from different perspectives. The first treats Ruxley's gain from the breach as the amount due from Ruxley to Forsyth. The second views the gain from the pool as the amount due from Forsyth to Ruxley.

Restitution as a Remedy for Breach of an Enforceable Contract

The patterns discussed so far in this chapter have generally involved claims to restitution by parties who couldn't make claims for breach of contract, either because there *was* no enforceable contract or because there was a good contract but the plaintiff is the one who breached it. But now suppose the parties do have a good contract and the defendant has failed to perform. That means the plaintiff has a claim for enforcement of the contract and a choice of remedies at the end. The most familiar of those remedies is expectation damages, but there are some other possibilities that might be described as restitutionary.

We say "might be described" because restitution as a remedy for breach of contract does not work exactly the same way, or follow from exactly the same premises, as restitution in the other situations just seen. It might seem obvious that if you fail to perform a contract for which you have been paid, I ought to be able to get restitution from you just as surely as I can get it if the contract is invalid. Either way you have been enriched at my expense. But that is not quite the case. Remember that restitution is, conceptually, the mirror image of tort law. For the most part it is a device for adjusting the rights of parties when they don't have a contract. If they *do* have a contract, the contract generally defines their rights—at least so far as economic losses are concerned—without any help from the law of restitution or tort.[49] Thus if you cause me financial losses by breaching our contract, everybody knows that I ordinarily cannot sue you in tort for damages.[50] My only remedy is in a suit on the contract, which settles our rights and displaces any notions of tort law that might have been in the air. The same principle usually prevents me from bringing a restitution claim. If you have breached a valid contract, my rights against you are settled by the contract itself, which will determine my right to damages and leave no room for a judicial inquiry into unjust enrichment.

What makes the matter confusing is that *within* a suit for breach of contract, the law does offer remedies called "rescission" and "restitution." Law students all hear about this. They are told that there are three kinds of damages a plaintiff can seek in a suit for breach of contract: expectation damages, reliance damages, and restitution (or "performance-based damages")[51]—and that is perhaps the last they hear about restitution during law school. There is a solid argument that the whole subject of restitution as a contract remedy should be left out of this book, which is mostly devoted to the *cause of action* known as "restitution"—that is, the cause of action based on unjust enrichment, not breach of contract. But the principles involved are similar enough in the two situations, and the usage of "restitution" in the contract setting is so familiar, that an account of restitution law probably should address this aspect of it as well.

Rescission

Here as elsewhere in the chapter, "restitution" can mean either rescission of the contract or (what is not always the same thing) restoration by the defendant of enrichment he received from the transaction. We begin with rescission—that is, rescission as a remedy for breach and as an alternative to enforcement of the bargain by an award of damages or specific performance. In that context, "rescission" generally means that the contract is set aside and each side returns to the other whatever he has received. Obviously this works only if each side's performance takes a form that can be returned more or less in full (with a cash payment or "accounting" made for whatever parts of the performance can't be given back).

As noted before, rescission may or may not be desirable to the plaintiff as a strategic matter. It merely returns the plaintiff to the position he had before the deal was made; but if the contract was a good one, he can do better than that. He can sue for damages that reflect the gains he expected to make from the deal—his expectation damages.[52] Still, suing to undo the deal might make sense if those expectation damages are hard to prove or if the contract turned out to be a losing proposition, even if those are not the facts of the typical contract case.[53]

Here are some simple examples. I pay you for widgets and you do not send them. I want my money back. I can seek rescission, meaning that I can seek recovery of the money I paid you rather than damages for the widgets you didn't send me. (Maybe damages are unattractive because the market price of widgets went down.) Or I pay you to paint my house and you don't do it. Or we agree to trade horses and I send you mine but you don't send me yours. Rescission in these cases allows me to get back what I have given you without need for proof of what your performance would have been worth to me. To be clear, rescission in this context does not mean the plaintiff has "specific" rights to the property the defendant has received. In other words, the plaintiff does not recover the property he seeks ahead of other creditors of the defendant. In noncontractual settings, or in a case of fraud or mistake, rescission sometimes does entitle a plaintiff to specific relief of that kind, as we have noted at various points. But when a plaintiff sues merely because the other side has committed a material breach of their contract, "rescission" just means that we measure what is owed to the plaintiff by looking at what the defendant received. The plaintiff gets an ordinary creditor's entitlement to its return.[54]

Rescission requires the defendant to hand back all that he has received. So if he has spent *some* time and money performing—even if not performing enough—rescission threatens to cause those expenses to be irrecoverably lost with no return on them. That would be severe. The severity is relieved partly by the rule that your breach must be "material" before I can seek rescission. But the greater relief comes from the rule that rescission will not be granted unless both sides can be restored to something like the status quo ante.[55] Anything else would also put the parties into troubling strategic positions. Imagine that after I pay you to paint my house, you do 90 percent of the work and then walk off the job. Damages for your failure to perform would naturally give me the cost of completion. Rescission, however, would work quite differently; it would give me 90 percent of the promised performance for nothing. So I can't have rescission. My right is just to collect from you the cost of hiring someone else to finish the last 10 percent of the work.

The requirement that it be possible to return both parties to their pre-contractual positions is not absolute. The rigors of it can be adjusted according to other facts in the case. If a seller commits a major breach, the buyer can generally get his money back without fussing about whether the seller is now out a little money for his initial efforts. So suppose I lease a house from you for a year then move out after the first week because I discover it is overrun with rats and is uninhabitable. I can rescind the lease and get back whatever I have paid you. There need not be any deduction for my one week spent there. Likewise if you pay for schooling and receive just a little of it before the defendant breaches.[56] If the breach is large enough, or sufficiently material in nature, it may justify rescission even with a loose end or two.

The examples just mentioned all involved breaching defendants who were allowed to be shortchanged a bit by rescission. But the law demands greater exactitude when approaching the problem from the other side and fashioning relief for the innocent plaintiff who was the victim of the breach. The defendant may have to not only return what he has received but also pay incidental damages to bring the plaintiff all the way back to where he was before the contract was signed. Thus in another swimming-pool case, *Bause v. Anthony Pools, Inc.*,[57] the plaintiff hired the defendant to build a pool, and the defendant did a terrible job; the pool contained cracks that leaked 150 gallons per day. The court awarded the plaintiff the entire amount he had paid the defendant plus the cost of removing the pool and refilling the hole where it had been. The result amounted not to damages but to rescission. The plaintiff got his money back and returned the pool at the builder's expense. This might seem a hard outcome, since the builder had spent significant time and money on the project. Unlike the partial painter of the house, though, he hadn't spent it doing anything that turned out to be of any value to the client.

The builder's obligation to remove the bad pool illustrates a point noted earlier: rescission for breach of a valid contract is not based—not very precisely, anyway—on the need to correct the defendant's unjust enrichment. If it were, the defendant would not be obliged to pay incidental damages to bring the plaintiff all the way back to his original position. Payments of that kind can be driven only by the wish to compensate, and have nothing to do with the defendant's enrichment. We find this discrepancy because here we are not dealing now with the law of unjust enrichment per se. We are dealing with the law of contracts, which occasionally awards remedies that it refers to as rescission and restitution and that proceed upon a similar and overlapping logic, but not an identical one.

Performance-Based Damages

Rescission calls for the return of whatever has passed between the parties—a refund of money paid or a handing back of things traded. So-called restitution when a contract has been breached can also take a different form: a demand by the plaintiff that the defendant pay over the value of the work the plaintiff has done (along with consequential and incidental damages). It is a bit misleading—though common—to call damages awarded on this theory in a contract case a form of "restitution," because courts awarding them make no real effort to figure out how much the defendant valued what he received from the plaintiff. Instead they basically just award the plaintiff the value of the performance he made, using its market value so long as that isn't any greater than the rate shown in the contract. When a plaintiff finds this remedy attractive, it is usually because expectation damages—that is, what he would have been due if the contract had been fully performed—are hard to prove. A plaintiff in that position has the option of seeking to recover the cost of the performance (reliance damages) or the value of it (performance-based damages). Those amounts will often be similar, but not always. Sometimes it is easier to show the market value of what the plaintiff did than to show what it cost the plaintiff to do it. And sometimes the plaintiff would like to recover the value of the performance (the "quantum meruit" measure) because it is greater than the contract rate, raising issues we will consider closely in a moment.

To start with the old and simple facts of *Brown v. St. Paul, Minneapolis & Manitoba R. Co.*,[58] the plaintiff performed lawyerly services for a railroad in return for the promise of a lifetime pass to ride its trains. The railroad repudiated the contract. The plaintiff sued for breach, and the railroad's liability was clear—but what should be the remedy? Assume, as the court did, that expectation damages would be hard to figure because lifetime passes are rarely given to anyone and there is no market for them. Rescission is no help here because the plaintiff gave the railroad nothing that it can return. So the plaintiff was permitted to recover in quantum meruit—that is, in restitution—a cash amount that reflected the reasonable market value of his services. Instead of a lifetime pass that could not easily be valued, the case might have involved a promised commission or royalty on a project that was never carried out, again making it hard to say what the plaintiff would have received if the contract had been fully performed. Since the plaintiff's expectation damages are hard to prove, he demands payment at a market rate for whatever he actually did.

Or expectation damages might be hard to prove because the plaintiff was fired in the middle of his work, and what his ultimate costs and gains would have been is a matter of conjecture. I hire you to build me a barn for $100,000; then I cancel and repudiate the agreement when you are a quarter of the way through the job. If your lost profits are hard to demonstrate, you can collect $25,000 in restitutionary damages (or whatever part of the $25,000 you haven't already received in progress payments).[59] This assumes all parts of the job were equally demanding, so that a reasonable payment for a quarter of the work is a quarter of the contract price. If the quarter that you finished is proven to have been especially hard or easy to perform, the amount due from me can be adjusted accordingly.[60] In any event, the initial benchmark for measuring the benefit received is the contract itself, which is convincing evidence of how much I thought your services were worth. Notice again that in none of these cases do we ask how much (or if) the performing party's labors were *actually* valued by the defendant. Maybe I really have lost all interest in the barn-building project, and the work you did has zero value to me. I nevertheless must pay the value of the work suggested by the contract or, if the contract is unhelpful, by the market.

So far none of this is controversial. But a difficulty can arise when we *do* know what the plaintiff's expectation damages would be and his claim for restitutionary damages is greater. The *Restatement* adapts the following example rather freely from the movie *Red River*:

> Boss hires Wrangler as one of 25 hands engaged to drive a herd of longhorns from Texas to Kansas. Wages are $5 per day, to be paid in gold if and when the cattle reach the railhead at Wichita; but no wages are earned if the herd is lost. After 60 days on the trail, Wrangler is wrongfully discharged for an alleged breach of discipline. One week later, the entire herd is lost in a stampede that Wrangler could have done nothing to prevent. Although Wrangler performed valuable services before the breach of contract by Boss, Wrangler has no claim to damages because the aleatory "contract rate" fixed by agreement calls for no compensation.[61]

The example is good because it puts the issue starkly. Wrangler did a lot of work, and (let us suppose) his sixty days of labor had some market value that could be determined easily enough. We might use that market value as a benchmark for restitutionary damages if his expectation damages were difficult to settle—if, for example, Boss had called off the entire project because he lost interest in the cattle drive. In that case, Wrangler would have been deprived of a chance that the cattle might make it to Wichita, and the value of that chance would be hard to calculate, so restitution (here simply the market value of the services rendered) becomes a natural measure of recovery. But that isn't what happened in the illustration. The herd was lost in a stampede. So we *do* know what Wrangler's expectation damages would have been: nothing. That is the amount he would have collected if he had not been wrongfully discharged and the contract had been fully performed. Why should he collect more than all the other wranglers just because he was wrongfully fired? He shouldn't. He should collect nothing, just like the rest of them.

This result is partly a matter of holding Wrangler to the method of valuing his services that he agreed to in the contract. But there is a point of policy as well. Suppose Wrangler realized that the cattle drive was not going well and that his prospects for collecting the gold were getting worse by the day. If a breach by Boss would entitle Wrangler to compensation on a daily basis regardless of the fate of the cattle, then it would be in Wrangler's interest to see such a breach occur. In fact, it would be in the interest of all the wranglers to see Boss breach, since then they all would get paid something. So the wranglers would have an incentive to provoke a breach if they could find some way to do it without seeming too blameworthy. This is not the sort of incentive the law wants to create. It would raise the cost of the enterprise.

In a better known and more controversial (if less cinematic) set of cases, the plaintiff seeks the value of benefits conferred rather than expectation damages because the benefits conferred are worth more. In other words, the plaintiff made a bad bargain, or a "losing contract." A famous example is provided by *Kehoe v. Rutherford*.[62] The plaintiff agreed to build a road for the defendants. The contract price for the work was 65 cents per foot for 4,220 feet, for an expected total price of $2,743. It later became evident that the job was more expensive to do than the plaintiff had expected; the cost of the work would be $5,044. The defendants called off the job when the plaintiff had finished about 3,500 feet. The plaintiff argued that since the defendants breached the contract, he should be able to recover the value of his work, and that the value should be measured by the actual cost of it. The court rejected this argument, concluding that the plaintiff was limited to recovery at the contract rate—which meant that he was to recover nothing. He already had been paid at the contract rate for the work he had done so far. And since the defendant's decision to stop work on the job did not cost the plaintiff anything (actually it saved him money, since he was performing at a loss; he had made a bad contract), he had no expectation damages. The plaintiff's logic would have allowed him to collect much more money when the defendant breached than he would have received if he had been able to perform the contract.

Kehoe v. Rutherford might look distant from the wrangler's case, but the logic is the same. The fact that the defendant breached does not mean that we now set the contract aside and start reasoning from scratch about how to value the benefits the plaintiff provided. The contract itself laid down a rate for the work, and that rate sets the terms of the plaintiff's entitlement whether the contract is performed or breached. And, again, the contract rate also is the right measure as a matter of policy. Otherwise the plaintiff in *Kehoe* would have an incentive, perhaps late in the performance period, to induce a breach on the defendant's part so that the plaintiff can collect the higher rate of market-measured restitutionary damages rather than the lower rate called for by the contract that the plaintiff no doubt regrets.

The *Restatement (Second) of Contracts* seems to take a different view than the one just described, suggesting that restitution might be used to recover more than the contract price of the work done. The case law in either direction is sparse, and the discussion in the contracts *Restatement* is brief and devoid of illustrations, so it is hard to build a robust debate from those materials. This different view, however, is probably supported by two intuitions. First is the nagging worry that defendants otherwise are unjustly enriched under the rule explained above and endorsed here. Boss breaches yet pays Wrangler nothing. But the worry is groundless. In the only cases where this issue matters, the plaintiff has made a losing contract. When the defendant's breach frees the plaintiff from the need to perform it, the *plaintiff* is the one who is enriched.[63] Thus Wrangler was lucky to be wrongfully fired, because at least he was then free to go find something else to do that had some money in it (unlike the cattle drive, which turned out to be a losing endeavor). The plaintiff in *Kehoe* was lucky that the defendants breached, because now there was no need for him to keep building the road at a loss. To the extent that the defendant gets to keep a valuable performance without paying for it, this is a result of the contract, not of his breach of it. Likewise, in the cattle-driving case it might seem annoying that Boss gets the benefit of sixty days of Wrangler's services without paying anything. But that again is just a result of the contract, which called for no payment to *anyone* unless the cattle made it to Kansas. When the cattle didn't make it, Boss turned out to get the labor of all of the wranglers without paying for any of it. This is sad for the wranglers but not unjust enrichment for the boss. It is just a consequence of the contract.

Others are tempted for a different reason to let a plaintiff recover more in restitution than he would have recovered under the contract if performed. They worry that the latter amount—the plaintiff's provable expectation—will not compensate him as fully as it should. As Professor Dobbs puts it, "A suspicion that the plaintiff has a losing contract because the defendant is in breach goes a long way toward justifying a recovery without an expectancy ceiling."[64] The concern evidently is that the defendant's breach will cause the plaintiff consequential damages that are hard to prove, especially in the complex manufacturing and construction settings where these problems tend to arise. The *Restatement (Third) of Restitution and Unjust Enrichment* reasonably suggests that these problems be handled by awards of "special damages," rather than by pretending they are matters of restitution.[65]

To summarize, a plaintiff's recovery of restitution for breach of contract should not exceed his provable expectation. Put differently, if it can be shown that the contract, if performed, would have lost money for the plaintiff, he should not be able to seek restitution to avoid that result and save himself from his bad bargain. (The same could be said, and is said more often, about reliance damages.)[66] This result fits our recurring theme: the workings of restitution as a contract remedy often have no rigorous connection to the defendant's unjust enrichment, but they make fine sense if restitutionary damages in a contract case are really meant as a second-best way to get at the loss of expectation that the plaintiff suffered from the breach.

Restitution for Opportunistic Breach

In one rare circumstance the law of contract does let the plaintiff seek restitution as a remedy in a stricter sense, including recovery that exceeds his own losses. These are cases where the defendant's breach is deliberate and profitable (it gains him more than honoring the contract would have done), and where the plaintiff can't use expectation damages to buy a full substitute for the defendant's performance.[67] To take a simple example, you promise to sell me your house for $100,000; then you sell it to someone else for $110,000. I can collect $10,000 from you.[68] Your breach was deliberate, it was profitable, and expectation damages cannot provide me with a full replacement for your promised performance. Here those expectation damages might theoretically be the difference—if such a difference could be proven—between the $100,000 contract price and my cost of buying an identical property from someone else. But we have to describe that measure as theoretical because the law generally regards each piece of real property as unique. This idea is more familiar from cases that award plaintiffs specific performance when the defendant breaches a contract to sell land. The similarity of analysis is no coincidence. The cases where a plaintiff can seek restitution of the defendant's gains from breach tend to be the same cases where specific performance would have been available if the plaintiff had been able to ask for it in time. The basic reasons for awarding specific performance or restitution are the same. Damages aren't enough to make the plaintiff whole, because they can't be used to buy a complete substitute for what the defendant had promised. So the plaintiff can choose to force performance by the defendant or (if it is too late for that) to strip the defendant of his gains.

It is the same if I rent an apartment to you with an agreement that you will not sublet the place—then you sublet it anyway, and I don't find out until afterward. Expectation damages probably will not be a satisfying remedy for your breach, because I am unlikely to be able to show any.[69] This is a common enough feature of cases where someone promises not to do something but then does it. (Another old example: you hire my company to protect your town against fires for twelve months; after the contract ends without incident and I have been paid, you find out that I had many fewer firefighters than were promised in the contract.)[70] In these situations the plaintiff is vulnerable to the defendant, who may perceive that he has a chance to breach the contract with impunity because the plaintiff will find damages impossible to prove. The defendant who deliberately breaches on that basis acts opportunistically. He takes advantage of a weakness in the usual rules of contract damages and so unjustly enriches himself at the plaintiff's expense. He therefore can be made to relinquish his gains, the better to deter him from such behavior.[71] Allowing the promisee to collect the promisor's gains makes their agreement more secure and more valuable in advance.[72]

A final example can be constructed from the famous facts of *Peevy-*

house v. Garland Coal & Mining Co.[73] A strip-mining company made a contract allowing it to tear up the plaintiff's property and take the coal buried there. In return the company promised to pay a royalty and to restore the land to its original condition. The company took the coal, paid the money, and then wouldn't restore the land. The court viewed the plaintiff's damages as the difference between the value of the property with and without the restoration—which turned out to be negligible. The contract damages might have been measured differently, of course. They could have been based on the cost of restoration, an alternative the court regarded as wasteful. But the case also lends itself to analysis under the framework considered here. If the cost of restoration was taken into account in setting the size of the royalty, then the strip-mining company would be unjustly enriched if it were able to take the coal and not restore the land. Its decision not to restore is then best viewed as opportunistic. The company made a choice detrimental to the plaintiff because it knew that the available measurements of damages would not fully capture the costs of performance. Or view it from the plaintiff's perspective: he will not be able to use the damages to get the very thing promised in the contract. This shortfall gives the defendant an incentive to commit a breach, a possibility which, if foreseen, might scuttle all such future contracts at their inception. The resulting enrichment—the company's savings in avoiding the restoration work—should be recoverable by the plaintiff as one possible remedy for the defendant's breach of contract.[74]

At first these rules might seem to sit uneasily with the notion of efficient breach.[75] This is the idea that sometimes it is best for a plaintiff to breach a contract—not just best for him, but best for the world. I make a contract with you; then along comes another bidder for my services who will pay me more than you did. With the money the new bidder offers me, I can breach our contract, pay your damages, and still have a profit left over. I will be better off after the breach, and so will the new buyer, and nobody will be worse off: an efficient outcome. The point of the theory is that such breaches of contract should be encouraged, not enjoined, and that position, whatever its merits, might seem inconsistent with letting the plaintiff take away the defendant's gains. But there really is no inconsistency. On the "efficient breach" facts just described, the defendant will not owe restitution to the plaintiff because his breach is not opportunistic. By hypothesis his payment of damages will make the plaintiff indifferent between breach and performance. That wasn't true in the strip-mining case, or the firefighters' case, or the real estate cases, which is why restitution was appropriate there. The breaches in those cases really *weren't* efficient. In the strip-mining case, for example, restitution is in order and it is not a case of efficient breach, and those two things are true for the same reason: there is a serious risk that damages wouldn't make the plaintiff indifferent between breach and performance. So we don't want the defendant to simply breach and pay damages. We want to make him negotiate with the plaintiff for some consensual way out of the contract that really *is* efficient. We induce those negotiations by making the defendant's breach valueless to him. We make the breach valueless to him by giving the plaintiff a restitution claim.

Few plaintiffs are ever really indifferent between performance by the defendant and a payment of damages. They typically would prefer the performance, because damages don't cover a plaintiff's legal expenses and various other inconveniences occasioned by a breach of contract. Some think that these points make the whole idea of efficient breach a mirage.[76] That debate is not quite our concern here, but it shows that there is an ambiguity when one talks about whether expectation damages are adequate or defective. For purposes of restitution—that is, in deciding whether a defendant's breach counts as opportunistic—the inadequacy of expectation damages has to be more severe than those routine disappointments just mentioned. The problem generally has to be that the plaintiff cannot use whatever money he would win in the lawsuit to buy a full substitute for whatever the defendant promised.[77] Which substitutes are good enough to count as "full" obviously is a judgment call, and there is room here for the court to think about not only the similarity between the replacement and the thing promised but also the good faith or ruthlessness of the defendant's behavior.

CHAPTER SIX

Money Remedies

Having surveyed the main ways that a plaintiff can win a restitution claim, we turn now to remedies. Some of the discussion in this chapter and the next will recapitulate points on the rules of liability made in the previous chapters, especially the chapter on takings. But the overlap has its advantages. It means these chapters can be brief and can tie together things that have been said in different places elsewhere; an overview of remedies shows relationships between different types of restitution claims that are harder to see when the claims are considered one at a time.

A successful claim for restitution can result, broadly speaking, in either of two kinds of remedies. One of them, only sometimes available, is the right to take back specific property from the defendant by means of various tools—the constructive trust, for example—originally developed by courts of equity. Those remedies are the subject of the next chapter. This chapter examines a simpler type of remedy available in every case: a money judgment that can be collected out of whatever assets the defendant has. This is known as a personal liability of the defendant because the plaintiff has rights against the defendant himself, not against any particular property in the defendant's hands.[1] The plaintiff in restitution recovers the money by the same methods of execution that are available at the end of a typical tort or contract suit.

Two Variables That Affect the Measurement of a Money Remedy

Sometimes the amount due at the end of a restitution case is an easy question. If the plaintiff mistakenly paid money to the defendant, then the amount the defendant owes is simply the amount he received, along with any interest he has earned on it.[2] The harder cases arise from two kinds of complications. First, sometimes a plaintiff provides benefits to a defendant that cannot be returned—perhaps a service, or an improvement of the defendant's property, or goods that get consumed. Deciding how much the defendant owes can then be difficult because there may be many ways to measure his enrichment. In roughly increasing order of generosity, those measures may include any expense the defendant was spared by the plaintiff's efforts, the cost the plaintiff spent to provide the benefit, the amount the defendant said he would pay for the benefit, the market value of the benefit, or all the benefits the transfer produced for the defendant, including not just the asset itself but any use value it had and any investment income it produced. (Early in that sequence we might also have mentioned another possibility that sometimes is available: the value of the plaintiff's work that the defendant realized in money when he later sold the property.) As a practical matter there is probably no case in which all of those options can be used, and in some cases more than one of them (such as market value and contract price) may yield the same outcome. But sometimes more than one measure is available and plausible, and much depends on the choice between them.

The second complication is that the defendant's responsibility for his own enrichment is greater in some cases than in others. The enriched defendant might bear no responsibility, as when he has received a mistaken payment that he never asked for; or partial responsibility, as when he receives benefits from a contract he signed that turns out to be invalid; or complete responsibility, as when he takes the plaintiff's property by fraud. Some of those defendants need to be deterred strongly, while others require no deterrence at all, and the law's sense of fairness calls for different treatment of them as well. The size of the payment the defendant makes at the end of a restitution case should be sensitive to these distinctions.

Conveniently enough, the two complications just shown—the different ways enrichment can be measured and the different responsibilities that defendants may have for the transfer—tend to take care of each other. The more responsibility the defendant has for his own enrichment, the more liberal the court will be in measuring it. That is not the only principle affecting the calculus; it has been argued, for example, that when the defendant's acts occurred in the context of a relationship with the plaintiff, courts are more generous than when the parties are strangers.[3] But the relationship between culpability and the assessment of a money remedy is powerful and will provide the organizing theme for the rest of this chapter. We will divide defendants according to the role they played in their own enrichment and see how the measure of recovery becomes more generous as their responsibility increases. In the chapter on takings we went through a smaller but similar exercise, putting all wrongs on a scale of culpability and then observing that conscious wrongdoers pay more than innocent ones. Here we extend the spectrum to include defendants who commit no wrong of any kind, and break down into more detail the remedial choices that apply to them.

Innocent Recipients

Begin with the innocent recipient of a mistaken transfer—that is, a defendant who received nonreturnable benefits that he never asked for and had no chance to refuse. Since the defendant in this position has no responsibility for his enrichment, he requires no deterrence and a court will measure the benefit he received by the most conservative method available. This typically means "value to the recipient": the plaintiff must prove how much the defendant actually valued the benefits he received, without relying on proxies such as the cost of providing the benefit or evidence of its market value.[4] In practice the plaintiff usually has to come up with evidence that the mistaken transfer spared the defendant some expense that he otherwise would have incurred—for example, that he would certainly have paid someone else to make the same improvement on his property if the plaintiff had not done it mistakenly. Or that the defendant realized the value of the improvement in a later sale. If the amount of the defendant's gain cannot be proven in these or other clear ways, the plaintiff collects nothing, even if it is evident that the defendant must have received some benefit of indeterminate size.

The principles just stated reflect traditional learning. But many courts will fashion an outcome more generous to the party who makes an expensive improvement to someone else's property in the good-faith belief that he has the right to do so. A classic example is the plaintiff who mistakenly builds on the defendant's property—perhaps an entire house. The traditional operation of the principles just shown would entitle the plaintiff to nothing unless he can make a fairly specific demonstration of the value of the improvement to the defendant. In a case of substantial hardship, however, courts sometimes use their equity powers to devise a more generous result, possibly even requiring a forced sale if the burden imposed on the defendant would be unusually slight. See the chapter on mistakes for closer consideration of these possibilities.

Lawson v. O'Kelley[5] illustrates the operation of the traditional principles in a more routine case. O'Kelley owned a building. Two of his tenants asked a roofer, Lawson, to put a new roof on it; O'Kelley had told the tenants not to do this, but Lawson was unaware of that. Lawson reroofed the building, O'Kelley refused to pay for the work, and Lawson sued him on a theory of "quasi-contract"—that is, restitution. The court found for O'Kelley. No doubt Lawson had conferred some benefit on him by installing a new roof, but the size of that benefit—the amount, if any, that O'Kelley would have been prepared to pay for it if he had been asked—was impossible to prove. It would have been different if Lawson had shown that his work enabled O'Kelley to cancel work by other roofers he had recently hired. Lawson would then have been entitled to whatever O'Kelley saved as a result of Lawson's labors. In the actual case O'Kelley sold the building soon after the work was done and received no extra payment on account of the new roof—for the buyer's plan was to tear the whole building down anyway.

Now suppose the plaintiff can prove that his mistaken improvement did save the defendant a substantial amount of money, but it cost somewhat less than that for the plaintiff to provide. Thus the mistakenly laid roof allowed the defendant to save $10,000 that he had been planning to spend, but cost the plaintiff $8,000 in labor and materials. Which of those amounts should the defendant be required to pay? The smaller one. As we have seen, the innocent defendant pays the value to him of the benefit received or the cost to the plaintiff of providing it, whichever is less.[6] Once the plaintiff has had his expenses covered, any remaining benefit the defendant enjoys may amount to enrichment, but it is not considered *unjust* enrichment. It might be viewed, rather, as enrichment of an innocent defendant without injury to the plaintiff, which the law does not find troubling.

Or we can view the choice from an economic standpoint and observe that awarding $10,000 might cause the plaintiff to turn a profit from his mistake. Insisting on the lesser recovery nudges the plaintiff (in the unlikely event that he needs a nudge) to take better care next time, whether by watching where he builds or more carefully consulting the defendant. This point also helps explain a similar and more general recurring principle: courts will not permit an award of restitution against an innocent defendant to be a source of profit to the plaintiff.[7] (Awards against culpable defendants are another matter.)

The law's protection of the innocent defendant is qualified when the value of the benefits he has received has been realized in cash. If the defendant turned profits as a result of a mistaken improvement, for example, the plaintiff can point to those as clear evidence of a benefit and might be able to collect them despite the defendant's innocence. Examples include those cases discussed earlier in the book where the plaintiff mistakenly builds a structure on the defendant's land, and the defendant then rents out the property or sells it for more than he would have obtained when the land was bare. But the defendant generally cannot be required to make that sale and cannot be forced to pay anything in advance of it. The reason is yet another protective principle for the innocent defendant: he cannot be made any worse off than he was before the mistaken transfer.[8] On a traditional view of the matter, the most the plaintiff might obtain is a lien to secure his recovery from the proceeds of any sale that may occur later.[9] But the amount of that recovery, secured or unsecured, is only what it takes to reimburse the plaintiff for his costs. If the sale yields profits beyond that amount, they are the defendant's to keep—always assuming that the defendant is innocent.

Defendants Who Requested the Benefits Received

Next is the defendant who did nothing wrong and had no contract with the plaintiff but at least did ask for the benefits he received. The law normally requires that such a defendant pay the market value of the benefits—the measure known as "quantum meruit." This will tend to be a more generous measure of recovery than would be had if the plaintiff were required to prove the value of the benefit to the defendant. The different rule here follows from the sensible assumption that if the defendant made clear he wanted the benefits but did not settle the price, he was ready to pay the going rate for them.[10] The same assumption is made about any other benefits that, even if not requested, the law presumes were valuable to the defendant, such as emergency medical services provided to him while unconscious.[11] Cases of that sort may involve no presumption about the defendant's actual intentions. He will have to pay market value even if he can later convince a court that he would not have wanted the emergency treatment at that price. The reason is that most people *would* want the treatment at that price, and the promise of compensation at a market rate makes the provider of the treatment more likely to supply it. (But in a restitution case one must be careful in talking of what the doctor needs by way of "compensation," for that is the language of tort law. To speak strictly, market value is used to measure the defendant's enrichment.)

Defendants Partly Responsible: Failed Contracts

Next in responsibility comes the defendant who received some benefits under a contract that cannot be enforced. He might not be at *fault* in a recognizable sense, but he bears substantial responsibility for the transfer since he did have a hand in making the contract. The measure of recovery against him will therefore tend to be a little larger—though as we saw in the chapter on failed contracts, the details of the remedy will depend on exactly why the contract is unenforceable. If the parties just didn't observe some formality, the courts will typically presume that the defendant valued the benefits at whatever price he had agreed to pay for them. The defendant may later have come to value the benefits less than that, but the contract price at least shows the minimum value he assigned to them when the agreement was made. If the defendant was never supposed to pay for the benefits but was instead supposed to *do* something, then the value of the benefits to him is presumed to be the market value of his performance.

Naturally the outcome may be different when the contract fails for less innocent reasons. If the parties' agreement was induced by fraud or duress on the plaintiff's part, then the price the defendant agreed to pay is not a good measure of his enrichment (and allowing that measure of recovery would fail to deter the fraud or other misconduct). The plaintiff, if entitled to recover at all, will have to prove how much the defendant actually valued what he received. And if the defendant acted in an opportunistic or otherwise objectionable way, the enrichment he is forced to give up may not be limited to the size of the plaintiff's expenses; it can then include any additional enrichment the defendant reaped, as it is all then considered unjust.[12]

Or suppose the plaintiff provided some benefits to the defendant under a contract that cannot be enforced because it is illegal. Again the plaintiff may not be able to recover anything; but if the rule forbidding enforcement of the contract is just a regulation with no strong policy of condemnation behind it, allowing the defendant to pay nothing for the benefits he received does seem to enrich him unjustly. On the other hand, letting the plaintiff recover the entire contract price might amount to the same thing as simply enforcing the contract, which the law has said must not be done. A typical compromise is to let the plaintiff recover just the costs he incurred by performing—better than nothing, but less than he would have been entitled to collect if the contract had been enforced. For more discussion of all the principles just mentioned, see the chapter on failed contracts.

Defendants Who Inadvertently Do Wrong; Secondary Sources of Enrichment

Next in culpability are defendants who commit legal wrongs without intending them, such as innocent trespassers or defendants who receive property that they did not know had been stolen. Defendants of this kind are always liable for at least the market value of whatever they received. That is the standard minimum recovery where a defendant has committed a legal wrong, whether deliberately or not—and this even if the actual value of the benefit to the defendant is shown to have been something less. So suppose the defendant has a contract with a supplier to receive coal at five dollars per ton. Unbeknownst to him, the supplier sends stolen coal that has a market value of six dollars per ton, which the defendant promptly burns. The liability of the defendant to the coal's owner is six dollars per ton.[13] The result might seem harsh. The defendant would be paying a price that outruns the value he put on the coal, and on these facts he had no intention of violating anyone's rights. But the harshness follows inevitably from the law's decision to treat the recipient of stolen property as a tortfeasor. Indeed, having the defendant pay the market value of the benefits received makes the liability in restitution look much like strict liability in tort.

If a wrongdoer had innocent intentions, this does entitle him to a few advantages compared to a wrongdoer of the deliberate variety. To see this requires a broader view of the elements of recovery. So far we have mostly been looking at how the defendant's culpability affects the way that courts value the property he receives: by its market value, its contract price, and so forth. But putting those specifics to one side, there are whole other categories of gains for which some defendants are held liable while

others are not. Suppose I receive property from you that I shouldn't—
never mind why. It might be an extra cow you sent with a delivery of
others I ordered, or an improvement you put on my property, or securities
that I stole. The receipt of any of these things could enrich me in several
respects. First is the value of the thing itself—the animal's market value,
for example, measured in any of the ways we have been discussing. But
other kinds of enrichment, which might be called "secondary," go beyond
the immediate value of the asset. To summarize:

Proceeds are the direct product of an asset—usually money received
upon the sale of it, but also anything the asset naturally produces: a calf
born to the cow, or dividends produced by shares of stock that were mistakenly received. They amount to the original property in new or ex-
panded form. Every restitution defendant who is liable at all is liable for
proceeds from the property in question.[14]

Use value refers to enrichment generated by using the asset. The most
common examples are interest earned on money or earnings from land
or other property when it is rented out. Every restitution defendant who
is liable at all is liable for use value realized in fact from an asset—that
is, for interest actually earned and rental income actually received.[15] But
the liability of an innocent defendant stops there, while a defendant who
is a wrongdoer of any sort (conscious or not) will typically be *presumed*
to have enjoyed the use value.[16] In other words, his liability will be based
on what the property could and should have earned if used prudently,
even if it wasn't. Notice that events can cause a defendant to change categories for these purposes. Suppose the defendant innocently acquires the
plaintiff's property but then will not return it when he is told that the
transfer was a mistake. For the period before he learned that the property
belonged to the defendant, he is liable for interest or other use value actually earned from it. For the period after he learned the truth, he is liable
for reasonable use value whether he actually earned it or not.

Consequential gains are benefits generated by the property in some
less direct and foreseeable way than was shown in the last two categories.
If the defendant sells the plaintiff's cow for its market price, the resulting funds are mere proceeds. If the defendant takes the plaintiff's money,
spends it on a lottery ticket, and wins, the resulting funds are better considered consequential gains. Think of proceeds, again, as the original property simply in new form and of use value as the property put to work
in obvious ways. Consequential gains, by contrast, are assets generated
through a chain with more links—additional and less obvious investment

decisions by the defendant or multiple transformations of the property that cause its value to grow in ways that aren't routine. These lines can be hazy. In the close cases, the difference between consequential and other gains is best understood by reference to its practical stakes. The general rule is that conscious wrongdoers are liable for consequential gains but other defendants are not.[17] So when deciding whether gains are "consequential," the judge is also likely to be examining the nature of the defendant's conduct and seeking an ultimate conclusion about how completely the defendant must pay over the gains obtained from having the plaintiff's property for a while. The degree of the defendant's misconduct and other equities of the case will influence difficult judgments about how to categorize his gains. The decision may not be expressed that way; it may be stated as a finding that the causation running between the transfer and the defendant's resulting enrichment was (or was not) too attenuated. But the driving force behind the analysis in a close case is likely to be the defendant's culpability or lack thereof.

With that overview in place, return to our question from a moment ago. How does the law measure the liability of a defendant who committed a wrong without knowing it? We saw earlier that the value of the property will be measured by its market value. Now we can add a few more conclusions based on the principles just shown. This sort of defendant will have to pay for any use value the property had in his hands, whether actually obtained or not, because he was a wrongdoer.[18] But he will not have to pay consequential gains because he was not a *conscious* wrongdoer. An important exception to all this is the fiduciary who breaches his duty, however inadvertently. As noted in chapter 4, rules governing that type of defendant tend to be idiosyncratic and often are severe, even when his intentions were good.

Blameworthy Defendants

We just saw that sometimes a defendant can commit an invasion of a plaintiff's legal rights without having a guilty mind. The opposite is also true. A defendant can commit an act that involves a bad mental state yet is not quite an "actionable" wrong that would result in prosecution or allow the plaintiff to sue for damages in tort. Perhaps the defendant saw his property being improved by the plaintiff, realized it was a mistake, but chose to say nothing. Such silence is not a wrong that allows the plaintiff to sue in tort, but it makes the defendant's enrichment unjust. And since the defendant had a culpable role in the transfer, the plaintiff is entitled to a generous recovery in restitution.[19] Or consider the abuse of a confidential relationship, as when the defendant has engaged in sharp practice when dealing with his dependent grandmother. Traditionally this gives the grandmother no right to recover damages in tort, but it does give her a restitution claim to recover the grandson's unjust enrichment.[20]

So to begin with our usual first question: How should the value of the transferred property itself be measured in cases like this? The culpable defendant pays market value or cost to the plaintiff, whichever is greater (the reverse of the rule for innocent defendants).[21] Further rules of measurement are hard to state precisely because the category can include so many different sorts of acts. Imagine a case like the one described a moment ago where the plaintiff built on the defendant's land, but where the defendant encouraged the plaintiff to build in the wrong place out of mere negligence. The defendant didn't realize the builder was mistaken but should have; the defendant's advice was not consciously bad and (let us suppose) is not actionable in tort but still was a minor wrong. A court might respond by making the defendant pay over to the plaintiff any increase in the market value of his property that resulted from the mistaken improvement—even if he isn't selling the land and doesn't plan to do so. This probably would be a more modest remedy than making the defendant pay the plaintiff's costs, which would be a more likely result in the earlier version of the same problem involving bad faith. But paying the increase in the property's market value is a more aggressive remedy than the payment of zero which likely would be due if the defendant had no responsibility for the incident at all. When confronted with defendants who have contributed to their own unjust enrichment by doing things that are blameworthy (but not actionable)—whether the acts are negligent, intentional, or somewhere in between—courts have flexibility to choose a measure of enrichment that seems sensible on the facts.

Now we also can ask the question introduced a moment ago about which other categories of gain a blameworthy defendant must return. Of course such a defendant will be liable for use value, whether actually earned or not. As for consequential gains, we know they are recoverable from defendants who have culpable states of mind—in other words, something worse than negligence. This can include some defendants in the category we are considering here: those who, though not violating the plaintiff's legal rights, behaved reprehensibly.[22] The law of restitution is hard on the conscious wrongdoer; he needs to be deterred, so the courts seek to ensure that his decisions produce no gains for him.

Defendants Who Deliberately Invade Another's Legal Rights

At the most culpable end of our spectrum is the deliberate invader of another person's legal rights as established under tort and criminal law, such as a thief, a defrauder, or an embezzler. This sort of defendant is in need of deterrence most of all and so will be liable for all benefits produced by the transfer, whether primary or secondary.[23] The remedy, again, is meant to make the defendant's act valueless to him. Restitution of this kind is known as "disgorgement" or an "accounting for profits." The property itself will be valued in ways generous to the plaintiff—usually by its market value. The disgorgement will also include every kind of enrichment we have discussed: proceeds, use value, and consequential gains. The defendant may also be denied a counterclaim for improvements or other value he has added to the property while it was in his hands, a point we will examine in more detail in a moment.

Problems of Causation

The measure of recovery against a defendant may also depend on principles of causation and on the credit the defendant may be due for adding value to the property at issue.[24] To begin with causation, the deliberate wrongdoer's obligation to disgorge consequential gains does not make his liability boundless. Eventually the gains from a transfer become too remote even to count as "consequential." Some of these matters were treated in the earlier chapter on takings; here we look at particular problems that arise in calculating money remedies. First, what if the chain of causation between the transfer and the enrichment includes not just one transaction but two or three? Here courts make another round of judgments about where to draw lines, and again the best guide to their location in a close case is the defendant's culpability.

Suppose, for example, that the defendant embezzles money from his employer to buy a house, then resells the house later at a profit. The employer is entitled to the embezzled money plus interest—and this regardless of whether the defendant actually earned any interest; for if he didn't, he should have.[25] And the employer is also entitled to the profit the defendant turned on the immediate investment of what he took: the increase in the value of the house. But now suppose the defendant took the profits from selling the house and invested them in yet another venture that doubled in value. Is his employer entitled to *those* profits as well? The question is whether the gains from the second investment are "attributable" to the defendant's wrong—that is, the embezzlement. In this case the defendant might well be liable for all the profits from both the first and second investments.[26] True, the gains were the result not only of the embezzlement but of the defendant's investment acumen, or perhaps of his good luck. But the law generally prefers to eradicate all benefits that flow from the wrongdoing. (If the defendant invests the embezzled money in a house and its value goes down, of course, he gets no relief. He remains liable for the entire sum taken.)

Yet our defendant might escape liability for those consequential gains after all if he can show that he would have made the second investment with other funds even if he hadn't had the ill-gotten gains from the first one.[27] This argument—that causation fails because the defendant would have ended up with the same assets even if he never committed the wrong—is a common source of difficulty in cases that involve the investment of wrongful gains. The replies that courts make tend to be much influenced, again, by the underlying equities of the case: the wrongfulness of the defendant's acts and whether disgorgement of all returns from his investment would work a hardship that seems disproportionate to his wrong.[28]

Now consider this variation. The second investment by the defendant was made partly with profits from the first investment but partly too—say 60 percent—with other money that he earned legitimately. This time a court might make a pro rata division, ordering payment to the plaintiff of 40 percent of the gains from the second investment.[29] But in some cases pro rata calculations do not work so well, as when stolen money is put into a pool with legitimate funds and the pool is applied to all sorts of purchases. Then decisions about whether a defendant's gains are too remote from his wrong to be recoverable often have to be based on rough approximations. We saw earlier that when suing an innocent recipient of benefits, the plaintiff must make precise showings of the defendant's enrichment or else lose the case. The same precision is not needed when suing a deliberate wrongdoer. Uncertainties generally are resolved against him; once the plaintiff has made a reasonable showing of the defendant's enrichment, the defendant has the burden of proving that the enrichment is less than it appears.[30] That burden of proof becomes important when the inquiries we have been discussing descend into uncertainties, as they often will.[31]

Credit for Value Added

Courts make a similar study of the policies behind the law when a defendant argues that his liability should be reduced to reflect what he spent to transform the property he stole into something more valuable. The argument for deducting those costs is plausible in principle, since the purpose of the exercise is to isolate the defendant's net enrichment. In practice, though, whether such credits are allowed will depend on whether they can be squared with the policies that require restitution in the first place. If the defendant deliberately harvests the plaintiff's wheat without permission and spends a lot of money refining it into flour that he subsequently sells, he will be liable for the proceeds of sale with no credit for his expenses in improving the stolen wheat.[32] Denying the credit can be defended in several ways.

First, a credit would mean, in effect, that the worst-case outcome for the thief is that he breaks even. He would therefore have positive expected returns from this kind of behavior, which would fail to discourage it (putting aside consequences that might be imposed by other bodies of law).

Second, a credit would allow the defendant to force a transaction on the plaintiff. In effect the defendant turns the plaintiff's wheat into flour and then the plaintiff has to pay a thief for milling services.

Lastly, if the defendant gets a credit, then formally this is best understood as the result of a restitution claim—actually a counterclaim—by him against the plaintiff.[33] When he has to give the flour to the plaintiff, he complains that this leaves the plaintiff unjustly enriched because his wheat was turned into flour at no cost to him. So the defendant demands a set-off to reflect his contribution to the final product. The court likely would say the defendant is equitably disqualified from making the counterclaim—for as noted in the chapter on failed contracts, equitable disqualification is not limited to cases that seek equitable relief. Sometimes this sort of denial is best explained as punitive, though punishment is not formally a purpose of restitution law.

Intellectual Property

Cases in which the defendant misappropriates the plaintiff's intellectual property frequently call for restitutionary recovery. Since ideas and other creative work can often be borrowed without reducing the owner's ability to also keep using them, the plaintiff's damages may well be minor while the defendant's gains are great. But the calculation of the remedy in such a case can present some special problems of measurement. The problems are frequently addressed by statute, which largely removes them from the scope of this book. A few generalizations might usefully be offered here, however, both about statutory tendencies and about the common-law principles that inform the interpretation of the statutes and fill in whatever gaps are left behind.[34]

As we have seen, "use value" is available as a matter of course to a plaintiff who brings a winning claim for restitution. That heading of recovery is the most common starting point in a case involving intellectual property, because typically the defendant is sued precisely for putting the plaintiff's idea or other creation to unauthorized use (as by exploiting a patent or incorporating copyrighted material into another work). The value of such uses will most often be measured by estimating the price of a reasonable royalty or license. Here as elsewhere, though, forcing a defendant to pay that amount may not adequately deter repetition of his conduct.[35] The law of restitution generally responds by letting the plaintiff alternatively collect any profits the defendant turned by acts of conscious wrongdoing. Federal statutes that protect intellectual property follow that principle roughly but often are more generous. Thus the Lanham Act, which covers trademark infringement and false advertising, allows recovery of the defendant's profits only when he has engaged in conscious wrongdoing, but no such showing is required in cases of copyright infringement, the infringement of a design patent, or the theft of a trade secret. Profits from those wrongs are subject to disgorgement by statute regardless of whether the defendant's invasion of the plaintiff's rights was deliberate, though no doubt measurement of recovery is more likely to be generous in fact in a case of purposeful infringement.

The most pervasive challenge in cases involving intellectual property is separation of what the defendant gained by infringing the plaintiff's rights from what the defendant would have gained legitimately without the infringement. In some cases this may involve complex problems of accounting. Thus in one famous case, *Sheldon v. Metro-Goldwyn Pictures Corp.*,[36] the defendants were found liable for deliberate infringement of the plaintiff's copyrighted play. Determining the amount of net profit earned by the infringing movie—one of dozens released by the studio that year— was a challenging task by itself, involving the allocation of overhead expenses between one production and another. Assume this number has been found; that still is not the end of the task, because the plaintiff must show what proportion of those net profits were attributable to the plaintiff's play, as opposed to all the other elements that made the film profitable: the stars, the advertising, and so on. Such calculations may be impossible to make with any certainty and so will often be decided as a result of presumptions and the burden of proof. These tend to resolve doubts against the wrongdoer, and so may force him, in effect, to pay more than he really gained. (This was almost certainly the case in *Sheldon*.) But such results accord with the longstanding legal principle that a defendant should not benefit from uncertainties that result from his own misconduct.

A more recent example is *Playboy Enterprises, Inc. v. Baccarat Clothing Co.*[37] The defendant created counterfeit blue jeans that included the rabbit-head logo associated with the plaintiff. The court found that the defendant committed willful infringement of the plaintiff's trademark, and so sought to devise a remedy that would make the wrong valueless. The court found that the defendant had sold twenty thousand pairs of the infringing trousers and had made a profit of at least $6 per sale. That produced a profit on the clothing of $120,000, all of which the plaintiff was entitled to recover. Perhaps the defendant might have purchased a license in advance for considerably less, but that was neither here nor there. The result is startling because it seems highly likely—obvious, even—that not all of the defendant's profits were attributable to the infringement of the plaintiff's logo. But establishing that difference was the defendant's job. Thus the *Restatement* rightly suggests that the award would properly have been reduced if the defendant had been able to show that it sold noninfringing jeans for only a little less than the infringing pairs. It would then be reasonably clear how much the infringement added to the defendant's gains and that those gains were considerably less than the entire net profit from the tainted jeans. The defendant in this case offered no such proof, however, and so was required to disgorge all of its profits to the plaintiff.

CHAPTER SEVEN

Equitable Remedies

Sometimes the plaintiff in a restitution case doesn't want a personal judgment that calls for the defendant to pay a certain amount of money. The plaintiff wants specific relief: a judgment awarding him particular property that the defendant holds or at least an interest in the property. The law of restitution offers four basic devices for taking property back from defendants in this way: a constructive trust, an equitable lien, subrogation, and rescission. This chapter explains how those devices work. We will consider each of them in detail in a moment, but it will help to start with a quick overview.

A *constructive trust* is an order stating that property to which the defendant holds title should and does belong to the plaintiff and must be delivered to him. It can be used simply to recover property to which the defendant obtained title wrongfully, as by fraud, but its more distinct use is to allow recovery of property that has changed form since it left the plaintiff's hands. Perhaps the defendant traded or sold the plaintiff's property for something else. The court imposes a constructive trust on the something else, and the plaintiff takes it ("takes it *back*," one often wants to say, though the thing he receives may not be exactly the thing that he lost).

Today the constructive trust can become important in the cases discussed in this book's chapter on takings: situations where the defendant has wrongfully made off with the plaintiff's property or has received it from a wrongdoer, and the plaintiff seeks the return of the very thing taken, not just the declaration of a judicially backed debt. The constructive trust also occasionally gets used in other circumstances: in cases of mistake, or when someone promises to transfer property in some way— for example, by including a provision in his will or by buying life insurance—in exchange for a certain act by the plaintiff. The plaintiff performs his side of the agreement, but the promising party does not—and then he dies. A constructive trust may be placed on the untransferred property for the plaintiff's benefit.[1]

Despite the name of the device, a constructive trust does not necessarily relate to the law of trusts. This body of law did begin with responses to breaches of fiduciary duty by trustees of express trusts; and while the modern applications are usually far afield from those facts, the device has been developed by analogy to those circumstances. The constructive trustee must not only hand over the property but also account for everything he earned with it. The analogy pretty much ends there, however; the constructive trustee does not have the duty of prudent management associated with real trustees of property, and in most other respects the practical operation of the constructive trust is not illuminated by ordinary trust law. The device is just a way to get property back to its owner. And the vocabulary of the constructive trust is potentially misleading in another way, too. Courts sometimes talk as if they are *creating* the arrangement—"a constructive trust is hereby imposed on the property for the benefit of the plaintiff," et cetera—when in substance the decision really amounts to recognizing that the plaintiff has, in good conscience, been entitled to the property all along.[2] The plaintiff thus has a claim to all proceeds the property has earned since the moment it was transferred to the defendant, not just what it has earned since the constructive trust was declared.

An *equitable lien* gives the plaintiff a security interest in the defendant's property: usually the right to force a judicial sale of it and to recover what he is owed out of the proceeds. This is a useful device when the plaintiff's property has been mixed with other assets. Suppose the defendant uses the plaintiff's money to add a fresh story to his house; after getting caught, he doesn't have enough money to pay back what he took. The plaintiff cannot fairly be made the house's owner. His assets only contributed to part of its value. But he can have an equitable lien on the house to the extent of the amount that was taken from him.

It is sometimes tempting, but misleading, to think of an equitable lien as representing a claim to part of the defendant's property, whereas a constructive trust represents a claim to the whole thing. Neither of those impressions is entirely right. It is quite possible to have a constructive trust on part of some piece of property; if you steal my money and combine it with yours to buy Blackacre, taking title in your name, we are equitable co-owners pro rata—a relevant distinction if Blackacre has increased in value before our dispute is resolved. Meanwhile an equitable lien does not make me a part owner of your property. It makes me a lienor. You own the entire thing, but I have a lien on the entire thing up to the value of my claim, and I will recover that amount as a secured creditor whether the value of Blackacre increases or decreases in the meantime.

Subrogation, as a remedy, may become available when you use my money to pay a debt that you owe to a third party. The debt you owed to him was secured by some piece of your property—perhaps a mortgage on your land. I can now step into the creditor's shoes and have all the same rights in your property that he had. To state the result fully, I am subrogated to his claim, his security, and his priority. I have the same right that he had to force a judicial sale of the property to collect what you owe me, and to take the proceeds ahead of any creditors who may be trying to pounce on your assets.

Rescission deserves a brief mention here. It means undoing an exchange, with each side returning what it has received. It need not be a specific remedy in the same sense as the other remedies just shown, but sometimes it is. The plaintiff may use rescission to regain ownership of land he passed to another by fraud or mistake. In some of those cases the effect of rescission may be just like the effect of a constructive trust, but lawyers sometimes adopt one equivalent formula in preference to another on various sorts of facts, as we will see.

The Function of Equitable Remedies

Two more preliminary notes. First, often the thing the plaintiff wants back is a piece of property: title to a disputed parcel of land, for example, rather than a cash substitute for it. But sometimes the "very thing" the plaintiff wants, and seeks by requesting specific relief, is money. At first this sounds odd because specific relief is usually described as an alternative to asking for money, not a different way of asking for it. In some cases, however, a court can say not that the defendant owes the plaintiff money but that the money rightfully belongs to the plaintiff already. The difference matters when the defendant is insolvent, because making a plaintiff the owner of the money lets him keep all of it. If the court just says the defendant *owes* money to the plaintiff, then the plaintiff has to get in line with all of the defendant's other creditors and settle for less than is due.

Second, when a plaintiff wants to get property back from a defendant, the defendant either has title to the property or he does not. "Title" for these purposes just means legally recognized rights of ownership.[3] If the defendant doesn't have title to the property that he holds and that the plaintiff seeks, he typically committed a tort in obtaining it (e.g., a theft or "conversion") or in refusing to give it up (e.g., if he found the property but then refused a legitimate demand for its return). Getting the property back from a defendant like that is easy, at least so far as legal rules are concerned. It isn't even a matter for the law of restitution. It *could* have been. One might very plausibly say that a thief who holds stolen property has been unjustly enriched and therefore suppose that a restitution claim is in order. But it just happens that historically the law has addressed that fact pattern with a different device known as replevin, which is the standard cause of action used by a plaintiff seeking to take stolen property back from a thief.[4]

The law of restitution is overqualified for cases of that kind. Its specific remedies address the more complicated problems that arise when the defendant does have title to the property he holds but the plaintiff has a better claim to it. This can come about in many ways. If a thief takes your car and then sells it, he has title to the money he made by the sale even if he had no title to the car (and the person he sold it to has no title to it, either).[5] If the defendant instead obtained the car in the first place by fraud rather than theft, then he likely has a kind of title to the car—the "voidable" kind[6] ("likely" because some frauds are so complete that they don't even convey voidable title).[7] If the defrauder then gives the car to a friend, the friend also has voidable title.[8] In all of these cases, getting back the car can be more disruptive and have more side effects than the simple use of replevin to take back stolen property from a thief. It requires a restitutionary remedy of one of the types to which we now turn.

Constructive Trusts Generally

"Constructive trust" is an obscure name for a fairly simple idea.[9] The court declares that property to which the defendant has legal title belongs in equity to the plaintiff, and orders that he be given possession of it. To express the idea in the simplest way, the judge looks at property held by the defendant, gestures toward the plaintiff, and says, in effect, "It is his; give it to him." The second instruction ("give it to him") is easy to understand. But the first part of the constructive trust—"it is his"—adds something important. It makes clear that the plaintiff has a better claim to the property than the defendant who has some sort of title to it.

The constructive trust can reach further than replevin does. It is the standard device for recovering proceeds from property that was stolen and then sold;[10] for equity allows a dispossessed owner to show what has been done with his property and to claim, as a substitute, the *product* of his original asset. This is the simplest version of a remedial mechanism often called "tracing." So suppose you steal my money and buy a car with it. I cannot take the car from you by means of replevin, because it is not mine and never was.[11] You bought it and have title to it. But the constructive trust allows the court to make me the owner of the car anyway by saying that I have a better equitable right to it than you do, since you bought it with money that was mine. The same would be true if, instead of stealing my money and buying a car, you stole my car and sold it for money. My ownership of the car is turned, by operation of the constructive trust, into ownership of the money you received for it. (To be technical about this, my legal title to the car produces an equitable claim to the money.) How far this process can go—how many transactions and transformations the property can endure and still be seized by the plaintiff—is the subject of more detailed rules about tracing that we will consider soon.

Reasons for a Constructive Trust

Maximizing the Value of the Recovery

Successful restitution plaintiffs can always get money judgments of the kind discussed in the previous chapter. When would they want a constructive trust instead? The answer may be the same reason why plaintiffs ever want a specific thing rather than money. The thing may not be replaceable with money; it may be a unique good—a painting, say, or a piece of land. Or it may be hard to quantify its value, or the property may be worth a lot to the plaintiff but much less in the market, or getting the property back may simply be cheaper than proving its value and executing a money judgment.[12] These are standard reasons for giving injunctive relief rather than an award of damages to an aggrieved plaintiff in a case where there is time to prevent the loss. There is "no adequate remedy at law," meaning that money damages are inadequate in some way. They are hard to prove or incapable of replacing the very thing the plaintiff has lost.[13] Those problems are common enough in restitution cases as well, since the plaintiff often seeks the return of property that once was his and that he may therefore value in some distinctive way.

Seizing property also can be a way to maximize the plaintiff's recovery in a case where that is appropriate. Suppose you embezzle $1,000 of my money and invest it in a stock. The stock goes up and is soon worth $2,000. I seek restitution, and rather than just demanding a money judgment for $1,000 plus interest, I request that a constructive trust be imposed for my benefit on the stock itself. In effect this will force you to disgorge the consequential gains from your receipt of the $1,000.[14] So whether I am entitled to a constructive trust depends on the rules about when disgorgement of such gains is appropriate. In short, if you acquired the money by committing a conscious wrong, I will be entitled to your gains from investing it and can seize those gains by means of a constructive trust imposed on the shares. The reason is not quite that I deserve those consequential gains. It is that you *don't* deserve them—that defendants should not profit from their wrongs.[15] If you acquired my money by mistake or in some other more innocent way—maybe I overpaid you and you didn't realize it—then your liability is limited to the initial $1,000. And since you don't owe me your consequential gains, it follows that I cannot have a constructive trust on the shares (since it would bring those gains my way). As we will see below, in these circumstances I also can seek an equitable lien on the shares for my $1,000, which will be preferable if they have gone down in value.

Rights against Third Parties

The points just mentioned explain why a plaintiff might want a constructive trust in a simple two-party contest between him and the defendant. But the full powers of the constructive trust become most evident in a case where third parties are in the picture. This might be so, first, because after a middleman somehow gained the plaintiff's property, he conveyed it to someone else. If the middleman is gone or insolvent, the plaintiff might like to seize the property from whoever now has it. Whether he will succeed depends on how the property moved from the plaintiff to the middleman, and how it moved from the middleman to the third party. If the middleman simply stole the plaintiff's property, he acquired no title to it. This means he has no rights to pass to a third party, and the plaintiff can take back the property wherever he finds it. But if the middleman first acquired the property by slightly less objectionable means—by fraud, say, or embezzlement, not to mention mistake—then he probably has "voidable" title, which means he does have something he can pass on to a third party. (In more traditional language, he has title subject to the plaintiff's equitable interest.) If the third party was a "bona fide purchaser," meaning that he gave value for the fraudulently obtained property and had no notice of the plaintiff's claim, then he is immune from any constructive trust the plaintiff might seek to impose on it.[16] If he did have notice of the plaintiff's claim, or if he received the property without paying for it—perhaps as a gift—then the plaintiff can take it back after all.[17] The details of these rules are discussed in the chapter on defenses. The general point is that a constructive trust sometimes allows a plaintiff to take property from someone who got it from a wrongdoer.

There is another set of third parties against whom a constructive trust can serve as a mighty weapon: creditors of the defendant. They are a common presence in a case where the defendant has taken the plaintiff's property in some wrongful way. Defendants who do that sort of thing, once caught, very often do not have enough money to cover all their liabilities to their victims and to people from whom they have borrowed. Such defendants frequently are bankrupt, in other words, and their creditors receive some number of pennies on the dollar. The constructive trust allows a plaintiff to avoid that fate. He takes back his property directly. It never goes into the pool of assets that will be distributed to the creditors on a pro rata basis. This at least is the traditional result. A few modern courts have not been willing to recognize constructive trusts in bankruptcy; to again say it in the older language, they resist the idea that general creditors take from the estate in bankruptcy only after equitable interests—such as those belonging to victims of the debtor's frauds—have been satisfied. But the still predominant view, and the view of the *Restatement*, is that the constructive trust does give its beneficiary priority over other creditors.[18]

We might reflect for a moment more on the difficult question of whether and *why* a restitution plaintiff should be treated as the owner of the property subject to a constructive trust, and not as just another creditor who should get into the queue with all others seeking satisfaction of their claims. A tempting explanation is that those other creditors typically chose to lend money to the defendant.[19] They made contracts and so had an opportunity to protect their rights; they hoped to be repaid in full but took their chances. They took a "solvency risk," we might say. The restitution plaintiff is different. In the most attractive case for use of a constructive trust, he was wronged. Possibly the benefits came to the defendant in some less nefarious way, but in any event they did not come to him consensually and by contract. Indeed, the constructive trust is not an appropriate remedy for breach of contract, and now we can see why. If it were, it really would give the plaintiff an unfair advantage over other creditors who also had contracts with the defendant. The constructive trust, rather, is for cases where the court is more sympathetic to the plaintiff than the defendant's other creditors because protection by contract was not available to him. Suppose by way of comparison that one of the defendant's other creditors *did* protect himself by contract. He reserved the right to seize certain property as collateral if the defendant didn't pay his debts—and the collateral is the same property the defendant obtained by fraud from the plaintiff. That is known as a secured creditor, and the constructive trust is no threat to him. A secured creditor amounts to a bona fide purchaser of property to the extent that he took a lien against it.

The previous paragraph offered an explanation of why the beneficiary of a constructive trust can avoid the queue in bankruptcy, and it described the explanation as "tempting"—but (alas) it is not entirely satisfying. There are features of the legal landscape that it doesn't explain. For example, victims of torts who have money claims against a debtor, and who likewise were innocent victims of wrongs, have to get in line with all the other general creditors; they can't avoid the queue like a plaintiff who obtains a constructive trust. Why are they different from the holder of a constructive trust who was victimized by fraud? The best answer is probably that the restitution plaintiff is asserting property rights, not just a right to payment of a debt. The winner of a tort claim is not asserting property rights. He is enforcing a money judgment. We should remember that we are not interested in the unjust enrichment of the debtor in cases of this kind. The debtor is out of money and out of the picture. We are interested in the possible unjust enrichment of the debtor's general creditors at the expense of the restitution claimant. The general creditors are entitled to be paid out of the debtor's assets, not out of assets that properly belong to someone else (the victim of theft, fraud, mistake, or whatever else) but that happen to be in the debtor's possession. The victim of a tort likewise has a claim against the tortfeasor's assets but not against the assets of an innocent bystander. If this train of thought sounds insufficiently rooted in clear distinctions of policy, perhaps that helps explain why the rule is controversial.

In any event, the law does favor the defendant's general (i.e., unsecured) creditors in one important way. We saw earlier that a constructive trust sometimes lets a plaintiff recover more than he originally lost. When the defendant is insolvent, that extra recovery comes not at his expense but at the expense of his creditors. Since *they* are not wrongdoers, the plaintiff should not profit at their expense. So to return to a story considered in the chapter on takings, suppose an embezzler dies and has a life insurance policy that pays a million dollars to his estate. But then it comes out that he paid all the premiums on the policy—$25,000 worth of them—using money he embezzled from his employer. (It could have been an outright theft rather than embezzlement; the issue is the same.) It might seem that the employer would have a good claim to a constructive trust on the policy and its proceeds: the $25,000, naturally, but also the $1 million. And if the estate is solvent, that is the result. But what if the embezzler's estate has creditors, or he has surviving dependents? The employer then gets a right, in the form of a lien, to $25,000 out of the benefits paid from the policy. Anything left over will probably go to satisfy the embezzler's creditors and then be paid to his dependents, if any.[20]

What the employer gets in the example just shown, then, is not quite a constructive trust but rather a remedy that goes part way in that direction: an equitable lien. We turn to that device now.

The Equitable Lien Generally

The logic of an equitable lien much resembles the logic of a constructive trust. Again the court recognizes the plaintiff's rights in property to which the defendant has title. But whereas the constructive trust causes the property to be transferred to the plaintiff, the equitable lien does not. It just gives the plaintiff a security interest in the property. Usually this means the right to force a sale and collect what is owed out of the proceeds.

When an equitable lien makes more sense than a constructive trust, it is typically because the plaintiff has only a limited claim to the defendant's property. Suppose, for example, that the defendant improved his own property by spending some of the plaintiff's money on it. Since the plaintiff's assets contributed just some fraction of the property's total value, it would be overkill to transfer all of the property in question to the plaintiff by means of a constructive trust. But since the plaintiff can follow his stolen money into the defendant's property, he surely should have some rights in it. An equitable lien reflects this mixed state of af-

fairs. If the defendant pays what he owes to the plaintiff, the lien is discharged and the property is no longer encumbered. The defendant has
exercised his "right of redemption." Otherwise the plaintiff can foreclose
the lien; that is, he can insist on a judicial sale of the property and satisfy
his claim out of whatever money it brings in. The defendant keeps whatever amount may be left over afterward. (The court has discretion to relax
these rules if the defendant was not a conscious wrongdoer, as by saying the plaintiff gets his money *if* the property is sold—but not ordering
the sale.)[21]

The facts giving rise to an equitable lien most commonly resemble
those just sketched. Assets from one person were used to improve or preserve property belonging to another, with the result that two parties now
have good claims to it. Maybe the defendant improved his property with
money he took from the plaintiff,[22] or maybe the plaintiff improved the
defendant's property while thinking it was his own or expecting that it
soon would be.[23] But other patterns are possible, too. Recall that a constructive trust typically is obtained when the defendant acquired the
property in question (or some prior version of it) in some objectionable
way—probably through an act of wrongdoing, though possibly in a manner just tainted by mistake. An equitable lien is easier to justify on a lesser
factual showing. It is only necessary that the plaintiff's property be traceable into the property on which the lien is sought or that there be some
other "nexus" between them. So let's say an insurance company pays out
benefits to a client who has lost a valuable diamond, but then the diamond is found. The diamond was not taken from the insurance company
or acquired wrongfully, so whether the company is entitled to have a constructive trust imposed on it might be questionable.[24] But the company
does have a sufficient interest to obtain an equitable lien on the diamond,
which will secure recovery of whatever amount the company mistakenly
paid out.

The Equitable Lien to Protect Value

An equitable lien is not just for cases where the plaintiff has a limited
right to the property held by the defendant. Another good occasion for
the device arises when the plaintiff could ask for a constructive trust but
would prefer to have a security interest in the property rather than possession of it. If the property has risen in value, then of course the plaintiff

probably would prefer to have it outright. But if the value of the property is fluctuating or going down, an equitable lien protects the plaintiff better; for even if the value of the property changes, the amount secured by the equitable lien is fixed. It is simply the amount owed under the rules discussed in the previous chapter on money remedies. When the plaintiff's remedy is a constructive trust, by contrast, the value of the remedy goes up and down with the value of the property at stake.

Suppose, then, that I embezzle $100,000 from you and invest it in a piece of land that doubles in value. You can have either a constructive trust or an equitable lien as your remedy. A constructive trust allows you to take the land. An equitable lien is inferior because it allows you to collect just $100,000 (not $200,000) when the land is sold. Now assume the same facts, but the land goes down in value after I buy it. You would rather have the equitable lien. If the property is no longer worth enough to satisfy your claim, you can get a deficiency judgment for the rest.[25] The constructive trust traditionally doesn't work that way. The plaintiff's money is identified *in* the property held by the defendant, so the property is all he gets as a replacement for the money. He is not generally entitled to a deficiency judgment if the value of the property is less than he lost, though that formality can be worked around; the plaintiff who gets a constructive trust can also be awarded an equitable lien, for example, which he can enforce in the alternative if he needs it.[26]

The Equitable Lien to Give the Plaintiff Rights against Third Parties

An equitable lien gives a plaintiff rights against third parties similar to those conferred by a constructive trust. The plaintiff's interest in the property takes priority over the interests of the defendant's general creditors.[27] We saw earlier that a *secured* creditor of the defendant amounts to a bona fide purchaser of the property used as collateral and that the rights of secured creditors thus come before those of a plaintiff with a constructive trust. The same is true here. An equitable lien is subordinate to a lien on the same property obtained by contract (a "consensual" lien) if the consensual lien was acquired without notice of the plaintiff's rights.[28] More generally, third parties are protected against equitable liens if they are good-faith purchasers of the property on which the liens are held.[29] If they aren't, their interests will be subject to the plaintiff's lien—but to whatever partial extent they may be innocent, the courts still can protect their interests by fashioning the terms of the lien with the sensitivity we have seen. The plaintiff will not be able to recover, at their expense, more than he originally lost, and there are some other protections as well.

Here is an example. A man embezzles $20,000 from his employer and uses it to buy a diamond ring for his wife, who understands nothing of what he has done. The embezzler is caught and jailed, leaving his wife to be sued in restitution by the employer. She was not a good-faith purchaser of the ring. She was a donee. So she has been unjustly enriched and is liable to the employer—but for what? For the value she received from the ring. Since she was an innocently minded wrongdoer, that value will be measured by the ring's market value. The employer thus can obtain an equitable lien on the ring for $20,000. But if the sale of the ring fails to produce that much money—suppose its value now as a "used" ring has gone down to $15,000—the employer must seek the rest of what it is owed from the employee, not from his wife. Since she is a kind of wrongdoer, she can be forced to sell the ring, but since she is an *innocent* wrongdoer (pardon the expression), she cannot be made to pay more than the ring is now worth.[30] How the defendant's culpability affects the amount she can be made to pay is not our exact concern now. Those questions were covered in the previous chapter. The point to see here is how those limits on recovery continue to be respected when the plaintiff seeks an equitable lien rather than a money judgment.

Subrogation Generally

Suppose a defendant acquires the plaintiff's money by fraud or mistake and uses it to pay off a creditor. The plaintiff has a good claim against the defendant for return of the money, but that just makes the plaintiff yet another creditor who may be competing with many others. The interesting question is whether the plaintiff can somehow get a specific claim to any of the defendant's property. A constructive trust or equitable lien will not work here, because the plaintiff's money has not been exchanged for property that the defendant can seize or seek to have sold. But another route may be possible. The plaintiff can step into the shoes of the creditor who was paid with his money. If that creditor had a security interest—a lien by contract—in the defendant's property, then the plaintiff now has that same lien with the same priority. If the defendant defaults, the plaintiff can foreclose the lien, force a judicial sale of the property, and get his money ahead of other creditors (though the defendant has the same defenses against the plaintiff that he would have had against the creditor in whose shoes the plaintiff now stands). Putting the plaintiff into the creditor's position this way is called "subrogation," which, as noted in the chapter on conferrings, is an old word for "substitution." It resembles the other devices just reviewed because again the plaintiff can gain rights in specific property held by the defendant. He just gets those rights less directly. He inherits them, so to speak, from the party who was paid with his money.

From the defendant's point of view, the effect of the subrogation is that he never paid his creditor after all. To be precise, he paid him with money that belonged to someone else, so now the someone else simply takes the old creditor's place. Notice that if the creditor who was paid off by the defendant was unsecured—in other words, if he had no lien on any of the defendant's property and the defendant merely owed him money—then the plaintiff still *could* step into his shoes, but there would be no point. It would just give the plaintiff a money claim against the defendant, which is what the plaintiff already has anyway when he wins his restitution suit. It is only worth bothering with subrogation as a remedy when it gives the plaintiff something more: not rights against the defendant, but rights in the defendant's property (and perhaps priority over other claimants).

Subrogation as a Theory of Liability Compared to Subrogation as a Remedy

We have been talking about subrogation as a remedy that can enable a plaintiff to get specific rights in a defendant's property. The chapter on conferrings also talked about subrogation, but as a theory of liability in restitution rather than as a remedy; in other words, it viewed subrogation as a way for a plaintiff to establish that he is owed money in the first place, not as a way to get a secured claim to the defendant's assets. These two different meanings of subrogation overlap, but they do not necessarily appear together and are best thought of as distinct. Subrogation as a theory of liability doesn't imply that anyone has a security interest in anyone else's property.[31] It just means that I have discharged some obligation you had, as by paying money that you owed to a creditor. Now I have

rights against you as subrogee of the creditor, but those rights will probably just enable me to win an ordinary money judgment against you for
the amount that I paid. There may well be no property in sight that I can
try to seize whether directly (by constructive trust or equitable lien) or by
subrogation to the rights of other creditors. I have to get in line with your
other creditors.

The flip side of this point is that subrogation as a remedy can be useful
in many sorts of cases, including some that rest on theories of liability like
mistake or fraud. The defendant might have stolen the plaintiff's money;
he might have acquired the plaintiff's money by breach of a fiduciary
duty; he might have acquired it by mistake.[32] If he uses the money, however acquired, to reduce his liabilities to someone with a security interest
in his property, then the plaintiff to whom the money rightfully belonged
now can get that same security interest. He is using subrogation as a way
to get what he is owed, not as a way to establish the substance of what he
is owed.

Equitable Limits on Subrogation

Like any equitable remedies, including the others already considered in
this chapter, subrogation can be denied if the court thinks it would be inequitable.[33] A court might so conclude because the plaintiff has acted in
bad faith or because the remedy would offend some other policy. Suppose I make a loan to you that is illegal and unenforceable. Perhaps the
interest rate is usurious. You use the money to pay off a secured creditor. Then you decline to repay me, and the illegality of the loan means
that I cannot sue to enforce its terms. So I bring a restitution suit claiming that you have been unjustly enriched. The question for this chapter
is whether I should be able to take the place of the secured creditor you
paid off, and thus whether I can use the rights he had in your property to
get my money back. Here is a possible compromise: if I made the loan
to you in good faith and if the secured creditor you paid off had lent you
money at a more appropriate rate of interest than I did, the court might
let me stand in that creditor's shoes enough to collect (out of your property) the amount I lent to you plus the lower interest rate the creditor had
charged.[34] Here as elsewhere, the court has discretion to fashion the remedy in a way that seems consistent with the policies that make the restitution claim appropriate in the first place.

Rescission Generally

"Rescission" is a potentially confusing word. Most often it is used to describe a remedy for breach of contract. But it also can be a way to unwind a transaction for other reasons besides a breach, as when a plaintiff wants to undo a contract that was the product of fraud or mistake. Rescission works differently in these two contexts. After a simple breach of contract, rescission may enable a plaintiff to get back whatever he gave to the defendant as opposed to collecting expectation damages that are harder to prove. But rescission does not give the plaintiff in a case of nonfraudulent breach of contract a way to take back his property or money ahead of other creditors the defendant may have.[35]

One reason for this limit involves respect for the body of law that governs secured transactions. Consider a simple case in which I sell you goods on credit and then you don't pay for them. If I can use rescission to take them back ahead of other creditors, then in effect the court will be giving me a security interest in the goods. I should not be able to achieve that result by judicial order. I should be required to negotiate for the security interest in our contract and then to comply with the statutory rules about perfecting such interests; otherwise those procedures end up gutted. Or reverse the facts: I send you money and you won't send the goods. I demand rescission, possibly because my expectation damages are too hard to prove to be worth the bother. (Getting my money back is even more attractive if I paid you more than the goods are worth—though in that case you are unlikely to breach.) Either way, rescission is fine as a way of measuring what I am due. But assuming, as usual, that this is a simple claim for breach of contract and not a claim for fraud, again I cannot use rescission to collect my money ahead of other creditors to whom you have debts. Specific relief in that strong sense is only available when you obtain my goods or my money in some way that conveys legal title to them but not equitable title. In other words, it has to be possible to say that you got the goods but never really had a full right to them. If you merely breach a contract, we cannot say those things. The sale of goods followed by delivery of them completes a valid transfer so far as the property rights at stake are concerned. Your breach of the contract afterward does not disturb the validity of the transfer or mean that you have legal title but not equitable title or any such thing. You simply owe me money because you didn't make good on your promise to pay. That makes me just another creditor. But rescission routinely does serve as a form of specific relief when a transfer is founded on a mistake, or duress, or fraud, or undue influence.[36]

Rescission and Constructive Trust Compared

The rationale for rescission just offered sounds much like the thought process used when a plaintiff seeks a constructive trust. Indeed, in any case where a plaintiff wants specific relief—that is, an ownership claim in property the defendant holds—because the plaintiff's transfer of the property was contaminated by fraud, mistake, or some other defect, he can seek rescission of the transaction or the imposition of a constructive trust on the disputed property, or he can ask for both. The results will be the same, though the two remedies tend to be invoked on slightly different facts. A constructive trust is the more natural choice if the defendant has creditors and the plaintiff wants to take back the property ahead of them. Constructive trust is also the more likely choice of remedy when the plaintiff seeks to recover not the very thing he transferred to the defendant but its traceable product. Tracing is done in a rescission case occasionally but not characteristically.

By contrast, rescission is the natural way to speak of the remedy if both parties are to return benefits to the other. True, an order of constructive trust can also be accompanied by a requirement that the plaintiff hand benefits back to the defendant,[37] but rescission puts more emphasis on the reciprocal nature of the restoration. Rescission also is most often invoked by plaintiffs who simply want their money back. If they use restitution to seek the return of other property, it is usually because that is easier than trying to prove damages, not because they are trying to beat out the defendant's creditors. In the end, however, when the same facts can be addressed either by rescission or constructive trust, the choice between them is best understood as rhetorical.

Tracing Rules Generally

"Tracing" assets can refer to two things, one general and one specific. First, it can refer generally to the process of following property into its product—that is, to the remarkable ways in which ownership rights in a thing can extend into substitutes for which the thing is exchanged or into whatever the thing may produce. Second, "tracing" assets can refer to the process of pursuing wrongfully taken money into a fund where it has been commingled with other money, and determining how much of the mixed money the pursuer can claim. We will start by briefly stating the principles that govern tracings in the first and more general sense, then turn to the narrower sense of the term.

Tracing: Common Complications

A plaintiff who wants rights in the defendant's property has to point to something specific the defendant holds and declare that it is his or the product of something that once was his. Tracing rules allow that showing to be made in some unexpected circumstances. The first and most basic principle is that property can be followed through any transfers and changes of form until it comes into the hands of a bona fide purchaser.[38] Thus suppose I defraud you out of one million dollars. I convert the money into bearer bonds. I give the bonds to my uncle, and he uses them to buy a house. The house is yours, or rather can be made yours by imposition of a constructive trust. Notice that you cannot seize the bonds from whoever sold the house to your uncle, because that seller was presumably the equivalent of a bona fide purchaser—a bona fide payee, to be exact. And you can seize the house from my uncle only because he *wasn't* a bona fide purchaser. I simply gave him the bonds. But as long as no bona fide purchase interrupts the sequence, there is, in principle, no limit to the number of times the property can be transferred or change form in the ways just shown and still be reached.

The difficulties in tracing assets arise because most cases aren't as clean as that one. First, of course, are factual complications. There may be serious problems of proof in showing that *this* money was converted into *those* bonds and that the house was bought with them. Second are two sorts of legal complications. The plaintiff's assets may have been mixed with others. Perhaps I combined your money with my own and then gave it all to my uncle. And the assets may have been spent on property— possibly an investment of some sort—that increased in value, raising questions about whether that increase belongs to the plaintiff or the defendant. When any of these wrinkles are present, is it right to point at the house and say that it simply amounts to your money in a new form? Notice that the answers may be less important to the defendant than to his creditors; for if the house is the traceable product of your assets, the result is that you will take it ahead of those creditors—and this is probably why you would bother to argue that the assets are traceable in the first place. In theory you also might want to trace assets because they have increased in value while in the hands of the defendant; he was shrewd or lucky in investing what he took, so you want the assets in their new and improved form rather than a mere money judgment against him. But that situation, though exciting when it appears, is rare. Wrongdoers usually are short on assets by the time they get caught, making the rights that their victims have in relation to one another the paramount question. Simply stated, tracing rules largely amount to judgments about how best to balance the interests of the defendant's creditors and the restitution plaintiff.[39]

Commingled Assets: The Rule of Lowest Intermediate Balance

Turning in more detail, then, to those complications just mentioned, we begin with assets of the plaintiff's that have been mixed, or "commingled," with others. If the defendant buys a house and pays for half of it with your money and half with his own, the problem is not bad. You can be said to own half the house and can obtain an equitable lien or constructive trust on it to secure your recovery—whichever works better.[40] The hard problem arises, rather, when your money is taken and put into an account with someone else's, and then some of the combined funds are withdrawn and spent. Never mind *how* it was spent (assume it cannot be traced). The trouble comes in saying how much of the money still left in the account is yours. Was the withdrawal made from your money, the embezzler's money, or a bit of both?

There is no literal way to answer that question. The balance in the account is just a number, not stacks of bills from different sources. The courts therefore use convenient presumptions and, as they are sometimes called, "tracing fictions" to answer these questions. Against a wrongdoer, the plaintiff gets every benefit of a doubt with respect to withdrawals. So suppose an embezzler of $10,000 of your funds combines it with $20,000 of his own money. If he then spends $20,000 out of the account in some untraceable way, leaving $10,000 behind, the courts will assume the entire $10,000 that remains is yours—that the wrongdoer spent his own money first.[41] If the wrongdoer instead takes out the $20,000 and invests it profitably, the courts will make the opposite assumption: that your $10,000 was the first chunk removed from the account, giving you a one-half interest in the investment he made.[42] In short, you get the benefit of favorable assumptions either way. If the money was used productively, it was yours. If it was squandered, it was his.[43]

But now take a different situation. The wrongdoer, again starting with $10,000 of your money and $20,000 of his own (for a total of $30,000 in the account), spends $25,000 of it—but then deposits another $10,000 of his own money at a later date. The account then contains $15,000, at which point you discover the entire scheme and demand your $10,000. You cannot identify that much of the account as your money, even though the account now contains more than he took from you. The reason is that when the wrongdoer spent $25,000, the balance in the account went down to $5,000. All of that $5,000 was rightfully yours. But future amounts the wrongdoer adds to the account are not presumed to restore the money you lost. To say it simply, a plaintiff's recovery from a mixed account can never be more than the lowest balance the account had between the time his money was added to it and the time of reckoning—the "lowest intermediate balance," as it is called.[44]

So let's say your money (any amount) is combined with the wrongdoer's in one account, and then he spends it all, leaving the account empty. But he adds more money to it later. As always, you can have a money judgment for whatever was taken from you and become another creditor of the wrongdoer. But you will not be able to claim that you are the rightful owner of any of the money in the account and should receive it ahead of the wrongdoer's other creditors. The funds in which your money was mixed were all spent before new money was added.[45] And if the wrongdoer, rather than spending all the money, had merely drained the account to $200 at one point before then rebuilding it to a healthier $10,000, your right to specific relief—to an ownership claim—would be limited to that $200 lowest balance. All the rest that you are owed would be awarded as an unsecured money judgment.

Additional Rules for Tracing against Innocent Defendants

We have been emphasizing claims against wrongdoers because they are the defendants against whom tracing rules are usually brought to bear: the defendant took the plaintiff's assets and spent them, traded them, or commingled them with others. But occasionally these rules also can be relevant when the recipient of the plaintiff's property is innocent, as when he receives an overpayment by mistake and deposits it in an account with other money. The "lowest intermediate balance" rule applies here just as it did when the defendant was a wrongdoer.[46] Differences in treatment arise, however, with respect to our other complication—that is, if the defendant withdrew money and invested it profitably, producing a final total that is greater than the plaintiff's losses. Clearly the plaintiff has a specific claim to the proceeds to the extent necessary to restore what he lost. But who gets the profits on the investment? Here the answer naturally can depend on the defendant's culpability or lack thereof.

There are two general principles to observe, both familiar enough by now. The first is that the plaintiff cannot have a recovery that gives him more than he originally lost if the defendant is innocent.[47] The second is that the plaintiff cannot have a recovery that gives him more than he originally lost if the extra recovery comes at the expense of the defendant's general creditors[48]—and this regardless of whether the defendant was innocent or a wrongdoer (for this rule really is not about him; it is about his creditors, and we are assuming that they, at least, are innocent). To return to our earlier example, suppose the defendant wrongfully took $10,000 of your money, combined it with $20,000 of his own, and then withdrew $5,000 and used it to buy lottery tickets that yielded $500,000. In a contest between you and the wrongdoer, you will be entitled to the entire $500,000.[49] But if the wrongdoer has other creditors, you will have to be content, at least in the beginning, with an equitable lien on the lottery winnings in the amount of $10,000—the amount you lost.[50] If there is money left over after the defendant's creditors are paid, you can claim it. You just cannot force those creditors to go unpaid so that you can collect more than you lost in the first place. But now assume the defendant was innocent, not a wrongdoer. In that case you are not entitled to collect anything more from him than $10,000 (plus interest, perhaps). Even if he has no other creditors, he prevails in a contest with you over the profits made by investing what he mistakenly received.[51]

The defendant's culpability may also be relevant to tracing in additional ways that again will be roughly familiar from other chapters. If he has spent time and money improving the plaintiff's property, he is likely to get a credit for his labors if he was innocent, and not if he was a wrongdoer. The extent of that credit is a matter of discretion for the court. And culpability also can matter at the fact-finding stage of the case. As noted earlier, it may not be so easy to prove that the money the defendant spent on something—whether it be insurance premiums, mortgage payments, or merchandise, et cetera—came from the plaintiff's assets. A court is likely to apply a more demanding standard of proof on these points when the defendant is innocent than it would if he were a wrongdoer.[52] If the plaintiff has shown that the defendant committed a conscious wrong and commingled the plaintiff's money with his own, some courts will even say the burden of proof then shifts to the defendant to show that property he acquired afterward *wasn't* bought with the plaintiff's money.[53] Courts are also likely to be more fastidious with the tracing rules when the recovery the plaintiff seeks would come at the expense of creditors. If it is just a question of capturing consequential gains from a crook, the pressure to be rigorous is not quite the same.

When an Account Contains Funds from Multiple Victims

Last, some nice problems of calculation can arise when a defendant mixes money from different victims in the same account. The basic rule is that the claimants are each entitled to a share of the account in proportion to the amount they (involuntarily) contributed to it, with the proportions measured at the time each deposit is made. So to follow the *Restatement*'s simplified example,[54] suppose the defendant takes $5,000 of your money and puts it into an account by itself. He spends $2,000 of it. Then he adds $5,000 from another victim. You and the other victim now share an ownership interest in the account. The proportion of shares is five for him and three for you. Now the defendant spends $4,000 of the money. The value of your interest was just cut in half; it is down from $3,000 to $1,500. Your fellow victim's interest was also sliced from $5,000 to $2,500. But of course the proportions you each hold are still the same: five to three. Finally the defendant adds $5,000 to the account from yet another victim. Now the total balance is $9,000. You have a $1,500 stake in that amount—the same as before. The second victim also has an unchanged stake of $2,500. The newest victim has a stake of $5,000. But since the defendant will probably be spending some of that money, the important question is the proportion of the account that each of you is entitled to claim. We can state the ratio in simple whole numbers by just doubling the basic amounts involved (so your $1,500 becomes a rounder $3,000, etc.). The resulting proportions are three, five, and ten for you, the second victim, and the third victim, respectively. Those are the shares that each will be allowed to take of whatever is left in the account and of whatever proceeds the investment of the money may produce. Notice that the earlier victim gains, by virtue of being early, no priority over the later ones.[55]

Lately some courts have departed from the traditional rules just described. In the recent federal decision *United States v. Durham*,[56] for example, a fraud was perpetrated on several claimants. The money taken from two of them—$83,000 of it—could be traced into a particular account. The money taken from the other victims had been spent. The usual rules would call for the traceable money to be returned to whoever lost it, on the ground that they never stopped owning the money and shouldn't have to share it with anyone else. It is like a case where a bank robber has stolen money from many banks, but when caught is found to just have bills that are still wrapped and labeled as coming from First National. First National takes those bills back directly, and the robber's other victims are out of luck. But in *Durham* the court "elected in the interest of equity, to distribute the $83,000 pro rata rather than giving the bulk of it to [the] victims whose funds had been traced." The court reasoned that giving the money back to the two claimants who could trace it would "elevate the position of those two victims on the basis of the actions of the defrauders."[57]

The third *Restatement* is critical of *Durham* and other recent cases like it, concluding that they are the result of "error and inattention"—and in particular a misunderstanding by the judges about the extent of their discretion under traditional principles of equity.[58] The basis of the criticism is that these cases depart from long-standing case law without clear justification and without evident recognition that the old rules even exist. But the new cases might nevertheless make sense as a matter of policy. The old rules allow the perpetrator of a fraud to favor some of his victims over others by keeping the funds of the favored ones separate and traceable. Then if the scheme collapses, the favored claimants take all their money back and the unfavored ones, whose money was spent, collect less or nothing. It might seem unlikely that a typical defrauder would have preferences of that kind about his victims or enough legal knowledge to give effect to such preferences in the way just described. But the authors of some well-known Ponzi schemes have conned their friends and family members as well as strangers, and in some cases they have shown sophistication in structuring their transactions. It is understandable that courts want to avoid rules that would reward such efforts.

Granted, one could object that this logic proves too much. It might imply that if the schemer almost fleeced his grandmother but stopped short at the last minute, she should share in the losses suffered by those he did fleece. After all, why should the defendant get to decide who suffers and who does not? But the old tracing rules don't just allow the defrauder to play favorites. In cases that involve Ponzi schemes, they also might encourage his friends to play along in the hope that they will have a better chance of getting all their money back if the scheme collapses. If it can be proven that those friends were collaborators, then they will be held liable regardless of the tracing rules. But the modern departures from those rules help to discourage the kind of silent and hopeful collaboration with a Ponzi schemer that is hard to prove.

CHAPTER EIGHT

Defenses

We have discussed some defenses to restitution claims in the course of earlier chapters. This chapter looks in detail at the two most important of them: change of position and bona fide purchase (as well as the related defense available to a bona fide creditor).[1]

Change of Position Generally

In *PaineWebber, Inc. v. Levy*,[2] the defendant, Levy, decided to sell some stock. The plaintiff handled the sale, made a miscalculation, and sent Levy $24,835 too much. Levy was not aware of the mistake and promptly spent the money paying his daughter's college tuition bill and buying her a computer. Then the plaintiff discovered its error and sought to take back the money. The plaintiff had a fine restitution claim against Levy—prima facie. But Levy had a defense: change of position, or what some lawyers might refer to as "detrimental reliance."[3] Because of the overpayment, Levy had done things that he would not have done otherwise, and that could not be undone; he had, for example, splurged on a computer that he would not otherwise have felt that he could afford. (The other expenses require a harder look, as we will see.) So forcing him to pay back the money now would make him worse off than he was before the payment arrived. Levy's defense was sound in theory. Whether it was sound in fact depended on how well the evidence supported the specific elements of the defense, which we must examine more closely.

Consider first why the defense works. Claims for restitution of mistaken payments are heavily influenced by two principles. The first is that the recipient is strictly liable for the payment's return, even if he had no responsibility for it and even if the claimant was negligent.[4] The second principle mitigates the harshness of the first: liability in restitution cannot make an innocent recipient worse off than he was before the transfer occurred.[5] The change-of-position defense is really just an application of this second principle. If Levy made decisions on account of the overpayment that cannot be taken back, then making him repay the money to PaineWebber would leave him poorer than he was before the mistake. He would be stuck with the decisions that the overpayment caused him to make but without the money needed to bear the consequences of them; in this case he will have a computer that he can't afford.

It helps to think about how the rules change when there is a loss to allocate between the parties. Holding Levy (or any recipient of a mistaken payment) liable without fault is fine if it requires nothing more than returning money. He is not then being asked to bear a loss—except for the bother, likely minor, of giving back what he shouldn't have received. A case that involves a change of position is different because now there *is* a loss that somebody will have to bear.[6] The defendant bought something that we now realize he shouldn't have bought—a bit of waste that will have to be allocated to one side or the other. The law allocates the waste to the party who was in the best position to prevent the misfortune—here, the claimant—in the name of fairness and perhaps for the sake of deterring the carelessness that leads to these fiascos.[7]

Limits on Change of Position as a Defense

Innocence

We can locate the limits of the defense by imagining a few variations on Levy's case. If Levy knew the payment was mistaken, the defense fails, for then *he* was in the best position to avoid the predicament. He knew that he had money the plaintiff was likely to demand back soon enough, so he should have done nothing that would make the return of it more difficult.[8] To put the point in the language of doctrine rather than policy, the defense requires a recipient who had no notice of the plaintiff's claim at the time he changed position. And of course the defense likewise fails if the person who asserts it was to blame for the mistake in the first place.[9] So if a plumber mistakenly sends an overstated bill and receives full payment of it, he cannot spend the money and then cry foul when the client demands it back.

The same theme drives both points just shown. When there is a loss to allocate, the law bases its decision on fault, so it takes a faultless defendant to claim a change of position as a defense. These conditions of the defense also mean more generally that it is only available in cases of mistake (by far its most common application) and of third-party fraud—in other words, cases where the defendant innocently benefited from someone else's wrongdoing. Change of position rarely is a good defense to the sorts of restitution claims discussed in the other chapters of this book (on conferrings, takings, or failed contracts), because in all of those cases the defendant is likely to have at least some responsibility for the transfer or some knowledge of the other side's claim to the money. In either circumstance he should not be changing position in reliance on his receipt of it.

Causation

The defense also fails if the recipient merely used the money to make a payment that he would have had to make anyway—and here is where Levy's case becomes difficult.[10] The point of the defense is not that the recipient spent the money he mistakenly received. It is that he spent the money in some way that he would not have done if it weren't for the overpayment.[11] An example is a widow who is mistakenly paid too much by her late husband's insurance company. She spends the overpayment, without realizing it *was* an overpayment, on a more lavish funeral than she otherwise would have ordered. When the insurance company demands back the money, it is too late. The widow changed position. To make her pay back the money would leave her worse off than if no overpayment had been made in the first place.[12] But if she had merely used the money to pay inevitable expenses, the insurer would have a winning restitution claim against her after all.

What, then, of Levy's expenditures? He said that the mistaken influx of money caused him to buy his daughter an expensive computer that he would not have purchased otherwise, and this evidently was not contested, so his defense was sound to that extent. But he also spent the mistaken payment on his daughter's tuition bill—and would he not have had to pay that bill anyway, regardless of PaineWebber's mistake? Levy had only just emerged from bankruptcy when he wrote the check. He claimed that he was spending money with unusual freedom because he unexpectedly had so much of it. What one would like to know, of course, is what Levy would have done about the tuition bill if the mistaken payment had never arrived. Might he have convinced the university to relieve him from payment of it on grounds of hardship? The court regarded these sorts of questions as matters for trial.

Other Changes of Position

A change of position can take other forms as well. The defendant invests the mistakenly received money and then the investment goes down.[13] This is a change of position. Making him pay back the entire amount he received would leave him worse off than before it arrived.[14] The result is the same in the simpler case where a thief steals the money from the mistaken recipient of it or where the property is demolished by accident. If the defendant obtained the money by fraud, he would bear the risk of any such losses; since he obtained it by mistake, the losses are assigned to the plaintiff. Or suppose the claimant thinks he is liable in tort for some loss the defendant has suffered (but actually he isn't liable for it). He therefore sends money to the defendant, and by the time this is discovered to be a mistake the statute of limitations has expired on any claims the defendant would have had against the parties who really are liable. The defendant's failure to go after those parties while there still was enough time is a change of position—assuming it was a reasonable choice, assuming he *would* have gone after them if the claimant had not mistakenly paid him, and assuming, finally, that the payment from the claimant was the claimant's idea.[15]

Sometimes the defendant's change of position can take yet another form. He hasn't quite spent the money, but he has paid it to someone else and cannot retrieve it. The easiest example is a case where the defendant is an agent and gives the mistaken payment to his principal.[16] The "agent" could be an individual or could be a bank that takes an overpayment and credits it to the customer to whom it was addressed. The agent would be liable in restitution if he still had the money when the claimant demanded its return. But once the money has left the agent's hands, he is not liable— assuming, as ever, that he acted innocently and also that he acted within his proper authority.[17] The reason might seem to be that the agent, if required to pay, would suffer a loss, for he doesn't have the money anymore. But that isn't necessarily so. He may be able to avoid that loss by then collecting reimbursement from his principal, who by assumption was unjustly enriched as well when the agent paid the money to him. The problem, rather, is that in the end someone will indeed need to collect from the principal, and this is itself costly; moreover, the principal may end up insolvent and thus unable to satisfy a judgment. The important question is who ought to bear those burdens and that risk. The answer, as usual, is the party most responsible for creating the situation—the claimant, not the agent.

Bona Fide Purchasers Generally

We have seen in earlier discussions—mostly in the chapter on equitable remedies—that a claimant whose property is taken from him by fraud can follow it through various changes of hands and still recover it until he runs into a bona fide purchaser. There the pursuit ends. The bona fide purchaser gains a title to property that cannot be disturbed by a claim for restitution; he can be asked neither to return it nor to pay its value.[18] The rule protects the stability of commercial expectations. It allows the buyer of a thing the comfort of knowing that he will not be surprised by a claimant to it who may appear later. But this immunity depends on the defendant's satisfaction of elements that we will consider one at a time. It is easiest to see them by translating the notion of a "bona fide purchaser" into a more precise English statement of what that phrase means: "an innocent purchaser for value," where "innocent" means "without notice."

Bona Fide Purchasers: Requirements

Notice

Let us begin at the end, with the idea of notice. "Bona fide purchaser" literally means "good-faith purchaser," but the expression "good faith" has the potential to confuse. It means here that the purchaser had no notice of competing claims to the property he was buying—that he did not know (and that it cannot be said he should have known) facts that would raise doubts about whether the seller had good rights to convey. The buyer is expected to draw reasonable inferences from what he can see and sometimes may be charged with knowledge without proof that he actually possessed it.[19] Paying a suspiciously low price and buying from someone who probably should not be selling are classic tip-offs that ought to tell the purchaser something may be amiss and that may spoil the bona fide purchaser defense if it is later asserted.

Purchase

Second, a bona fide purchaser must be—no surprise here—a purchaser. A purchase in this setting need not mean buying a thing in the usual sense (though it most often does).[20] It also includes leasing property or taking a lien on it. To return to an example from the chapter on equitable remedies, suppose someone takes your property by fraud and then uses it as collateral to obtain a loan. Obviously you have a good restitution claim against him, but you do not have good rights against the bank that agreed to use the property as collateral. When the bank made a contract with the wrongdoer that gave it a security interest in the property, it was not quite a buyer of the property, but it was a "purchaser" in our sense—and a bona fide purchaser, assuming the bank had no reason to know the property was acquired fraudulently. "Purchases," however, notably do not include rights obtained by operation of law.[21] So if a statute gives you an automatic lien against property to collect your fees when you perform repairs on it—a "mechanic's lien"—this does not make you a bona fide purchaser.[22] To attain that status, the lien must be the subject of a contract between you and the holder of the property.

Value

Last, the purchase must have been made for value.[23] This is not a requirement that the recipient pay full market price. A failure to pay the market rate may be relevant to whether the buyer had notice that the transaction was fishy, as we have seen. But that goes to the good-faith requirement, not to the element of value. "Value" just means the recipient has to give *something* up in return for the property received. In most cases this is easy. A simple purchase of property in the ordinary course of business is "for value." A simple gift is not. (Oddly enough, a gift *is* counted by the common law as a kind of purchase. Its recipient is not a bona fide purchaser, though, because he gives no value for it.)[24]

All this might make value sound the same as the requirement of consideration that makes a contract enforceable. The ideas overlap almost entirely, though not quite.[25] Consideration is merely meant to distinguish enforceable promises from some others that the law does not care to enforce for various reasons, so just about anything will do.[26] A promise in return for a promise is enough. The requirement of value serves a different purpose. It is part of an effort to balance the interests of innocent victims of a defrauder and the interests of innocent buyers *from* a defrauder. The common law carries out that balancing by sometimes declining to find "value" and refusing to protect a later buyer when the buyer received goods in exchange not for money but for a promise—and had not yet performed the promise when the victim appeared to reclaim his property.[27] But the Uniform Commercial Code has put aside most skepticisms about whether value is given in cases of that kind, preferring to err on the side of stability in commercial expectations; it resolves doubts in favor of the purchaser on facts like those just described and in many similar cases.[28] So suppose I fraudulently take your goods and give them to a creditor of mine to help pay a debt that I owe to him. Then you appear and demand your goods back. Does my creditor count as a purchaser for value? The common law held that he did not, but the UCC says that he does.[29] The UCC contains its own complications, however, as do the common-law rules that apply where the UCC doesn't. One has to take a detailed look—more detailed than we will discuss here—at any case where the defense of bona fide purchase is asserted by a creditor or anyone else who took the property in return for something besides conventional payment.

Bona Fide Purchasers: Consequences

With the elements of bona fide purchase now broadly explained, we turn to its consequences. As seen in the previous chapter, a buyer, even if a bona fide purchaser, cannot get title from a seller unless the seller had some sort of title to pass on in the first place. So if you steal property and sell it to me, the victim can seize the property regardless of whether I was a purchaser for value or had notice of his claim. The defense of bona fide purchase applies, rather, to cases where the buyer gets the property from a seller who does have a kind of legal title to convey, but one that is subject to an equitable claim by another. The equitable claim is enough to overcome the seller's rights but not the rights of a bona fide purchaser.[30] Sellers with these sorts of intermediate rights will include most who obtain property by fraud or embezzlement. If a thief steals property but then sells or trades it, he had no title to the stolen property but does have title to whatever new property he got in exchange for it. He can transfer that new property to a bona fide purchaser, who will take it with immunity from any victim's claims. Sellers with title also include, of course, any who obtained property by mistake or in some other more or less innocent way.

To be clear, any of those sellers may lose to a claimant who sues them to recover the property. But buyers *from* those sellers can be bona fide purchasers who take the property with immunity from restitution claims by the original owner.

The distinction just drawn between thefts and frauds may seem arbitrary, but it contains a core of functional sense. Here, as in many cases involving a change of position, there is a loss to allocate. Either the victim will get nothing in return for what he lost or the bona fide purchaser will have to give up something he paid for (or pay for it twice—once when he bought it and then again when he pays restitution). Here, as before, the loss would ideally be allocated on the basis of fault. The difficulty is that it often is not so easy to say which side is more to blame: the victim of a fraud or the person who buys from the defrauder. The law doesn't analyze this question case by case. It relies on generalizations. The rules may reflect a view that the potential victim of a fraud typically has a greater ability to protect himself than the victim of a theft, maybe because the victim of a fraud is more likely to know the wrongdoer and have chances to size him up. If the victim of a fraud failed to do that effectively, perhaps it makes sense for the suffering that later results to be allocated to him rather than to the innocent buyer of the thing who comes along later.[31] But if the claimant was a victim of a *theft*, his ability to protect himself may not have been so great (the wrongdoer more likely was a stranger and may have used force), so the law does not allocate the loss to him. The law looks to the later purchaser, rather, to make sure he is not buying stolen goods.

This line of reasoning is undeniably speculative and tentative. When no more clear-cut defense of a legal rule is available, it is no surprise to find that the rule is sometimes different in other countries—as is the case here.[32] And it is no surprise, either, that courts sometimes relax these rules when the rationales for them give out. Thus as explained in chapter 5, the victim of a fraud who had no realistic ability to protect himself may be allowed to take his property back from a bona fide purchaser, just as though he were the victim of a theft.

Bona Fide Creditors

Now consider a case where the thing taken by fraud, or stolen, was not some sort of property that could be sold. It was cash. And then the cash was used to buy a car that has since vanished. Where does that leave the original owner of the money—and the final recipient, or "payee," of it? The car dealer who receives the money is not quite a bona fide purchaser. One almost wants to say that he did "purchase" the money in return for the car, but that usage is too strained. Since he received money rather than some other sort of property, we instead call him a bona fide creditor, or payee: a party who received money in satisfaction of a debt he was owed and without notice of any mistake or other problem with the payment. His rights are robust, much like the rights of a bona fide purchaser. He has a solid defense against claims made by the money's original owner.[33]

Turning to other examples, then, think of a bank robber who steals money and uses it to pay his taxes.[34] Or a trustee, in breach of his fiduciary duty, takes money out of the trust to pay his own creditors.[35] Or a creditor is paid with a check, and the debtor's bank honors the check before discovering that the debtor doesn't have enough money in his account to cover it or that the account has been closed. In each of these cases the recipients of the money have clear title to it. There may be prima facie claims against them for restitution, but they all have good defenses as bona fide creditors, assuming they had no notice of the victim's claim until after the payment from the wrongdoer had become irrevocable. ("Irrevocable" here means that the robber's payment to the creditor was final rather than tentative; once the robber has no right to change his mind and take the money back, the creditor has it securely.)[36]

Note that creditors—that is, people paid money—get more protection than purchasers of real estate or goods. A creditor who receives *money* in good faith keeps it even if it was stolen.[37] The best explanation for that rule lies in the importance of treating money payments as final for the sake of reducing uncertainty in their recipients.[38] Someone who receives money generally will find it harder than the recipient of a car, a painting, and so on, to research whether the money came into the payor's hands unlawfully. And perhaps it is true that money received tends to be combined quickly with other money and then spent, invested, and so forth, so that the burden of trying to show an actual change of position in every case would be costly and usually not necessary. A danger in thinking about rationales of this kind, though, is that they can be beguiling enough to make the rule sound inevitable. It isn't. Until fairly recently New York's courts required a showing of an actual change of position before allowing the recipient of a mistaken payment to keep it.[39] This did not cause the wheels of commerce to come to the halt that the rationale for the usual rule might suggest.

The most surprising application of the bona fide creditor defense works as follows. A hospital treats you in an emergency. It sends the bill to an insurance company that is thought to provide your coverage, and the company pays the hospital the full amount due—say, $50,000. Then the insurance company discovers that the payment was a mistake. You do not have insurance there; maybe your policy had lapsed, or they confused you with someone else who had a similar name. The insurance company has a good restitution claim against you because it paid a debt that should have been yours. But you might not be able to satisfy the claim, so the insurance company demands its money back from the hospital. Yet the hospital wins in a majority of jurisdictions.[40] True, it is a case of mistake. Reimbursement came from a party who had no legal responsibility to pay, so the insurance company has a good prima facie case for the return of the money. But the hospital defends against the claim successfully by describing itself as a bona fide creditor. The outcome might be defended on the ground that reliance (i.e., change of position) by the hospital is conclusively presumed on such facts because it is so likely, or it might be said that the hospital was not unjustly enriched by the payment. After all, it did provide expensive services to you. Now it merely has been reimbursed, though from a source that had no obligation to pay.

A strong argument the other way is that a hospital and insurance company, if bargaining in advance about this scenario, would presumably make a different arrangement. They typically *do* make different arrangements. A mistaken payment by an insurance company to a hospital is common enough, and it usually results in a reimbursement or set-off for the insurer under the terms of their contract. The law of restitution never enters into it. Cases like the one mentioned a moment ago, where the insurer sues and loses, tend to come up only when the parties don't deal with each other often enough to have made a contract to deal with the situation. It is unfortunate for a rule of restitution law to run contrary to the practice of well-advised parties who make contracts about the same point. In effect that discrepancy forces the parties to make such contracts about it rather than relying on the background rule. Some might say it is a good thing to make parties do this, because then they have to pay attention to the issue and craft a solution that fits their circumstances better than any background rule would.[41] But in this case a sensible background rule seems so easy to devise that there isn't much to be gained by forcing people to worry about it when they write their contracts. The result is just an increase in transaction costs and outcomes that seem unattractive in the cases that get litigated.

Against that argument there admittedly is a comeback of uncertain strength. It is that in cases where the parties don't have enough dealings to warrant making a contract, the costs of undoing a mistaken payment are likely to weigh more heavily on the hospital. Parties with lots of dealings can easily rectify mistakes with offsets against other payments that may be made later the same day. A hospital that rarely deals with a particular insurance company, however, may change its position in reliance on the payment in ways that aren't as easy to fix.

A final interesting application of our current theme involves victims of Ponzi schemes. In the standard pattern a swindler persuades a series of victims to invest in a phony investment program. One of the early investors—Victim 1—later asks to withdraw his money. The swindler, hoping to keep the scheme running longer, pays Victim 1 with money taken from a later investor—Victim 2. When the scheme collapses soon thereafter, and the swindler has no money left, Victim 2 seeks to collect restitution from Victim 1, who was paid with his money. Victim 2 reasons that his money was taken by fraud. But Victim 1 may reply that he was a bona fide payee: he was not unjustly enriched because he really was owed the money he received from the swindler. Of course Victim 1 must show that he lacked notice of the fraud behind the repayment he received, and courts define "notice" in a range of ways for these purposes. If the lucky investor who got his money back had reason to suspect the fraud behind the scheme, that may be enough to spoil the defense. But assume Victim 1 had no reason to think anything was amiss. What to do?

The hard doctrinal question in such a case is whether Victim 1 gave up value in return for his payment from the swindler. He wasn't quite a creditor of the swindler's in the usual sense; he thought he was, but since the scheme was fraudulent he really just had an "inchoate" claim against the swindler for rescission and restitution. The payment to Victim 1 from the swindler did satisfy or eliminate that claim, so Victim 1 was indeed a bona fide creditor—but only to the extent of his original investment. If the swindler paid back to Victim 1 not only Victim 1's investment but also fictitious returns on it, those returns were not received "for value" and must be relinquished, perhaps to the receiver who is collecting the swindler's assets for distribution to Victim 2 and others like him.[42] And do not forget that Victim 1 may have another defense as well: change of position. All of this assumes, however, that the case is being analyzed as a matter of common law. In practice, state and federal statutes often take center stage in the unwinding of a Ponzi scheme—though not always because they

must. Sometimes the parties do not appear to realize how useful the doctrines of restitution law can be.

The implications of this discussion reach beyond Ponzi schemes. The
deeper question is whether the defense of bona fide payee should be
available to a defendant who received money not as part of the purchase
of anything but just to pay off a debt he was owed. A defendant in the
latter position was not unjustly enriched by his receipt of the money, but
it often will be the case that he did not change position in reliance on it,
either. He merely scratched an entry from his ledger. He therefore might
well be able to return the money without upsetting his affairs; in short, he
is not so likely to have changed position. When we consider whether to
recognize him as a bona fide payee—and whether to treat him as having
received payment in return for "value"—we really are asking whether the
"value" element of the defense is a placeholder for a change of position
that we expect the recipient of money will inevitably (or not so inevitably) commit. The analysis sketched above follows the majority rule that
canceling a debt in response to payment of it does amount to a giving of
value for the money received. But that conclusion might be questioned,
and some have indeed questioned it, if one has doubts about the practical difficulties imposed on such a recipient of money who is later asked
to return it.

Absence of Unjust Enrichment

The cases just considered bear a family resemblance to a related batch
of decisions in which defendants receive mistaken payments but fend off
restitution claims because they aren't unjustly enriched. These patterns
can take simpler forms than the cases just shown. You owe me $10,000
and send me that amount—but it was a mistake. You meant to send it to
another creditor. You nevertheless cannot get the money back, because
I was not unjustly enriched.[43] You cannot get the money back even if I
had notice that you were making a mistake (perhaps you enclosed a nice
note addressed to someone else), because this time the payment was directly from you to me, not via an intermediary like an insurance company.
The result is the same if one party pays a real debt to another because he
thinks he is legally obliged, but then isn't—whether because the statute
of limitations had expired on the underlying claim or the claim was unenforceable for some reason. If the recipient of the assets is not unjustly enriched, the sender of them has no claim for recovery in restitution.[44]

This principle invites us to consider a variation on *Webb v. McGowin*, a case discussed early in the book.[45] Webb was an employee at a mill; he saved McGowin from a dreadful accident but was maimed in the course of the rescue. McGowin was grateful to Webb, promised him regular payments for as long as Webb lived, and started to make them; then McGowin died and his executor stopped paying. Webb successfully sued to enforce McGowin's promise. But now suppose McGowin had made the payments under the false impression that he was legally responsible for Webb's injuries. Later McGowin learns that he wasn't legally responsible, and a court finds that he need not pay Webb anything more. Can McGowin then get back the amounts he already paid to Webb? They were paid because McGowin was laboring under a mistake. But the suit would still likely fail—so asserts the *Restatement*, in any event—because under these circumstances Webb was not unjustly enriched.[46]

Notes

Preface

1. Andrew Kull, *Rationalizing Restitution*, 83 Calif. L. Rev. 1191, 1195 (1995).
2. George E. Palmer, The Law of Restitution (1978).

Chapter One

1. Moses v. Macferlan [1760], 97 Eng. Rep. 676 (2 Burr. 1005).
2. John P. Dawson, Unjust Enrichment 3 (1951); for discussion, see Mark Gergen, *What Renders Enrichment Unjust?* 79 Tex. L. Rev. 1927 (2001).
3. The publication of Peter Birks's *An Introduction to the Law of Restitution* (1985) was a major event in the theoretical exploration of the subject. Hanoch Dagan's *The Law and Ethics of Restitution* (2004) contains a helpful bibliography and is a significant entry in its own right.
4. See, e.g., Chaim Saiman, *Restitution in America: Why the US Refuses to Join the Global Restitution Party*, 28 Oxford J. Leg. Stud. 99 (2008).
5. For history and discussion, see Andrew Kull, *Three Restatements of Restitution*, 68 Wash. & Lee L. Rev. 867 (2011); Andrew Kull, *Rationalizing Restitution*, 83 Calif. L. Rev. 1191 (1995); Douglas Laycock, *The Scope and Significance of Restitution*, 67 Tex. L. Rev. 1277 (1989).
6. An idea most prominently advanced in Peter Birks, Unjust Enrichment (2005).

Chapter Two

1. Amoco Product Co. v. Smith, 946 S.W.2d 162 (Tex. App. 1997).
2. See, e.g., Bank of Alex Brown v. Goldberg, 158 B.R. 188 (E.D. Cal. 1993) (de-

fendant received two refund checks when one was due); *In re* Berry, 147 F. 208 (2d Cir. 1906) (bookkeeper's error caused defendant to be credited twice for amount due once).

3. See Restatement (Third) of Restitution and Unjust Enrichment § 48 (2011) [hereinafter Restatement].

4. See Amoco Product Co. v. Smith, 946 S.W.2d at 164 (The action "is not premised on wrongdoing, but looks only to the justice of the case and inquires whether the defendant has received money which rightfully belongs to another."); United States v. Nw. Nat'l Bank & Trust Co., 35 F. Supp. 484, 486 (D. Minn. 1940) ("[I]f a benefit is bestowed through mistake, no matter how careless or inexcusable the act of the bestower may have been, the recipient of the benefit in equity must make restoration, the theory being that the restitution results in no loss to the recipient. He merely received something for nothing."); Sentry Ins. v. ClaimsCo Int'l., Inc., 608 N.W. 2d 519, 524 (Mich. App. 2000); Restatement § 5 cmt. f.

5. See *Ex parte* AmSouth Mortg. Co., 679 So.2d 251, 255 (Ala. 1996) ("If all persons who negligently confer an economic benefit upon another are disqualified from equitable relief because of their negligence, then the law of restitution, which was conceived in order to prevent unjust enrichment, would be of little or no value.").

6. See, e.g., *In re* Berry, 147 F. at 210 ("Stripped of all complications and entanglements we have this naked fact that Raborg & Manice by mistake paid Berry & Co. $1,500, which they did not owe and which Berry & Co. could not have retained without losing the respect of every honorable business man."); W.B. Hibbs & Co. v. First Nat. Bank of Alexandria, 112 S.E. 669, 673 (1922) (W.D. Va. 1990) (mistaken payments must be returned *ex aequo et bono*—i.e., according to equity and good conscience).

7. Restatement § 50(3).

8. As in Sears v. Grand Lodge A.O.U.W., 57 N.E. 618 (N.Y. 1900). The plaintiff's husband had been missing for many years and was presumed dead. The defendant promised to pay the plaintiff $666 "not to be returned in any event," with an additional amount held in escrow for later payment if the husband still hadn't appeared some years later. After the parties made this agreement but before the defendant paid anything, the husband reappeared. The defendant resisted payment of the $666; the court held for the plaintiff, that the contract was explicit on the defendant's obligations and on its assumption of the risk of a reappearance.

9. Pilot Life Ins. Co. v. Cudd, 36 S.E.2d 860 (S.C. 1945).

10. *Id.* at 864.

11. New York Life Ins. v. Chittenden & Eastmen, 112 N.W. 96 (Iowa 1907).

12. *Id.* at 99.

13. Tarrant v. Monson, 619 P.2d 1210 (Nev. 1980); see Restatement § 5(2)(b).

14. Tarrant v. Monson, 619 P.2d at 1211.

15. United States v. Systron-Donner Corp., 486 F.2d 249 (9th Cir. 1973).

16. Restatement § 5(3)(a) cmt. b(1).

17. See Silano v. Carosella, 172 N.E. 216, 218 (Mass. 1930) ("Subsequent conditions which cast an appearance of injustice over the transaction as a gift do not afford ground for legal liability. A gift flowing from unalloyed good will commonly promotes friendship and stimulates thankfulness, but ingratitude cannot transmute a gift into an obligation enforceable at law."); Horn v. Owens, 171 S.W.2d 585 (Mo. 1943); Restatement § 5 cmt. c.

18. Hutson v. Hutson, 177 A. 177 (Md. 1935).

19. Mott v. Iossa, 181 A. 689 (N.J. Eq. 1935).

20. E.g., Bank of America v. J. & S. Auto Repairs, 694 P.2d 246 (Ariz. 1985); or see Restatement § 9 illus. 1.

21. Dept. of Human Services *ex rel.* Palmer v. Unisys Corp., 637 N.W.2d 142 (Iowa 2001).

22. For acknowledgment of the "whichever is less" principle in various contexts, see Madrid v. Spears, 250 F.2d 51, 54 (10th Cir. 1957); Washington v. Claassen, 545 P.2d 387, 391 (Kan. 1976); Beavers v. Weatherly, 299 S.E.2d 730 (Ga. 1983); Restatement § 10 cmt. h.

23. Restatement § 50(3).

24. Olin v. Reinecke, 168 N.E. 676 (Ill. 1929); Blowers v. S. Ry., 54 S.E. 368 (S.C. 1906); Restatement § 9 cmt. c.

25. See TVL Associates v. A & M Const. Corp., 474 A.2d 156 (D.C. 1984); Golob v. George S. May Intern. Co., 468 P.2d 707, 712–13 (Wash. App. 1970).

26. Mich. Cent. R. Co. v. State, 155 N.E. 50 (Ind. App. 1927); Restatement § 9(c)–(d) & illus. 6.

27. See, e.g., United States v. Pegg, 782 F.2d 1498, 1500 (9th Cir. 1986) (government mistakenly conveyed to defendant a lot with a house on it rather than a vacant lot; defendant was required to remit the additional value received when he later resold the property); Restatement § 9(b). Cf. Lawson v. O'Kelley, 60 S.E.2d 380 (Ga. App. 1950) (no claim for unjust enrichment where subsequent buyer of building did not pay more on account of the mistaken improvement the plaintiff had made to it; the new buyer intended to raze the building). The *Restatement* suggests that a court might even give the improver a lien on the house—in other words, a partial property interest in it—until such time as it ever is sold. See Restatement § 9 cmt. d & illus. 5.

28. See Shick v. Dearmore, 442 S.W. 2d 198 (Ark. 1969); Pull v. Barnes, 350 P.2d 828, 830 (Col. 1960); Atchison, T. & S. F. R. Co. v. Morgan, 21 P. 809 (Kan. 1889).

29. Producers Lumber & Supply Co. v. Olney Building Co., 333 S.W.2d 619 (Tex. App. 1960).

30. Restatement § 10.

31. See Soma v. Zurawski, 772 N.W.2d 724 (Wis. App. 2009); Somerville v. Jacobs, 170 S.E.2d 805 (W.Va. 1969); Hardy v. Burroughs, 232 N.W. 200 (Mich. 1930).

32. For discussion, see Restatement § 10 illust. 19 & reporter's note.

33. See Fitzpatrick v. Allied Contracting Co., 182 N.E.2d 183 (Ill. 1962); Mulholland v. Jolly, 17 S.W.2d 1109 (Tex. App. 1929).

34. Bank of America v. J. & S. Auto Repairs, 694 P.2d at 248; Restatement § 10 cmt. g.

35. See, e.g., Doyle v. West Temple Terrace Co., 152 P. 1180 (Utah 1915).

36. See Ollig v. Eagles, 78 N.W.2d 553 (Mich. 1956); Olin v. Reinecke, 168 N.E. at 678.

37. See Brown v. Davis, 493 So.2d 523 (Fla. App. 1986) (where the defendant, acting in reliance on a mistaken survey, built a house on the plaintiff's land; when plaintiff sought to eject defendant, the court ordered the parties to exchange their lots, which were identical). For examples of courts shutting the door on claims brought by plaintiffs who made improvements without a plausible basis for believing the property was theirs, see O'Marr v. McLean, 238 N.Y.S. 443 (App. Div. 1930); Schaffner v. Schilling, 6 Mo. App. 42 (1878).

38. Voss v. Forgue, 84 So.2d 563 (Fla. 1956).

39. See, e.g., Alaska Stat. § 09.45.640 (2009); N.J. Stat. § 2A:35-3 (2009); N.Y. Real Prop. Acts. Laws § 601 (2009); Annot., 137 A.L.R. 1078; Restatement § 10 cmt. b.

40. See Goulding v. Cook, 661 N.E.2d 1322 (Mass. 1996); Winthers v. Bertrand, 396 P.2d 570, 571 (Or. 1964).

41. See Goulding v. Cook, 661 N.E.2d. at 1325.

42. Bank of America v. J. & S. Auto Repairs, 694 P.2d at 246; Restatement § 9 illus. 3.

43. Ochoa v. Rogers, 234 S.W. 693 (Tex. App. 1921).

44. See, e.g., State Farm Mut. Auto. Ins. Co. v. Northwestern Nat. Ins. Co., 912 P.2d 983 (Utah 1996); Restatement § 7, cmt. b.

45. Partipilo v. Hallman, 510 N.E.2d 8, 12 (Ill. App. 1987).

46. See Taylor v. Roniger, 110 N.W. 503 (Mich. 1907); Detroit & N. Mich. Bldg. & Loan Ass'n v. Oram, 167 N.W. 50 (Mich. 1918); Brookfield v. Rock Island Improvement Co., 169 S.W.2d 662 (Ark. 1943); Restatement § 8 illus. 3.

47. Sykeston Township v. Wells County, 356 N.W.2d 136 (N.D. 1984).

48. See Restatement § 7 illus. 9.

49. See Restatement § 7 illus. 2; cf. Buckett v. Jante, 767 N.W.2d 376 (Wis. App. 2009).

50. See Restatement (Second) of Judgments § 27 (1982).

51. See Restatement § 27.

52. As in Beavers v. Weatherley, 299 S.E.2d 730 (Ga. 1983); see also Farnum v. Silvano, 540 N.E.2d 202 (Mass. App. 1989).

53. Restatement § 27 illus. 2.

54. E.g., Renner v. Kehl, 722 P.2d 262 (Ariz. 1986).

55. Cf. Burton Imaging Group v. Toys "R" Us, Inc., 502 F. Supp. 2d 434, 440 (E.D. Pa. 2007) (both promissory estoppel and unjust enrichment claims failed

when other party's statements were too vague to make reliance on them reasonable); Restatement § 28 cmt. b.

56. See McCloud v. AmSouth Bank, 540 So. 2d 75 (Ala. App. 1989).

57. See Dixon v. Smith, 695 N.E.2d 284 (Ohio App. 1997); Evans v. Wall, 542 So. 2d 1055 (Fla. App. 1989).

58. See, e.g., Doe v. Burkland, 808 A.2d 1090, 1095 (R.I. 2002).

59. As in Evans v. Wall, 542 So. 2d. 1055.

60. As in Salzman v. Bachrach, 996 P.2d 1263 (Col. 2000); Bramlett v. Selman, 597 S.W.2d 80 (Ark. 1980).

61. Restatement § 28.

62. Johnston v. Estate of Phillips, 706 S.W.2d 554 (Mo. App. 1986); Tapley v. Tapley, 449 A.2d 1218 (N.H. 1982); Restatement § 28 cmt. d.

63. Restatement § 28 illus. 8. Cf. Meyer v. Meyer, 620 N.W.2d 382 (Wis. 2000); Pyeatte v. Pyeatte, 661 P.2d 196 (Ariz. App. 1982).

64. See discussion in chapter 6.

65. Compare Restatement § 28 cmt. e & illus. 13.

Chapter Three

1. See, e.g., Bailey v. State, 500 S.E.2d 54, 60 (N.C. 1998); Powell v. Henry, 592 S.W.2d 107, 109 (Ark. 1980) ("[I]nadequate compensation will cause attorneys who are competent to handle this type of litigation to shun it, or if they accept it, fail to devote sufficient time to adequately prepare or present the case."); see also Annot., 38 A.L.R.3d 1384 § 5.5 (1971 & Supp.); Restatement (Third) of Restitution and Unjust Enrichment § 29 cmt. b, & illus. 1 & 7 (2011) [hereinafter Restatement].

2. For discussion, see John P. Dawson, *Lawyers and Involuntary Clients: Attorney Fees from Funds*, 87 Harv. L. Rev. 1597 (1974); Daniel Friedmann, *Unjust Enrichment, Pursuance of Self-Interest, and the Limits of Free-Riding*, 36 Loy. L.A. L. Rev. 831, 860 (2003); Annot., *Amount of Attorney's Compensation in Absence of Contract or Statute Fixing Amount*, 57 A.L.R.3d 475 (1974 & Supp.); Annot., *Method of Calculating Attorney's Fees Awarded in Common-Fund or Common-Benefit Cases-State Cases*, 56 A.L.R.5th 107 (1998); Restatement § 29 cmt. c.

3. Felton v. Finley, 209 P.2d 899 (Idaho 1949).

4. For more authority to the same effect, see Security Nat'l Bank & Trust Co. v. Willim, 180 S.E.2d 46 (W. Va. 1971). Compare Estate of Pfoertner, 700 N.E.2d 438 (Ill. App. 1998), which the *Restatement* rejects as "contrary to the rule and spirit of § 29." Restatement § 29 reporter's note to cmt. g.

5. Felton v. Finley, 209 P.2d at 901.

6. See Petition of Crum, 14 S.E.2d 21 (S.C. 1941) (allocating attorney fees to parties who were present during the litigation but "stood aloof and without coun-

sel"); Shamblin v. Sylvester, 304 S.W.3d 320 (Tenn. App. 2009) (ordering the "passive beneficiary" of a wrongful death suit to pay a reasonable attorney fee); Restatement § 29 cmt. d & illus. 9.

7. As in Domenella v. Domenella, 513 N.E.2d 17 (Ill. App. 1987) (refusing to award attorney's fees out of share collected by relatives who were never informed of the legal action); see Restatement § 29 cmt. g & illus. 23.

8. For discussion, see Restatement § 29.

9. Ulmer v. Farnsworth, 15 A. 65 (Me. 1888).

10. See Howard R. Williams and Charles J. Meyers, Oil and Gas Law § 204 (2010); Dean Lueck, *The Rule of First Possession and the Design of the Law*, 38 J.L. & Econ. 393, 403 (1995).

11. Wendover Road Prop. Owners Ass'n. v. Kornicks, 502 N.E.2d 226 (Ohio App. 1985); see also Dinosaur Dev., Inc. v. White, 265 Cal. Rptr. 525 (Cal. App. 1989).

12. Songbird Jet Ltd. v. Amax, Inc., 581 F. Supp. 912 (S.D.N.Y. 1984); Restatement § 30 cmt. c & illus. 11.

13. Cotnam v. Wisdom, 104 S.W. 164 (Ark. 1907); for additional authority, see Piggee v. Mercy, 186 P.2d 817 (Okla. 1947); *In re* Chrisan Estate, 107 N.W.2d 907 (Mich. 1961); K.A.L. v. S. Med. Bus. Serv., 854 So. 2d 106, 108 (Ala. App. 2003); Restatement § 20.

14. Cotnam v. Wisdom, 104 S.W. at 167; *In re* Chrisan Estate, 107 N.W.2d at 908; Restatement § 20 cmt. c & illus. 8.

15. See Ladd v. White, 92 N.W. 365, 367 (Wis. 1902).

16. See Ross Albert, *Restitutionary Recovery for Rescuers of Human Life*, 74 Calif. L. Rev. 85, 86 (1986); Geoffrey R. Watson, *In the Tribunal of Conscience: Mills v. Wyman Reconsidered*, 71 Tul. L. Rev. 1749, 1800 (1997); Restatement § 20 cmt. b & illus. 7.

17. See Osterlind v. Hill, 160 N.E. 301, 302 (Mass. 1928); Yania v. Bigan, 155 A.2d 343 (Pa. 1959).

18. Webb v. McGowin, 168 So. 196 (Ala. App. 1935).

19. See Annot., 98 A.L.R.5th 353 (2002); Restatement (Second) of Contracts § 86 cmt. d & illus. 7 (1981).

20. As in Chase v. Corcoran, 106 Mass. 286 (1871) (allowing recovery where plaintiff came upon defendant's empty boat and saved it).

21. As in Berry v. Barbour, 279 P.2d 335 (Okla. 1954).

22. Trott v. Dean Witter & Co., 438 F. Supp. 842 (S.D.N.Y. 1977).

23. E.g., First Federal Savings & Loan Ass'n of Warren v. A & M Towing & Road Service, Inc., 711 N.E.2d 755 (Ohio App. 1998).

24. E.g., Hartford Fire Ins. Co. v. Albertson, 298 N.Y.S.2d 321 (Cty. Ct. 1969); see also Allstate Ins. Co. v. Reeves, 440 So. 2d 1086 (Ala. App. 1983).

25. Bailey v. West, 249 A.2d 414 (R.I. 1969).

26. See Restatement § 21 cmt. c; Glenn v. Savage, 13 P. 442 (Or. 1887) ("The law will never permit a friendly act, or such as was intended to be an act of kindness or benevolence, to be afterwards converted into a pecuniary demand."); Sparks v.

Gustafson, 750 P.2d 338 (Alaska 1988) ("Courts will allow the defendant to retain a benefit without compensating plaintiff in several situations, one of which is relevant to the case at hand: where the benefit was given gratuitously without expectation of payment.").

27. See also Keith v. DuBussigney, 60 N.E. 614 (Mass. 1901); Morse v. Kenney, 89 A. 865 (Vt. 1914).

28. Tice Towing Line v. James McWilliams Blue Line, 51 F.2d 243, 246 (S.D.N.Y. 1931), aff'd in relevant part and modified, 57 F.2d 183, 184 (2d Cir. 1932) (L. Hand, J.) (holding a negligent tug operator liable for salvage efforts which assisted in mitigating damages); Restatement § 21 cmt. f & illus. 11. The maritime law of salvage may also be a source of recovery for a rescuer of property (though not of life); the recovery then follows rules that sometimes depart from principles of restitution. See William M. Landes and Richard A. Posner, *Salvors, Finders, Good Samaritans, and Other Rescuers: An Economic Study of Law and Altruism*, 7 J. Legal Stud. 83 (1978); cf. Peninsular & Oriental Steam Navigation Co. v. Overseas Oil Carriers, Inc., 553 F.2d 830 (2d Cir. 1977) (plaintiff's vessel detoured to rescue fireman who was ill on defendant's vessel; plaintiff was allowed to recover its costs on "quasi-contract" theory).

29. McNeilab, Inc. v. North River Ins. Co., 645 F. Supp. 525 (D.N.J. 1986).

30. See also Klein v. Fidelity & Deposit Co. of Am., 700 A.2d 262, 278 (Md. 1997); Saul Levmore, *Obligation or Restitution for Best Efforts*, 67 S. Calif. L. Rev. 1411 (1994); Restatement § 21 cmt. f.

31. See Restatement § 23 cmt. a.

32. Yellow Cab of D.C., Inc. v. Dreslin, 181 F.2d 626 (D.C. Cir. 1950).

33. See Annot., 25 A.L.R.4th 1120 (1983); Annot., 92 A.L.R.3d 901 (1979).

34. See Restatement § 26.

35. See Restatement § 26 cmt. b.

36. See Joyce v. Pearce, 641 P.2d 1170 (Or. App. 1982); Restatement § 26 cmt. e.

37. Stockwell v. Mut. Life Ins. Co. of New York, 73 P. 833 (Cal. 1903); *In re* Montgomery's Estate, 149 A. 705 (Penn. 1930); Restatement § 23 cmt. b & e, & illus. 11 & 22.

38. Compare Whirrett v. Mott, 601 N.E.2d 525 (Ohio App. 1991) (requiring contribution from one co-owner to another for payment of utility bills and taxes but not lawn care).

39. Restatement § 26 cmt. a.

40. Whirrett v. Mott, 601 N.E.2d at 527.

41. See, e.g., W. Am. Ins. Co. v. Yellow Cab Co. of Orlando, Inc., 495 So.2d 204 (Fla. App. 1986); Restatement § 24.

42. Am. Surety Co. v. W. Surety Co., 22 N.W.2d 429, 431 (S.D. 1946); see 16 Couch, Cyclopedia of Insurance Law § 61:18 (1959).

43. See Restatement § 24 cmt. b.

44. See, e.g., Oxford Production Credit Ass'n v. Bank of Oxford, 16 So. 2d 384, 390 (Miss. 1944); Restatement § 24 cmt. g.

45. See Restatement (Second) of Torts § 920A (1979); Helfend v. S. California

Rapid Transit Dist., 465 P.2d 61 (Cal. 1970) (discussing the rationale for the rule and criticisms of it); Annot., 77 A.L.R.3d 415 (1977); Restatement § 24 cmt. c.

46. Rawson v. City of Omaha, 322 N.W.2d 381 (Neb. 1982).

47. See Restatement § 24 cmt. e.

48. See Rivers v. Roe, 4 Upper Can. C.P. 21 (1854). For related modern applications, see Mut. Service Cas. Inc. Co. v. Elizabeth State Bank, 265 F.3d 601 (7th Cir. 2001) (insurer entitled to equitable subrogation against bank for enabling embezzlement); Fidelity Ins. Co. v. Arthur Andersen & Co., 552 N.E.2d 870 (N.Y. 1990); Restatement § 24 cmt. g.

49. See City of New York v. Keene Corp., 505 N.Y.S.2d 782 (Sup. Ct. 1986), aff'd, 513 N.Y.S.2d 1004 (App. Div. 1987).

50. See, e.g., *In re* Estate of Boyd, 972 P.2d 1075 (Col. App. 1998); Osborne v. Osborne, 683 N.E.2d 365 (Ohio App. 1996); Estate of Kemmerrer, 251 P.2d 345 (Cal. App. 1952).

51. Estate of Cleveland v. Gorden, 837 S.W.2d 68 (Tenn. App. 1992). See also Estate of Bends, 589 S.W.2d 330 (Mo. App. 1979); Annot., 35 A.L.R.2d 1399 (1954); Restatement § 22 cmt. b & f.

52. See Restatement § 22 cmt. e.

53. See United States v. Consolidated Edison Co. of New York, Inc, 580 F.2d 1122 (2d Cir. 1978).

54. See Hurdis Realty, Inc. v. Town of N. Providence, 397 A.2d 896 (R.I. 1979).

55. See Tipper v. Great Lakes Chem. Co., 281 So. 2d 10 (Fla. 1973); Aqua-Terra Const. & Eng'g Sys. v. Oak Harbor Inv. Props., L.L.C., 2008 WL 3539728 (E.D. La. 2008); Restatement § 22 cmt. h & illus. 22.

56. See Restatement § 22 cmt. e.

57. Hazelwood Water Dist. v. First Union Management, Inc., 715 P.2d 498 (Or. App. 1986).

58. Bacon v. Bacon, 89 P. 317 (Cal. 1907); Caskie v. Philadelphia Rapid Transit Co., 184 A. 17 (Penn. 1936); College Park v. E. Airlines, Inc., 300 S.E.2d 513 (Ga. 1983); Restatement § 48.

59. Wayne Cty. Produce v. Duffy-Mott Co., 155 N.E. 669 (N.Y. 1927); Harrison Sheet Steel Co. v. Lyons, 155 N.E.2d 595 (Ill. 1959) (customers were entitled to restitution for the additional costs imposed for the Retailers' Occupation Tax after it was ruled that the tax did not apply to the retailer); Cohon v. Oscar L. Paris Co., 149 N.E.2d 472 (Ill. App. 1958); Restatement § 48 cmt. e & illus. 9.

60. Wilson Area Sch. Dist. v. Skepton, 895 A.2d 1250 (Penn. 2006) (school district was not entitled to restitution from a contractor after permit fees were ruled illegal; since the contractor had a written contract based on a single total bidding price, the court found that the refunds were simply an unexpected cost savings for the contractor); Restatement § 48 cmt. e & illus. 10.

61. Gutierrez v. Madero, 564 S.W.2d 185 (Tex. App. 1978).

62. For similar authority, see Brunnenmeyer v. Massachusetts Mut. Life Ins. Co., 384 N.E.2d 446 (Ill. App. 1978); Faulknier v. Shafer, 563 S.E.2d 755 (Va. 2002).

63. Ontiveros Insulation Co. v. Sanchez, 3 P.3d 695 (N.M. App. 2000) (subcontractors were entitled to compensation from home owners after general contractor filed for bankruptcy); Annot., *Building and Construction Contracts: Right of Subcontractor Who Has Dealt Only with Primary Contractor to Recover against Property Owner in Quasi Contract,* 62 A.L.R.3d 288 § 2 (1975); Restatement § 25 cmt. b & illus. 2.

64. Commerce P'ship 8098 Ltd. P'ship v. Equity Contr. Co., 695 So. 2d 383 (Fla. App. 1997); Ontiveros Insulation Co., Inc., v. Rawson, Inc. Builders Supply, 3 P.3d at 700 (noting that a payment of 52 percent of the total contract was not sufficient to deny recovery to the subcontractor); Restatement § 25 cmt. b & illus. 1.

65. Callano v. Oakwood Park Homes Corp., 219 A.2d 332 (N.J. App. 1966).

66. Pepi Corp. v. Galliford, 254 S.W.3d 457, 462 (Tex. App. 2007) (subcontractor's valid contractual claim against the general contractor barred an action in quantum meruit against the property owner); Annot., *Building and Construction Contracts: Right of Subcontractor Who Has Dealt Only with Primary Contractor to Recover against Property Owner in Quasi Contract,* 62 A.L.R.3d 288 § 2 (1975); Restatement § 25 cmt. b & illus. 3.

67. See Flooring Sys., Inc., v. Radisson Group, Inc., 772 P.2d 578 (Ariz. 1989); Paschall's, Inc., v. Dozier, 407 S.W.2d 150, 155 (Tenn. 1966) (limiting subcontractor's recovery to a "reasonable value of his services"); Guarantee Elec. Co. v. Big Rivers Elec. Corp., 669 F. Supp. 1371, 1380 (W.D. Ky. 1987) (noting that in order to have a valid restitution claim against a landowner a subcontractor must have exhausted his contractual claims without having received the reasonable value of his services); Restatement § 25 cmt. c & e.

68. Puttkamer v. Minth, 266 N.W.2d 361 (Wis. 1978); Restatement § 25 cmt. c.

69. See Gen. Leasing Co. v. Manivest Corp., 667 P.2d 596 (Utah 1983); Restatement § 25 cmt. c & illus. 7.

Chapter Four

1. See discussion in Ablah v. Eyman, 365 P.2d 181, 192 (Kan. 1961); Olwell v. Nye & Nissen, 173 P.2d 652, 653 (Wash. 1946) ("It is uniformly held that in cases where the defendant *tort feasor* has benefited by his wrong, the plaintiff may elect to 'waive the tort' and bring an action in assumpsit for restitution."); see also John D. McCamus, *Disgorgement for Breach of Contract: A Comparative Perspective,* 36 Loy. L.A. L. Rev. 943, 945 (2003); Arthur Corbin, *Waiver of Tort and Suit in Assumpsit,* 19 Yale L.J. 221 (1910).

2. E.g., CAMAS Colo., Inc. v. Bd. of Cnty. Comm'rs, 36 P.3d 135, 140 (Col. App. 2001) (comparing limitations periods); Mich. Educ. Emps. Mut. Ins. Co. v. Morris, 596 N.W.2d 142, 152 (Mich. 1999) (laches).

3. See Restatement (Second) of Torts § 874 (1979).

4. See United States v. Carroll Towing Co., 159 F.2d 169, 172 (2nd Cir. 1947);

for discussion, see Doug Rendleman, *Common Law Restitution in the Mississippi Tobacco Settlement: Did the Smoke Get in Their Eyes?*, 33 Ga. L. Rev. 847, 905 (1999).

5. See, e.g., 17 U.S.C. § 504(b); 35 U.S.C. § 259; Dane S. Ciolino, *Reconsidering Restitution in Copyright*, 48 Emory L.J. 1, 13 (1999); Caprice L. Roberts, *The Case for Restitution and Unjust Enrichment Remedies in Patent Law*, 14 Lewis & Clark L. Rev. 653, 678 (2010); Restatement (Third) of Restitution and Unjust Enrichment § 42 cmt. a & c (2011) [hereinafter Restatement].

6. See, e.g., Blanchard v. Norman-Breaux Lumber Co., 57 So.2d 211 (La. 1952) (liability for product less expenses of creating it); McGee v. SECO Timber Co., 350 So.2d 1265, 1268 (La. App. 1977) (similar); Kennedy v. Perry Lumber Co., 52 So.2d 847 (La. 1951) (liability for entire value of finished product); Nutting v. Raub, 7 Cal. Rptr. 227 (Cal. App. 1960) (similar).

7. See Annot., 69 A.L.R.2d 1335 (1960); 52 Am. Jur. 2d *Logs and Timber* § 107.

8. See Morgan v. Fuller, 441 So.2d 290, 298 (La. App. 1983).

9. De Camp v. Bullard, 54 N.E. 26 (N.Y. 1899).

10. *Id.* at 28.

11. See EarthInfo, Inc. v. Hydrosphere Res. Consultants, Inc., 900 P.2d 113 (Colo. 1995); Andrew Kull, *Disgorgement for Breach, the "Restitution Interest," and the Restatement of Contracts*, 79 Tex. L. Rev. 2021, 2030–31 (2001).

12. On which see County of San Bernardino v. Walsh, 69 Cal. Rptr. 3d 848, 856 (Cal. App. 2007); Warren v. Century Bankcorporation, Inc., 741 P.2d 846, 852 (Okla. 1987).

13. Restatement § 40 cmt. d.

14. See Corey v. Struve, 149 P. 48, 49 (Cal. 1915), overruled on other grounds by Maben v. Rankin, 358 P.2d 681, 684 (Cal. 1961); Fratt v. Clark, 12 Cal. 89, 90 (1859) (awarding farmer price received from sale of meat after butcher wrongfully converted the cattle, slaughtered them, and then sold them).

15. Silsbury v. McCoon, 3 N.Y. 379 (1850).

16. *Id.* at 381–82.

17. *Id.* at 385–86; see also Atlas Ins. Co. v. Gibbs, 183 A. 690, 692 (Conn. 1936) (allowing the innocent defendant to retain his engine he put into the plaintiff's stolen car); Meyers v. Gerhart, 103 P. 1114, 1117 (Wash. 1909).

18. Ochoa v. Rogers, 234 S.W. 693, 694 (Tex. App. 1921) ("[I]f the one in wrongful possession be an innocent or unintentional trespasser, and in good faith improves and enhances the value of the property, and such improvements and additions exceed, or even substantially approach, the value of the article in its raw state when found, the property in dispute becomes merely accessory to the resulting product, and title thereto passes to the purchaser, who is liable to the original owner only for the market value of the lost article at the time it is found."); see also Capitol Chevrolet Co. v. Earheart, 627 S.W.2d 369 (Tenn. App. 1981).

19. Jewett v. Dringer, 30 N.J. Eq. 291 (N.J. 1878).

20. Jewett v. Dringer, 30 N.J. Eq. at 291 (citing Docker v. Somes, (1834) 2 Myl. & K. 674).

21. See Restatement § 58 illus. 26; Janigan v. Taylor, 344 F.2d 781, 787 (1st Cir. 1965) ("[I]f an artist acquired paints by fraud and used them in producing a valuable portrait, we would not suggest that the defrauded party would be entitled to the portrait, or to the proceeds of the sale.").

22. As in Potter v. Mardre, 74 N.C. 36, 41 (1876) ("[I]f the owner of the trees can recover the staves made from them, why not the casks made from the staves; and if in replevin he can recover the planks, why not the ship built with the planks, etc.?").

23. Jacque v. Steenburg Homes, 563 N.W.2d 154 (Wis. 1997).

24. See Restatement § 40.

25. Quality Excelsior Coal Co. v. Reeves, 177 S.W.2d 728, 732 (Ark. 1944) (calling this kind of damages the "wayleave" or "haulage royalty"); see also Pomposini v. T.W. Phillips Gas & Oil Co., 580 A.2d 776, 780 (Pa. Super. 1990) (charging defendant the market value for similar storage space after the defendant illegally stored natural gas on the plaintiff's property).

26. Cf. State Farm Mut. Auto. Ins. Co. v. Campbell, 538 U.S. 408 (2003); Exxon Shipping Co. v. Baker, 554 U.S. 471, 515 (2008).

27. America Online, Inc., v. Nat'l. Health Care Discount, Inc., 174 F.Supp.2d 890 (N.D. Iowa 2001).

28. Roberts, *supra* note 5, at 679; Restatement §§ 40 & 42.

29. See, e.g., McGinnis v. Rogers, 279 A.2d 459, 470 (Md. 1971).

30. See, e.g., Vrooman v. Hawbaker, 56 N.E.2d 623, 626 (Ill. 1944).

31. Restatement § 43 cmt. h.

32. See *id.* at § 41 cmt. d & illus. 5, & § 51.

33. See *id.* at § 41 cmt. e & § 60; Hanoch Dagan, *Restitution in Bankruptcy: Why All Involuntary Creditors Should Be Preferred*, 78 Am. Bankr. L.J. 247, 267 (2004).

34. G & M Motor Co. v. Thompson, 567 P.2d 80 (Okla. 1977).

35. See Brown v. N.Y. Life Ins. Co., 152 F.2d 246 (9th Cir. 1945); Restatement § 41 cmt. d & illus. 5, & § 61 cmt. b & illus. 3.

36. See First Nat'l Bank of Mobile v. Pope, 117 So.2d 174, 177 (Ala. 1959); Mullikin v. Pedersen, 71 N.W.2d 485, 488 (Neb. 1955); Annot., 24 A.L.R.2d 672 (1952).

37. G & M Motor Co. v. Thompson, 567 P.2d at 83.

38. Riggs v. Palmer, 22 N.E. 188 (1889).

39. *Id.* at 190; see also *In re* Estate of Macaro, 699 N.Y.S.2d 634, 638 (N.Y. Sur. 1999).

40. See Ronald M. Dworkin, Taking Rights Seriously (1977).

41. As in Estate of Troxal v. S.P.T., 851 N.E.2d 345, 349 (Ind. App. 2006); see also Annot., 27 A.L.R.3d 794 (1969).

42. See Angleton v. Estate of Angleton, 671 N.E.2d 921, 927 (Ind. App. 1996).

43. See, e.g., Crawford v. Coleman, 726 S.W.2d 9, 11 (Tex. 1987) (proceeds go to the insured's nearest relative).

44. See Cook v. Grierson, 845 A.2d 1231, 1233 n.3 (Md. 2004) (collecting examples).

45. See Jacobson v. Jacobson, 370 A.2d 65, 68 (N.J. Sup. 1976).

Chapter Five

1. See Restatement (Third) of Restitution and Unjust Enrichment § 31 cmt. e (2011) [hereinafter Restatement]; Wolf v. Malevani, 343 So.2d 949, 950 (Fla. App. 1977); Misisco v. La Maita, 192 A.2d 891, 892 (Conn. 1963).

2. As is Montanaro Bros. Builders, Inc. v. Snow, 460 A.2d 1297, 1301 (Conn. 1983). See Restatement § 31 cmt. d.

3. See Restatement § 34 cmt. c; Cent. Baptist Theological Seminary v. Entertainment Communications, Inc., 356 N.W.2d 785, 789 (Minn. App. 1984); Frigillana v. Frigillana, 584 S.W.2d 30, 33–34 (Ark. 1979).

4. Restatement § 34 illus. 17; see also Turner Falls Lumber Co. v. Burns, 45 A. 896 (Vt. 1899).

5. Restatement § 34 cmt. e; Great S. Life Ins. Co. v. Emp. Fringe Benefits, Inc. 420 So.2d 407, 410 (Fla. App. 1982).

6. Parker v. Arthur Murray, Inc., 295 N.E.2d 487, 489 (Ill. App. 1973).

7. Restatement § 34 cmt. d.

8. See Restatement § 31 cmt. d; Meaney v. Conn. Hosp. Ass'n, Inc., 735 A.2d 813, 825 (Conn. 1999); Engelbrecht v. Prop. Developers, Inc., 296 N.E.2d 798, 801 (Ind. App. 1973); Creative Servs., Inc. v. Spears Constr. Co., 202 S.E.2d 581, 583 (Ga. App. 1973).

9. National Recovery Systems v. Ornstein, 541 F.Supp. 1131, 1133 (D.Pa. 1982); see also Sea Air Support, Inc. v. Herrmann, 613 P.2d 413 (Nev. 1980); Nat'l Recovery Sys. v. Feltman, 511 A.2d 1307, 1310 (N.J. Super. 1986); Nat'l Recovery Sys. v. Bryer, 507 A.2d 1226 (Pa. Super. 1986); Restatement § 31 cmt. a.

10. Womack v. Maner, 301 S.W.2d 438, 439 (Ark. 1957). See also Clark v. United States, 102 U.S. 322 (1880); Sinnar v. Le Roy, 270 P.2d 800 (Wash. 1954).

11. Restatement § 32 cmt. d & illus. 11; see also Restatement § 62. Hartman v. Harris, 810 F.Supp. 82, 86 (S.D.N.Y. 1992); Stone v. Freeman, 82 N.E.2d 571, 572 (N.Y. 1948).

12. State v. Pettit, 698 P.2d 1049 (Or. App. 1985).

13. *Id.*; see also State v. Garcia, 866 P.2d 5 (Utah App. 1993); Restatement § 32 cmt. c & illus. 2. These cases typically involve application of statutes that require criminals to make "restitution" to their victims. Those statutes often produce recovery that compensates the victim for harm suffered and is not restitutionary in the sense used in this book, but in this case the recovery does indeed amount to restitution and could be sought under the common law without recourse to the statutes.

14. Restatement § 32 illus. 10; Clark v. United States, 102 U.S. at 332.

15. Cohen v. Radio-Electronics Officers Union, 679 A.2d 1188, 1199 (N.J. 1996); for a variation, see Restatement § 32 illus. 7.

16. Sceva v. True, 53 N.H. 627, 630 (1873); Porter v. Wilson, 209 A.2d 730, 732 (N.H. 1965); Restatement § 33 cmt. f.

17. Magnolia Courts, Inc. v. Webb, 470 S.W.2d 16, 18 (Tenn. App. 1970); Gregory v. Lee, 30 A. 53 (Conn. 1894); see generally Annot., 68 A.L.R. 1185; Restatement § 31.

18. See Annot., 33 A.L.R.3d 1164; Restatement § 33 cmt. f.

19. Restatement § 33 cmt. f & illus. 22; see discussion in KunkleWater & Elec., Inc. v. City of Prescott, 347 N.W.2d 648, 648 (Iowa 1984).

20. Restatement § 13 cmt. c; Wood v. Kalbaugh, 114 Cal.Rptr. 673, 676 (Cal. App. 1974); In re Clark's Estate, 253 N.Y.S. 524, 528 (App. Div. 1931); Canadian Agency v. Assets Realization Co., 150 N.Y.S. 758, 767 (App. Div. 1914) (finding that a contract may be rescinded due to innocent mistake of a material fact).

21. E.g., Pedersen v. Bibioff, 828 P.2d 1113 (1992).

22. E.g., Connors v. Fawn Mining Corp., 30 F.3d 483 (3d Cir. 1994).

23. See Restatement § 13 cmt. e; Brett v. Cooney, 53 A. 729, 731 (Conn. 1902).

24. Gray v. Baker, 485 So. 2d 306, 308 (Miss. 1986); Restatement § 13 illus. 7.

25. See Restatement § 13 cmt. h.

26. Farnsworth v. Feller, 471 P.2d 792 (Or. 1970).

27. Id. at 797 (quoting McGowan v. Willamette Valley Irr. Land Co., 155 P. 705 (Or. 1916)).

28. See Restatement § 13 cmt. h.

29. See id. at cmt. a.

30. See Kausky v. Kosten, 179 P.2d 950, 953 (Wash. 1947); White v. White, 519 S.W.2d 689, 693 (Tex. App. 1975); Earl v. Saks & Co., 226 P.2d 340, 344 (Cal. 1951); Restatement § 13 cmt. f.

31. See Restatement § 15 cmt. b. Matter of Estate of Welch, 534 N.W.2d 109 (Iowa App. 1995); Bank v. Waggoner, 117 S.E. 6 (N.C. 1923).

32. See Restatement § 15 cmt. c; McDonald v. Hewlett, 228 P.2d 83, 87 (Cal. App. 1951); Folsom v. Buttolph, 143 N.E. 258, 262 (Ind. App. 1924); Worsham v. Johnson, 164 So. 381, 382 (Ala. 1935).

33. Webster v. Lehmer, 742 P.2d 1203 (Utah 1987).

34. Rubenstein v. Rubenstein, 120 A.2d 11, 13 (N.J. 1956); Beamer v. Clayton, 96 S.E. 969, 972 (W. Va. 1918); Samuels Shoe Co. v. Frensley, 3 P.2d 216, 222 (Okla. 1931).

35. See Restatement § 14 cmt. g.

36. Id. at cmt. d (addressing "restitution to the extent of unjust enrichment"). Wilbur v. Blanchard, 126 P. 1069 (Idaho 1912); Nelson v. Leszczynski-Clark Co., 143 N.W. 606, 608 (Mich. 1913).

37. See Restatement § 14 cmt. g.

38. See Peters v. Halligan, 152 N.W.2d 103, 105 (Neb. 1967); Restatement § 36 cmt. a.

39. See Halle v. C.I.R., 83 F.3d 649, 651 (4th Cir. 1996).

40. See Annot., 134 A.L.R. 1064; Restatement § 36 cmt. d.

41. See Restatement § 36 cmt. b & c; see Britton v. Turner, 6 N.H. 481, 486 (1834).

42. Restatement § 36 cmt. b(3) & illus. 2.

43. Dodge v. Kimball, 89 N.E. 542 (Mass. 1909).

44. See Restatement § 36 illus. 19; Smith v. Brady, 17 N.Y. 173 (1858).

45. For additional authority, see Lynch v. Culhane, 129 N.E. 717 (Mass. 1921).

46. Ruxley Electronics & Constr. Ltd. v. Forsyth, 1 App. Cas. 344 (H.L. 1995).

47. See Posner, Economic Analysis of Law § 4.9 (7th ed. 2007).

48. Restatement § 36 illus. 20.

49. See Restatement (Third) of Torts: Liability for Economic Harm § 3 (Tentative Draft 2012).

50. *Id.* Put aside complications that may arise when the breach of contract is also the breach of an independent duty imposed by the law of torts, as in cases where a plaintiff sues a defendant for malpractice.

51. See Restatement (Second) of Contracts § 22 (1981).

52. Restatement § 37 cmt. b. Tongish v. Thomas, 840 P.2d 471, 473 (1992) (awarding the difference between the contract price and the market value when the seller breaches the contract).

53. Restatement § 37 cmt. c.

54. E.g., Puskar v. Hughes, 533 N.E.2d 962 (Ill. App. 1989).

55. See, e.g., Britton v. Turner, 6 N.H. at 481.

56. See Timmerman v. Stanley, 51 S.E. 760, 762 (Ga. 1905).

57. Bause v. Anthony Pools, Inc., 23 Cal. Rptr. 265 (Cal. App. 1962).

58. Brown v. St. Paul, Minneapolis & Manitoba R. Co., 31 N.W. 941 (Minn. 1886); Restatement § 38 illus. 4.

59. See Restatement § 38 illus. 6; Britton v. Turner, 6 N.H. at 481.

60. See Clark v. Manchester, 51 N.H. 594 (1872); Restatement § 38 cmt. c & illus. 8.

61. Restatement § 38 illus. 16. See also Stark v. Magnuson, 2 N.W.2d 814, 815 (Minn. 1942); Bailey v. Furleigh, 208 P. 1091, 1092 (Wash. 1922).

62. Kehoe v. Rutherford, 27 A. 912 (N.J. Sup. 1893).

63. See Restatement § 38 cmt. c; Amber Res. Co. v. United States, 73 Fed. Cl. 738 (Fed. Cl. 2006), *aff'd*, 538 F.3d 1358 (Fed. Cir. 2008).

64. 3 Dan B. Dobbs, Law of Remedies § 12.7(5), at 183 (2d ed. 1993); see also Mark Gergen, *Restitution as a Bridge Over Troubled Contractual Waters*, 71 Fordham L. Rev. 709 (2002); Restatement § 38 cmt. e & reporter's note.

65. Restatement § 38.

66. See, e.g., Citizens Fin. Serv. v. United States, 57 Fed. Cl. 64 (Fed. Cl. 2003); 3 Dobbs, Law of Remedies § 12.3(2) (2d ed. 1993).

67. See Restatement § 39.

68. See *id.* at illus. 1; Coppola Enter., Inc. v. Alfone, 531 So. 2d 334 (Fla. 1988); Warren v. Century Bankcorp., Inc., 741 P.2d 846, 852 (Okla. 1987).

69. See, e.g., Long Bldg, Inc. v. Buffalo Anthracite Coal Co., 74 N.Y.S.2d 281 (N.Y. Sup. Ct. 1947).

70. See Restatement § 39 illus. 7; the *Restatement*'s view reverses the result in City of New Orleans v. Firemen's Charitable Ass'n, 9 So. 486 (La. 1891).

71. See Restatement § 39 illus. 8; Long Bldg, Inc. v. Buffalo Anthracite Coal Co., 74 N.Y.S.2d at 281.

72. See Restatement § 39 cmt. b.

73. Peevyhouse v. Garland Coal & Mining Co., 382 P.2d 109 (Okla. 1962).

74. See, e.g., Groves v. John Wunder Co., 286 N.W. 235 (Minn. 1939); Am. Standard, Inc. v. Schectman, 439 N.Y.S.2d 529 (N.Y. Sup. Ct. 1981); Restatement § 39 illus. 5.

75. On which see Richard A. Posner, Economic Analysis of Law § 4.9 (7th ed. 2007).

76. See, e.g., Daniel Friedmann, *The Efficient Breach Fallacy*, 18 J. Leg. Stud. 1 (1989).

77. See Snepp v. U.S., 444 U.S. 507 (1980); Attorney General v. Blake, [1998] Ch. 439 (C.A. 1997), *app. dismissed*, [2001] 1 A.C. 268 (H.L. 2000); Restatement § 39 cmt. e.

Chapter Six

1. See Restatement (Third) of Restitution and Unjust Enrichment § 49 (2011) [hereinafter Restatement].

2. See *id.* at § 53.

3. See Hanoch Dagan, *Restitution and Relationships*, 92 B.U. L. Rev. 1035 (2012).

4. Restatement § 50 cmt. c.

5. Lawson v. O'Kelley, 60 S.E.2d 380 (Ga. App. 1950).

6. See Massey v. Tyra, 234 S.W.2d 759, 763 (Ark. 1950); Beavers v. Weatherley, 299 S.E.2d 730, 732 (Ga. 1983); Restatement § 50(2)(a).

7. See Madrid v. Spears, 250 F.2d 51, 54 (10th Cir. 1957); Restatement § 50 cmt. f.

8. See Restatement § 50 (3).

9. See *id.* at § 50 cmt. g.

10. See, e.g., Anderson v. Schwegel, 796 P.2d 1035 (Idaho App. 1990); Restatement § 50 cmt. d.

11. See discussion of *Cotnam v. Wisdom* in chapter 3.

12. See Bendix v. Ross, 238 N.W. 381, 382 (Wis. 1931).

13. This example is adapted from Michigan Cent. R. Co. v. State, 155 N.E. 50 (1927), which did not involve a theft.

14. See Restatement § 53 cmt. c.

15. See *id.* at cmt. b & illus. 5.

16. See Mackie v. Rieser, 296 F.3d 909 (9th Cir. 2002); Restatement § 53 cmt. b.

17. See Restatement § 53 cmt. a & d.

18. See, e.g., Plack v. Baumer, 121 F.2d 676, 679 (3d Cir. 1941).

19. See First Nationwide Savings v. Perry, 15 Cal.Rptr.2d 173, 176 (Cal. App. 1992).

20. See, e.g., Sack v. Feinman, 413 A.2d 1059 (Pa. 1980).

21. See Guyana Telephone & Telegraph Company v. Melbourne International Communications, 329 F.3d 1241, 1249 (11th Cir. 2003).

22. See, e.g., Cross v. Berg Lumber Co., 7 P.3d 922, 935 (Wyo. 2000).

23. See, e.g., Estate of Jones v. Kvamme, 449 N.W.2d 428 (Minn. 1989); Sheldon v. Metro-Goldwyn Pictures Corp., 106 F.2d 45, 51 (2d Cir. 1939).

24. For general discussion, see Daniel Friedmann, *Restitution for Wrongs: The Measure of Recovery*, 79 Tex. L. Rev. 1879 (2001).

25. See, e.g., Bank of America National Trust and Savings v. Ryan, 24 Cal. Rptr. 698 (Cal. App. 1962).

26. See Restatement § 53 illus. 8 & 9.

27. See *id.* at cmt. d & illus. 11.

28. See, e.g., Levin Brothers v. Davis Manufacturing Company, 72 F.2d 163, 165 (8th Cir. 1934).

29. See Edwards v. Lee's Administrator, 96 S.W.2d 1028, 1033 (Ky. App. 1936).

30. See Nickel v. Bank of America National Trust and Savings Association, 290 F.3d 1134, 1139 (9th Cir. 2002).

31. See Restatement § 51 cmt. i.

32. See Pine River Logging and Improving Company v. United States, 186 U.S. 279, 295 (1902).

33. See Restatement § 51 cmt. h.

34. For more in-depth analysis, see *id.* at § 42, which the discussion here follows.

35. See Taylor v. Meirick, 712 F.2d 1112, 1120 (7th Cir. 1983); Iowa State Univ. Research Foundation, Inc. v. American Broadcasting Cos., 475 F. Supp. 78, 83 (S.D.N.Y. 1979).

36. Sheldon v. Metro-Goldwyn Pictures Corp., 106 F.2d 45 (2d Cir. 1939), *aff'd*, 309 U.S. 390 (1940).

37. Playboy Enterprises, Inc. v. Baccarat Clothing Co., 692 F.2d 1272 (9th Cir. 1982).

Chapter Seven

1. E.g., Brown v. Brown, 152 S.W.3d 911, 918 (Mo. App. 2005).

2. See, e.g., United States v. Fontana, 528 F. Supp. 137, 146 (S.D.N.Y. 1981).

3. See Black's Law Dictionary 1622 (9th ed. 2009); see also Maverick Motorsports Group, LLC v. Dep't of Revenue, 253 P.3d 125, 132 (Wyo. 2011).

4. See Restatement (Third) of Restitution and Unjust Enrichment § 55 cmt. f (2011) [hereinafter Restatement].

5. Hardware Mut. Cas. Co. v. Gall, 240 N.E.2d 502, 506–7 (Ohio 1968) ("A thief cannot convey valid title to a stolen motor vehicle to a bona fide purchaser for value without notice ... absent any question of estoppel arising from an act of the owner."); see Allstate Ins. Co. v. Estes, 345 So. 2d 265, 266 (Miss. 1977).

6. See, e.g., West v. Roberts, 143 P.3d 1037, 1044 (Colo. 2006) (en banc); see Charles Evans BMW, Inc. v. Williams, 395 S.E.2d 650, 651 (Ga. App. 1990).

7. See, e.g., NXCESS Motor Cars, Inc. v. JPMorgan Chase Bank, N.A., 317 S.W.3d 462, 470 (Tex. App. 2010).

8. See, e.g., Costell v. First Nat'l Bank of Mobile, 150 So. 2d 683, 686 (Ala. 1963).

9. On the origins of the term and concept, see George E. Palmer, *The History of Restitution in Anglo-American Law*, in 10 International Encyclopedia of Comparative Law: Restitution-Unjust Enrichment and Negotiorum Gestio 17 (Peter Schlectriem ed., 1989).

10. See Annot., 38 A.L.R.3d 1354 (1971); Restatement § 55 cmt. f.

11. See Vogt Mfg. & Coach Lace Co. v. Oettinger, 34 N.Y.S. 729, 731 (Sup. Ct. 1895).

12. For discussion of these theories, see, e.g., Am. Family Care, Inc. v. Irwin, 571 So. 2d 1053, 1061 (Ala. 1990); Locken v. Locken, 650 P.2d 803, 805 (Nev. 1982); Fitz-Gerald v. Hull, 237 S.W.2d 256 (Tex. 1951).

13. See Douglas Laycock, The Death of the Irreparable Injury Rule (1991).

14. See Mourad v. Coupounas, 361 So. 2d 6, 10 (Ala. 1978); Peine v. Murphy, 377 P.2d 708, 714 (Haw. 1962).

15. See Clark v. Pullins, 341 P.2d 73, 76 (Cal. App. 1959); St. Paul Fire & Marine Ins. Co. v. Cox, 583 F. Supp. 1221, 1227 (N.D. Ala. 1984).

16. See, e.g., Cox v. Waudby, 433 N.W.2d 716 (Iowa 1988); Rogers v. Pahoundis, 897 N.E.2d 680, 689 (Ohio App. 2008).

17. See, e.g., Simonds v. Simonds, 380 N.E.2d 189, 194 (N.Y. 1978).

18. See, e.g., *In re* Morris, 260 F.3d 654 (6th Cir. 2001); *In re* Mill Concepts Corp., 123 B.R. 938, 944 (Bankr. D. Mass. 1991) ("The beneficiary of a constructive trust has priority over creditors of the title holder, even a creditor who obtains a judicial lien without knowledge of the underlying circumstances.").

19. See United States v. Andrews, 530 F.3d 1232, 1237 (10th Cir. 2008); Andrew Kull, *Restitution in Bankruptcy: Reclamation and Constructive Trust*, 72 Am. Bankr. L.J. 265, 277–90 (1998); Emily L. Sherwin, *Constructive Trusts in Bankruptcy*, 1989 U. Ill. L. Rev. 297, 335–37, 350–55 (1989); Hanoch Dagan, *Restitution in Bankruptcy: Why All Involuntary Creditors Should Be Preferred*, 78 Am. Bankr. L.J. 247 (2004).

20. See Restatement § 61 cmt. b & illus. 3.

21. See 1 Dobbs, Law of Remedies § 5.8(3), at 798 (2d ed. 1993).

22. As in Carlson Orchards, Inc. v. Linsey, 296 B.R. 582, 590 (Bankr. D. Mass. 2003); cf. Curtis Sharp Custom Homes, Inc. v. Glover, 701 S.W.2d 24, 25 (Tex. App. 1985) (although plaintiff held an equitable lien on defendant's property improved with funds embezzled by the defendant, the state homestead exception prevented foreclosure).

23. See Stevens v. Crowder, 273 So. 2d 793, 794 (Fla. App. 1973).

24. Restatement § 56 cmt. e & illus. 17; for a case recognizing a constructive trust on such facts, see In re Angus, 9 B.R. 769, 771 (Bankr. D. Or. 1981).

25. See Jud Whitehead Heater Co. v. Obler, 245 P.2d 608, 615 (Cal. App. 1952); Restatement § 56 cmt. c.

26. See Briceno v. Briceno, 2007 WL 4146280, at *7 (Tenn. App. 2007); cf. Butler v. Wilkinson, 740 P.2d 1244, 1262 (Utah 1987).

27. See, e.g., Carr v. Burgess, 623 A.2d 1384, 1388 (N.J. Ch. Div. 1991); In re Webb, 160 F. Supp. 544, 548 (S.D. Ind. 1958).

28. See Wells v. Davis, 198 So. 838, 840 (Fla. 1940); Restatement § 56 cmt. e.

29. See Hunnicutt Constr., Inc. v. Stewart Title and Trust of Tucson No. 3496, 928 P.2d 725, 729 (Ariz. App. 1996); cf. Cox v. Waudby, 433 N.W.2d 716 (Iowa 1988) (finding defendant not entitled to the benefit of this rule because she was a gratuitous transferee).

30. See In re Marriage of Allen, 724 P.2d 651, 660 (Colo. 1986); Jud Whitehead Heater Co. v. Obler, 245 P.2d at 615.

31. See Restatement § 57 cmt. a.

32. See id.

33. Dix Mut. Ins. Co. v. LaFramboise, 597 N.E.2d 622, 624 (Ill. 1992); In re Co-Build Co., 21 B.R. 635, 636 (Bankr. E.D. Pa. 1982); Restatement § 57 cmt. g.

34. See Restatement § 57 illus. 23; St. Germain v. Lapp, 48 A.2d 181 (R.I. 1946).

35. See Restatement § 54 cmt. a.

36. See, e.g., Osterberger v. Hites Constr. Co., 599 S.W.2d 221, 227 (Mo. App. 1980); Hicks v. Clayton, 67 Cal. App. 3d 251, 264 (Cal. App. 1977).

37. See, e.g., Isenhower v. Duncan, 635 P.2d 336, 339 (Okla. App. 1981).

38. See Restatement § 58.

39. See Restatement § 58 cmt. b; for discussion, see Dale A. Oesterle, *Deficiencies of the Restitutionary Right to Trace Misappropriated Property in Equity and in U.C.C. § 9-306*, 68 Cornell L. Rev. 172 (1983); James Steven Rogers, *Negotiability, Property, and Identity*, 12 Cardozo L. Rev. 471, 491 (1990).

40. See In re Comm'r of Banks & Real Estate, 764 N.E.2d 66, 100–101 (Ill. App. 2001); Restatement § 59.

41. See In re Kountze Bros., 79 F.2d 98, 101–2 (2d Cir. 1935).

42. See Mitchell v. Dunn, 294 P. 386, 389 (Cal. 1935) (holding that where misappropriated commingled funds have been either invested or dissipated, defendant holds investment in constructive trust for plaintiff because the law prohibits defen-

dants from saying their personal funds paid for the investment while the plaintiff's funds were dissipated); *In re* Erie Trust Co., 191 A. 613, 617–18 (Pa. 1937); see also Restatement § 59 cmt. d & illus. 5.

43. See Primeau v. Granfield, 184 F. 480, 484 (S.D.N.Y. 1911) (L. Hand, J.) ("[I]f the first withdrawals be invested in losing ventures, then the beneficiary is to have a lien, if he likes, till he uses up that whole investment, and then may elect to fall back for the balance upon the original mixed account from which the withdrawal was made . . . . [H]e may elect to accept the investment if he likes, or to reject it."); Restatement § 59 cmt. d & illus. 8.

44. See Conn. Gen. Life Ins. Co. v. Universal Ins. Co., 838 F.2d 612 (1st Cir. 1988); *In re* Catholic Diocese of Wilmington, Inc., 432 B.R. 135, 151 (Bankr. D. Del. 2010); Restatement § 59(2)(c).

45. See Conn. Gen. Life Ins. Co. v. Universal Ins. Co., 838 F.2d at 619.

46. See *In re* Mahan & Rowsey, Inc., 817 F.2d 682, 685 (10th Cir. 1987); *In re* Berry, 147 F. 208, 211 (2d Cir. 1906); Restatement § 59 cmt. e. & illus. 14.

47. See L.E. Zannini & Co. v. Jenkins & Boller Co., 512 N.E.2d 89, 91 (Ill. App. 1987); Nat'l City Bank, Norwalk v. Stang, 518 N.E.2d 241, 243 (Ohio App. 1992); Restatement § 59(3).

48. Andrew Kull, *Restitution in Bankruptcy: Reclamation and Constructive Trust*, 72 Am. Bankr. L.J. 265, 289 n.62 (1998).

49. See *In re* Stix & Co., 27 B.R. 252 (Bankr. E.D. Mo. 1983).

50. See Dale A. Oesterle, *Deficiencies of the Restitutionary Right to the Misappropriated Property in Equity and in U.C.C. § 9-306*, 68 Cornell L. Rev. 172, 194 (1983); Restatement § 58. cmt. b & i.

51. See Merrill Lynch, Pierce, Fenner & Smith, Inc. v. Clayton, 488 F.2d 974, 975 (5th Cir. 1974); Daniel Friedmann, *Restitution for Wrongs: The Measure of Recovery*, 79 Tex L. Rev. 1879, 1921 (2001).

52. See Restatement § 58 cmt. e.

53. See *In re* Estate of Wallen, 633 N.E.2d 1350, 1360 (Ill. App. 1994); Clancy v. Coyne, 244 F.Supp.2d 894 (N.D. Ill. 2002); Smith v. Mottley, 150 F. 266, 268 (6th Cir. 1906).

54. See Restatement §59 illus. 18; the illustration is adapted from *In re* Walter J. Schmidt & Co., 298 F. 314, 316 (S.D.N.Y. 1923) (L. Hand, J.).

55. See Cunningham v. Brown, 265 U.S. 1 (1924); *In re* Walter J. Schmidt & Co., 298 F. at 316 ("There is no reason in law or justice why his depredations upon the fund should not be borne equally between them. To throw all the loss upon one, through the mere chance of his being earlier in time, is irrational and arbitrary . . . .").

56. United States v. Durham, 86 F.3d 70 (5th Cir. 1996).

57. United States v. Durham, 86 F.3d at 72 (affirming the district court's decision).

58. The reporter's note to Restatement § 59 cmt. g regards the result of *Dur-*

ham as "inconsistent with the fundamental rules of property." The note prefers the "orthodox approach to multiple-fraud cases," which "returns identifiable assets to their owners, turning to pro rata distribution only when specific identification or transactional tracing is impossible."

Chapter Eight

1. The defense known as "passing on" is not considered here, as it is limited to a very narrow set of cases; see Restatement (Third) of Restitution and Unjust Enrichment § 64 (2011) [hereinafter Restatement]. Statutes of limitations are likewise omitted because the analysis of them is so specific to the relevant jurisdiction.

2. PaineWebber, Inc. v. Levy, 680 A.2d 798, 799 (N.J. Super. 1995).

3. See, generally, Restatement § 65.

4. See Shearson/Am. Exp., Inc. v. Mann, 814 F.2d. 301 (6th Cir. 1987); United States v. Smith, 182 F. Supp. 503, 504 (S.D.N.Y. 1960).

5. See Mut. Life Ins. Co. of Baltimore v. Metzger, 172 A. 610 (Md. 1934); Lincoln Nat. Life Ins. Co. v. Rittman, 790 S.W.2d 791, 793–94 (Tex. App. 1990).

6. See Restatement § 65 cmt. a.

7. See State *ex rel.* Steger v. Garber, 1979 WL 207282 (Ohio App. 1979); Home Ins. Co. v. Honaker, 480 A.2d 652, 655 (Del. 1984).

8. See Akerson v. Gupta, 458 F. Supp. 189, 190 (E.D. Mo. 1978); Western Cas. & Sur. Co. v. Kohm, 638 S.W.2d 798 (Mo. App. 1982).

9. See Restatement § 65 cmt. g.

10. For additional cases on the issue, see Sharp v. Bowling, 511 So. 2d 363, 365 (Fla. App. 1987); United States v. Reagan, 651 F. Supp. 387, 389 (D. Mass. 1987).

11. See Restatement § 65 cmt. c.

12. Mut. Life Ins. Co. of Baltimore v. Metzger, 172 A. at 612.

13. See Restatement § 65 cmt. d.

14. Hilliard v. Fox, 735 F. Supp. 674, 678 (W.D. Va. 1990).

15. See CSX Transp., Inc. v. Appalachian Railcar Servs., Inc., 509 F.3d 384, 388 (7th Cir. 2007); Messner v. Union County, 167 A.2d 897, 900 (N.J. 1961); Atl. Coast Line R.R. Co., v. Jacob S. Schirmer & Sons, 69 S.E. 439, 440 (S.C. 1910).

16. See Restatement § 65 cmt. b.

17. See Hullett v. Cadick Milling Co., 168 N.E. 610 (Ind. App. 1929).

18. See, generally, Restatement § 66.

19. Compare Touchstone v. Peterson, 443 So. 2d 1219, 1224 (Ala. 1983), and First Fiduciary Corp. v. Blanco, 276 N.W.2d 30, 33 (Minn. 1979).

20. See Restatement § 66 cmt. c; it explains that "purchase" here follows the definition in U.C.C. § 1-201(b)(29) (rev. 2001), which includes "taking by sale, lease, discount, negotiation, mortgage, pledge, lien, security interest, issue or reissue, gift, or any other voluntary transaction creating an interest in property."

21. See Restatement § 66 cmt. c.

22. See Restatement § 66 illus. 3; Neil v. Kinney, 11 Ohio St. 58, 70 (1860).

23. See, generally, Restatement § 68.

24. See Groza-Vance v. Vance, 834 N.E.2d 15, 29 (Ohio App. 2005); Corp. of President of Church of Jesus Christ of Latter-Day Saints v. Jolley, 467 P.2d 984, 985 (Utah 1970).

25. See Restatement § 68 cmt. b.

26. See Restatement (Second) of Contracts § 71 (1981).

27. See Hongsermeier v. Devall, 744 N.W.2d 481, 491 (Neb. App. 2008); Restatement § 68 cmt. e.

28. See Restatement § 68 cmt. d & e.

29. See *id.*

30. See *id.* at § 66.

31. See, e.g., Davison v. Morgan, 50 F.2d 311, 313 (D.C. Cir. 1931).

32. See Levmore, *Variety and Uniformity in the Treatment of the Good-Faith Purchaser*, 16 J. Legal Stud. 43 (1987).

33. See Restatement § 67.

34. As in Transamerica Ins. Co. v. Long, 318 F. Supp. 156, 161 (W.D. Pa. 1970).

35. See Chiquita Brands, Inc. v. Micbruce, Inc., 800 F.Supp. 1521, 1525 (N.D. Ohio 1992).

36. See Restatement § 67 cmt. h.

37. See, e.g., Ohio Cas. Ins. Co. v. Smith, 297 F.2d 265, 266 (7th Cir. 1962); Weiner v. Roof, 122 P.2d 896, 899 (Cal. 1942) (Traynor, J.).

38. See Stephens v. Bd. of Educ. of City of Brooklyn, 79 N.Y. 183, 187 (1879).

39. See Banque Worms v. BankAmerica Int'l, 570 N.E.2d 189, 195 (N.Y. 1991).

40. See, e.g., Federated Mut. Ins. Co. v. Good Samaritan Hosp., 214 N.W.2d 493, 495 (Neb. 1974); Nat'l Benefit Adm'rs, Inc. v. Miss. Methodist Hosp. & Rehab. Ctr., Inc., 748 F. Supp. 459, 466 (S.D. Miss. 1990).

41. See Ian Ayres & Robert Gertner, *Filling Gaps in Incomplete Contracts: An Economic Theory of Default Rules*, 99 Yale L.J. 87 (1989).

42. See Restatement § 67 cmt. f.

43. See Restatement § 62 illus. 2; Banque Worms v. BankAmerica Int'l, 570 N.E.2d at 195.

44. See Restatement § 62 illus. 1; *In re* S. Shore Co-op Ass'n, 103 F.2d 336, 338 (2d Cir. 1939); Clifton Mfg. Co. v. United States, 76 F.2d 577 (4th Cir. 1935).

45. Webb v. McGowin, 168 So. 196 (Ala. Ct. App. 1935).

46. See Restatement § 62 illus. 5.

Index

www.ingramcontent.com/pod-product-compliance
Lightning Source LLC
Chambersburg PA
CBHW020835210326
41598CB00019B/1913